The Businessman's Guide to Washington

The Businessman's Guide to Washington

by
WILLIAM RUDER
and RAYMOND NATHAN

MACMILLAN PUBLISHING CO., INC.
New York

COLLIER MACMILLAN PUBLISHERS
London

Macmillan Publishing Co., Inc.
866 Third Avenue, New York, N. Y. 10022
Collier-Macmillan Canada Ltd.

Library of Congress Cataloging in Publication Data

Ruder, William.
The businessman's guide to Washington.

Includes index.
1. United States—Executive departments.
2. Independent regulatory commissions—United
States.   I. Nathan, Raymond, joint author.
II. Title.
JK424.R8   1975b   353'.0002'433   74–31352
ISBN 0–02–605910–0

FIRST PRINTING 1975

Printed in the United States of America

CONTENTS

86859

THE DEPARTMENTS

THE REGULATORY AGENCIES

THE SCIENCE AGENCIES

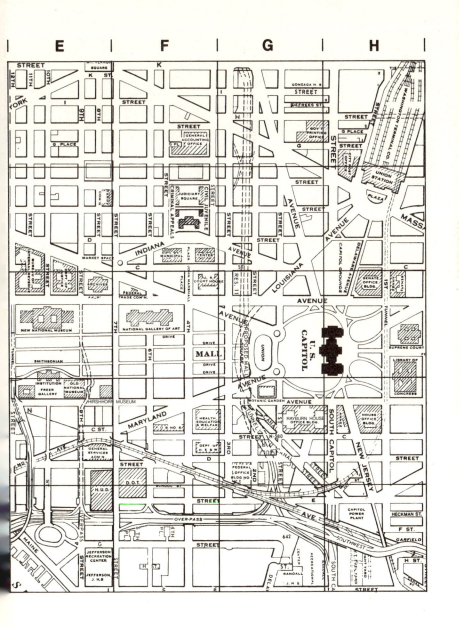

FOREWORD

By Senator Charles H. Percy

One of the most frequent questions asked me by my former business colleagues when I went into public life was: "What is the difference you find between business and public life?" This is an easy question, for it did not take me long to find the difference; namely, decision-making. In corporate life, once the chief executive officer had made a decision, usually in company with his senior officers and the board of directors, most of the battle was over and from then on it was simply a matter of implementing the decision, with very little resistance ever being experienced.

In politics, once a decision has been made by a public official, the battle has barely begun. There is no authority that stems from the top, even in the office of the President, sufficient to implement that decision without a great deal of persuasion all the way through the process. The bureaucracy can grind an idea of the President's into pulp without his knowing it. A legislator who has an idea faces a battle of anywhere from two years to twenty years or longer to see it actually appear in law, and then an indefinite period of time to see it implemented.

A basic understanding of this difference is essential to the businessman when he comes to Washington. If he understands that the wheels of democracy, by design, grind exceedingly slowly, and that the same process that deliberately prevents a public official of evil intention from imposing his will upon the republic also works to prevent a man of good will from quickly implementing his ideas or thoughts, it will help relieve some of the frustration so frequently expressed by my business colleagues who exclaim, "Why can't government be run like a business?"

Just as business today is becoming more responsive to the democratic processes and is beginning to feel the impact of consumerism, the pressure forces of the environmentalists, and is adjusting to them as it did to organized labor decades ago, so too, the processes of government can be responsive to business procedures and techniques. I was aghast when I arrived in Washington in 1967 to find literally no budgetary process in the Congress, though the Congress was supposed to control the purse strings of the Treasury. It has taken seven years and a lot of hard work with some of my colleagues to introduce the process. When we did ultimately prove successful in this effort in 1974—and created for the first time in congressional history budget committees in both the House and the Senate and an entirely new set of procedures and budgetary practices—we discovered that it was the first major reform of the budgetary process undertaken by the Congress since 1921.

So things can and do change in Washington. Change is also taking place in the delicately balanced relationship between government and business. Sometimes, unfortunately, the relationship is an adversary one, often to the detriment of both. At the other extreme, the businessman and the public official may engage in exchanges so close as to be suspect.

For our nation to prosper economically and morally, business executives should make full use of the services and information that are available from government to all citizens. In order to do so, they must know exactly what benefits the government can provide.

Surprisingly few citizens, businessmen included, are aware of the remarkable range of activities conducted by their government. Perhaps the great variety of government functions and the complexity of the organizations carrying them out discourage the average American from digging into this treasure lode.

Since he has paid for it with his tax dollars, however, he would be foolish not to share in its riches. This book can help all Americans, and especially those engaged in business and industry, to locate more readily the wealth of assistance to be found in their government.

In the present Washington climate, there may be some tendency for the businessman to lean over backwards and stay away from the government, lest he accidentally overstep the line of propriety. This would be unfortunate for business and a great waste of the taxpayers' money.

The businessman should feel free to communicate his point of view to government. It is always welcomed, though not always accommodated. And he certainly should not feel the slightest hesitancy about asking government for the information and assistance to which he is entitled.

This book will provide him with a road map to the many sources of legitimate help for the citizen–businessman. I hope that it will be used to build a better relationship between government and business.

ACKNOWLEDGMENTS

During the years that the two of us have spent in Washington as public servants, we have been able to participate in one of the great experiences of a lifetime. The satisfaction of working in the public interest and of flexing one's intellectual muscles in the biggest arena in the world is infinite and endless. We wish to acknowledge the great debt that the both of us owe to our colleagues and former colleagues in government.

Most particularly, we would like to point out that the basic idea for writing this book came from the thinking that former Secretary of Commerce Luther H. Hodges often expressed— namely, that one of the crying needs of the business community is to get real practical help in making use of the government services and aids that are available to them. Likewise, it is a great waste that there is so much valuable material and so many willing hands available in the government just waiting to be tapped to be at the service of the private sector. It is our hope that this book makes a contribution in this direction.

This volume is a complete revision of and a successor to *Businessman's Guide to Washington*, which we wrote to meet this need in 1964. That book is now out of print, and we thank

Prentice-Hall for graciously permitting us to proceed with the present project.

Great changes have taken place in government in these ten years. In terms of organizational structure, two entirely new cabinet departments have been created; major new agencies and regulatory commissions have been established; other agencies have been abolished or consolidated.

Even more important, government has moved into new activities with major impact on business. Consider the work of the Consumer Product Safety Commission, for example, or the Environmental Protection Agency.

Special acknowledgment and sincere thanks are due for the helpfulness of the public information officers of the various departments and agencies. They supplied great masses of raw material and reviewed for accuracy the end-product we distilled from that material and other sources. We did not, however, ask or receive official approval for any statements made in this book. The authors themselves bear sole responsibility for the contents.

Credit also should be given to Janice Berger for research assistance on two chapters, and to Eleanor Anderson, Marie Dobson, Louise Feuerstein, and Beverly Keith for secretarial help.

And we thank our wives for their forbearance during our months of labor pains on this book.

WILLIAM RUDER
RAYMOND NATHAN

NOTE ON

GOVERNMENT PUBLICATIONS

Throughout this book, you will find government publications listed with a price and the acronym GPO. (Other publications listed are available free from the issuing departments and agencies.) This means that to order the book you should send the amount indicated to Superintendent of Documents, Government Printing Office, Washington, D.C. 20402. Do not send an order and ask to be billed.

Many publications can be bought at GPO bookstores in the following cities:

Washington, D.C. (in six locations: 710 N. Capitol St.; Commerce Department, 14th & E N.W.; Forrestal Bldg., 1000 Independence Ave. S.W.; Pentagon Bldg., Main Concourse; State Department, 21st & C N.W.; USIA, 1776 Pennsylvania Ave. N.W.)

Atlanta, Ga., Federal Office Bldg., 275 Peachtree N.E.

Birmingham, Ala., 2121-8th Ave. N.

Boston, Mass., John F. Kennedy Federal Bldg.

Canton, Ohio, 201 Cleveland Ave., S.W.

Chicago, Ill., Federal Office Bldg., 219 S. Dearborn St.

Cleveland, Ohio, Federal Bldg., 1240 E. 9th St.

Dallas, Tex., New Federal Bldg., 1100 Commerce St.

Denver, Colo., Federal Bldg., and U.S. Courthouse, 1961 Stout St.

Detroit, Mich., Federal Office Bldg., 231 W. LaFayette Blvd.

Kansas City, Mo., Federal Bldg., 601 E. 12th St.

Los Angeles, Calif., Federal Bldg., 300 N. Los Angeles St.

New York, N.Y., Federal Office Bldg., 26 Federal Plaza

Philadelphia, Pa., U.S. Post Office and Courthouse, 9th & Chestnut Sts.

San Francisco, Calif., Federal Bldg., 450 Golden Gate Ave., P.O. Box 36104

Pueblo, Colo.

The Businessman's Guide to Washington

GOVERNMENT—OUR
BIGGEST PARTNER

The authors of this book have both been businessmen. Each of us has had the experience of having worked for some years in the federal government. Each in his own way, after beginning to work for the government, realized that he came with a vast body of ignorance as to the impact of the government on his own capacity to make a living and on the ability of his business to turn a profit.

Each of us feels that he is much better off for having learned about the federal establishment—how it affects his livelihood and the success of his business planning. It seemed to us that we should try to share some of the knowledge about the relationship of government to business, both big and small, with our associates in the free enterprise system.

The government is the biggest partner we have. First, of course, the government takes a huge slice of our profits in corporate taxes. Second, the government is the largest single influence on the fundamental economic conditions that control our business environment. Third, the federal government, either by act of Congress or by an administrative ruling of an executive department or regulatory agency, can mean literally life or

1

death to a business enterprise. It can reduce profits to a trickle, or eliminate them entirely; on the other hand, it can, by a stroke of a pen, create windfalls. Finally, the vast government machinery truly operates—or tries to—in the interest of the total economy. As a result, it produces aids and services which are incredibly valuable to the individual business. Many of these aids and services are hard to come by, far-ranging, and expensive. It would be impossible for an individual business to provide them for itself. Unfortunately, most businessmen do not know about the magnificent services available to them from various government agencies.

The aim of this book is to present to the businessman—agency by agency, function by function—the broad array of the federal government's interest in his business; control of his operations; and most importantly, assistance that can be rendered to him.

It should be pointed out very early in the game that although this particular volume is addressed to the question of what the businessman ought to know about the federal government, he should be informed also about state and local government. Because of its sheer size, the federal government is likely to be much more important to the businessman. In a given case, however, it is entirely possible that his state or local government can have as much impact on his business as the federal government—through local taxes, Sunday closing laws, city ordinances concerning truck deliveries, real-estate regulations, and an assortment of other controls.

There is an interesting point of fundamental economic waste involved in this general question of the relationship between businessman and federal government. Our annual federal budget is approximately $300 billion. Subtract about 30 percent of that for the defense establishment and this leaves $210 billion in federal government expenditures. It is impossible to determine exactly what part of that sum goes into turning out information, services, assistance, and programs which are of potential aid to any given businessman. We do know, however, that a big proportion of federal programming results in just this kind of final product. To the extent that this product is unknown to the businessman, or not used by him to its maximum, the taxpayer doesn't get his money's worth. When, for example, the Bureau of the Census turns out statistics on population, the taxpayer does not get the total value of his investment unless the information is used, not only for its fundamental demographic and sociological purposes, but also for market research by the business community.

There is a two-way responsibility here. First, the government has the responsibility of marketing its output of information, data, services, and assistance to the potential user in the business community (and to other users—welfare workers, housewives, farmers, etc.). Second, the businessman has the obligation of educating himself as to what he can get from his government— and we don't mean "get" in the sense of a handout. He should know what he is entitled to by virtue of being a citizen, a taxpayer, and the operator of an enterprise that makes an economic contribution to society.

There are, we believe, three fundamental points involved in the businessman's relationship with government. The first is that to get your due and to reap your normal interest from your personal and business dollar investment in government requires not one iota of influence or wire-pulling. The businessman does not have to know any specific person in government. He does, however, have to know how the system works. It is just the same as in your own business. One does not have to know the president of your company to do business with it. The man who knows the structure of your business and the "fit" between different jobs can wend his way through your organization chart and put his finger on the right man to solve any particular problem. The government works the same way.

If you know how the system works; if you know what the executive-branch responsibility is, the hierarchy within a particular department; if you know what the legislative responsibility is, the operation of various committees and subcommittees in the Senate and the House of Representatives; then you can find your way through the government maze to the right man to help you with a particular problem.

The second point is that the time to build a communications path to the federal government is before you really need it. Often, businessmen come down to Washington when they are almost purple with apoplexy. A particular piece of legislation or an administrative ruling has been either passed or under consideration for weeks, months, or perhaps even a year. When it is about to be completed—or even after it has been passed—the businessman shows up in Washington for a last-ditch effort. He must necessarily be aggressive and antagonistic, in conflict with a policy or a program whose cement has virtually hardened. How much better for him if he makes himself known to people in government in advance, building an easy access and a ready communication with them before things reach a crisis stage in terms of any particular problem. Our experience has been that the government official is anxious to know about your business before he considers a problem in which the government has an interest. For instance, when the Treasury Department is undertaking a revision of depreciation schedules, industry by industry, its economists want to know all about, say, the shoe industry, its manufacturing and machinery problems, so that they can do an intelligent job. This little example is repeated tens of thousands of times in government. In this book we will be laying out for you those special interests the different federal agencies have, so that you can determine for yourself who in government should be informed about your business and its problems before any federal issues arise.

The third critical point for the businessman to realize is that he does not have to be afraid of government, nor deal with government people at arm's length. The curious fact is the federal bureaucrat responds just as any ordinary human being. A man likes to feel that he is appreciated, that he is making a contribution, that his work is important, that somebody is interested in his point of view. He likes to be asked questions, for he has the normal instinct to be helpful to his fellow man. When the businessman comes with a problem and asks for help, when the businessman lets the bureaucrat know that it's important that the bureaucrat know something about his business, that the businessman wants to be understood by the bureaucrat, much of the difficulties tend to fade.

It seems to us that the government must make its contribution by actively marketing its output to the business community. In turn, each member of the business community has to develop the ability to build a sound relationship with the government, just as he would with one of his customers. Relationships are worked out and usually don't come by accident. Good communication is a skill; businessmen have that skill. They must decide to apply it to their relationship with the government.

THE BUSINESSMAN
AND CONGRESS

The low plateau lying on the eastern fringe of Washington's downtown area known as Capitol Hill has, in the years since World War II, become increasingly familiar ground to the businessman.

It is here—on "the Hill"—that the operations of the entire federal structure are first given life by way of legislative authorization. It is here that the means for carrying out these operations are provided—i.e., funds must be appropriated before a wheel can turn. It is here that any weaknesses or abuses in government or business are aired by investigating committees, and it is here that the businessman can often get the most effective help for all his government problems, whether they center in the legislative or executive branches.

In the course of normal business affairs, these are the most common occasions for contacting one or more members of Congress:

- To express support or opposition regarding pending legislation;
- To appear before one of the congressional committees, or to submit testimony;

- To enlist congressional guidance and assistance in a matter with one of the departments or agencies in the executive branch of the federal government; and
- To voice views regarding policies and practices within the federal structure.

Every businessman faced with such problems has at least four good starting points in the legislative branch of the government: the two senators from his state, the congressman from the district in which his business is headquartered, and, usually, the chairman of the committee that concerns itself with the legislative interest most intimately related to the businessman's particular enterprise.

From this, one branches out, because committees in Congress have subcommittees with even more specialized interests; congressmen have administrative assistants; committees and subcommittees have staff personnel. In addition, both parties have congressional policy committees composed of leading members of Congress and a professional staff.

At the end of this chapter, you will find a complete listing of congressional committees, a very brief delineation of the particular interest, authority and scope of each, and the names of the chairman, ranking minority member, and staff director (with his telephone number). You should be familiar with the committees that are important to your business. It is almost unthinkable that there should be only one committee of interest to you. For instance, let us suppose that you are in the garment manufacturing business. This means that you are affected by the price of cloth, which takes you into the Agriculture Committee and its consideration of cotton subsidies, wool imports. Your business is affected by transportation costs. This takes you into the Interstate and Foreign Commerce committees. Your business is affected by labor legislation, which comes before still another committee. Your business is affected by labeling, by packaging, by copyright. It is a good idea to be familiar with the total congressional road map.

Your own prompt attention to your problem is essential. The longer you put off enlisting the aid of your senator or representative, the more your chances diminish of getting the help needed. If the senator or representative is contacted as a last resort, the course of events will, more often than not, be too far along for him to be able to work effectively for you—as much as he surely wants to.

Last-minute appeals rarely change a vote. The process through which every legislative proposal must move is long and painstakingly thorough. By the time a bill comes to a vote, it has been before the legislator for a long time. Probably he has already determined how he will vote. Remember, this man is human! Just like the rest of us, he is most reluctant to change a position once he has taken it, especially if he has announced it or otherwise made it known.

Furthermore, the most effective work for, or in opposition to, a particular legislative item can most often be done while the bill is still in the mill—not after it reaches the floor. After a bill has been drafted and introduced, it must move through committees and subcommittees of each house. At each step in its journey through Congress, a bill can be bottled up, or amended, or moved along to the next hurdle. Keeping a bill moving demands constant attention. The member of Congress who is convinced of the need and worth of a particular piece of legislation is in a unique position to give it just that. Similarly, his position as a member of Congress gives him many opportunities to help kill, delay, or amend a bill. How vigorously a congressman applies his energies and influences to particular legislation depends upon how thoroughly convinced he is. Your job is to convince him thoroughly—and to do so early in the fight.

Ordinarily, bills move consecutively through the House of Representatives and the Senate. Only rarely will one house begin consideration of a bill until it has had final action in the other chamber. After a bill is introduced, it is sent to the appropriate committee, where the chairman's disposition toward it can mean life or death for the measure. The chairman may assign it to one of his subcommittees for hearings and recommendations, or he may retain it in the full committee where he will have virtually complete control over its future.

If your congressman is a member of the committee to which the bill has been assigned, his personal assistance can mean much to your interests in the measure. If he is not a member of the committee, he can nevertheless lend a very effective hand, enlisting the support of his colleagues who do serve on it. Cooperation among members of Congress is very often the key to the doors that have to be opened, or locked, on Capitol Hill. It frequently cuts across party lines and goes beyond provincial interests.

Weeks and months often pass before a measure reaches its first vote on the floor. Success there is only half the battle. Before it can go to the president for his signature or veto, it must be passed by both houses of Congress and any differences compromised by a Senate–House conference. Then the compromise itself must be approved by both chambers. The opportunities to shape and determine the outcome of legislation are numerous. The measure of your success in promoting your interests as they may be affected by pending legislation will likely be in direct proportion to how early your efforts have started—and how sustained they have been. (For a revealing, fast-moving account of how one bill was nursed into law, we recommend Eric Redman, *The Dance of Legislation* [New York: Simon and Schuster, 1974].)

More often than not, a direct and straightforward approach to the representative from your home district, your senators, or both will be one of the most valuable and effective efforts you can make in dealings with the federal government. Effective ways to enlist the aid of representatives and senators vary as widely as do their individual personalities and backgrounds. Obviously, if you already know your senators or representative, the problem of initial contact is considerably lessened, for you will only be calling on an old friend. If you are not acquainted with them, you have been missing a good bet and neglecting an important duty of citizenship. But fortunately that problem can be remedied quickly and easily by letter, through introduction by a mutual friend, or by a call and visit when the congressman is in your community. This doesn't mean that you have to be his supporter or endorse his goals or methods, but it does mean that you should get to know as much as possible about him and about his interests. Reflect a moment! You are sure to realize that he is anxious to know you. You, as one of his constituents, are important to him. He represents you in Washington, and in order to serve you best, he must know your problems, your thoughts, your interests, and your goals. Just as you may not approve of everything he does or stands for, he may not always go right down the line with you. It would be surprising if you were to find yourselves in constant and complete agreement. But your acquaintance, however slight it might be, will prove of mutual benefit.

The relative informality of the House of Representatives as compared with the more austere Senate should not lead you to think that your representative will be less valuable to you than your senator. Local interests and issues will usually be of more direct concern to your representative than to your senator, whose interests range more widely. The representative himself, as a general rule, is more accessible and approachable than a senator, whose ear is sought by five times as many people. Both, though, have the ability, the know-how, and experienced staff personnel to give the help it would be impossible to find elsewhere.

If your business on Capitol Hill is legislative, it is imperative that you work with both the House and the Senate. The two legislative bodies are completely separate and independent in their legislative activities. Certain subjects—revenue and spending, for instance—by rule and tradition must originate in the House of Representatives. On the other hand, the Senate has exclusive jurisdiction over such matters as treaty ratifications and the confirmation of presidential appointees. Each chamber of Congress is jealous of its independence and jurisdiction.

In deciding which senators and representatives to approach on legislative matters, keep in mind that some have developed personal identifications with particular subject areas, which may coincide with your area of interest and impel them to be especially helpful to you. One member, for example, is especially identified with the pharmaceutical field. Another has expert knowledge of atomic energy, while a third has built up a near franchise on safeguarding the rights of small businessmen.

Whichever congressman you go to, following certain basic ground rules will help achieve maximum results. If you can lay out your problem in such a reasonable way that he feels yours is not merely a case of special interest, but rather one representative of a broad category of businessmen with a problem that properly can be solved by legislation, you have a good chance of enlisting his support. One of the most widely held misconceptions about Capitol Hill is that its decisions are controlled exclusively by pressure, pull, and partisanship. While these play a role, just as they do in almost every facet of business and private life—and probably a somewhat larger role—the overriding element is usually the persuasiveness of sound reasoning and logical presentation. The man who relies on influence alone is in for the same disappointment that would result in business if he depended only on "contacts" and offered a poor product.

The man who makes his case on the basis of reason will avoid the common error of "demanding" that the legislator work and cast his vote for or against a particular bill. Frequently, this is coupled with an implied threat that if he does not follow instructions the congressman will find himself out of office after the next election. Few people have the political muscle to make good such a threat, and the congressman knows it. Consequently, the net result will be either a polite brushoff or a brusque showing to the door, with a strong likelihood that the congressman will take a position opposite to that sought.

Far more effective is the positive approach of trying to be helpful to the man whose assistance you want. One thing a businessman often can do for a congressman is give him publicity, which is the lifeblood of a man who must keep his name before the voters. Suppose, for example, you are going to open a new plant. It is both good politics and good public relations to invite your representative and your senators to participate in the ceremonies. In some cases, it might also be appropriate to invite an out-of-state congressman who has taken a special interest in your industry through his work on a committee or otherwise.

Campaign Contributions

Should the businessman make campaign contributions to a congressman? Only the businessman himself can make the final decision, but certain considerations may be helpful:

1. Contributing to a candidate's campaign fund or to a party or committee is certainly not illicit for an individual businessman, though it is forbidden for a corporation. Since the law sets a maximum as well as other restrictions on contributions, it is well to check with an attorney before proceeding.

2. The costs of conducting a campaign are extremely high. A congressional salary, taking into account the expenses of maintaining households in Washington and the home district, can't begin to cover them. Understandably, then, fund-raising is of major importance to members of Congress. Contribution records are carefully compiled, so if you have contributed to the campaign of a senator or representative, you can be sure he knows it. While a contribution does not guarantee his giving you a hand, he would be less than human if he did not react a little faster and a little more favorably for those who had responded to his needs when it counted the most.

3. A campaign contribution is the one way most businessmen find it possible to participate in politics. If made openly and held within reasonable limits, it is a legitimate expression of the businessman's interest in government and a means of cementing relationships between himself and political leaders.

Committee Hearings

At some stage in the legislative life of a bill you are interested in, hearings will be held on it, unless, of course, it has been introduced merely as a gesture with no expectation of action. It may or may not be useful for you to testify. This will depend on such factors as whether the committee has active opponents to your position who could pepper you with tough questions; your own effectiveness under fire; and whether the committee is anxious to keep the hearings short. Your congressman, or your Washington representative if you have one, is best able to advise you whether a personal appearance is desirable. If it is, your congressman's request to the committee chairman ordinarily will assure your being listed as a witness; in some cases, just writing to the clerk of the committee and asking to be scheduled, whenever hearings are held, will be sufficient. When oral testimony is not practical, a written statement may be submitted before the hearings for insertion in the printed record.

It is not necessary to be accompanied by an attorney at a committee hearing, but you have the right to be represented by counsel if you feel more comfortable that way.

It can be especially helpful to the successful promotion of your interests before a congressional committee if your senators or representative will go with you to the hearing and introduce you to the members. This is a legitimate service to a constituent that your congressman is willing to perform, provided he can work it into his schedule and there are no conflicting interests (or other circumstances) that would make it inappropriate for him to do so.

The closest possible attention should be given to preparation of testimony. Keep it as brief as possible, bringing out clearly all the points you want to make. If you can document how the voters will be affected by the legislation in terms of jobs, earnings, prices, or other specifics, you will make a far greater impression than the man who talks in generalities. Your formal statement should be completed in time to reproduce copies for committee members, staff, and press representatives attending the hearing. Be sure, however, not to offend the committee by giving copies to the press before giving it to them. One of the committee staff will see that copies are distributed to the press at the time you begin testifying. Charts or other exhibits keyed to your statement can help drive home your major points, but be sure these materials are on a scale large enough to be read easily at a distance.

A witness should expect to be closely questioned; usually, the members of the committee will inject their queries and comments long before the prepared statement has been made in full. One way to arm yourself for the ordeal is a rehearsal in which your associates shoot questions at you that a congressman might conceivably ask. It is impossible to anticipate every question, but this method is a good test of whether you have done your homework and are prepared to discuss the subject in depth.

Perhaps your trade association or other businessmen in your field are going to testify along similar lines. It may be possible to coordinate your efforts so that you do not duplicate each other's material. You may find that you can save a trip to Washington altogether, unless the strategy of your side is to throw in as many witnesses as possible in order to delay action on a bill you oppose. Even if you don't testify, however, you have several other ways to make your views known. In addition to submitting a statement for the committee hearing record, you can write to your own senators and congressman and to members of the full committee who may not attend the subcommittee hearings or read the voluminous record. You might also consider writing letters to the editor of your newspaper and to the newspapers of the towns from which the chairmen of the appropriate congressional committees come. This will serve two important purposes: give exposure to your point of view and let key congressmen know that the issue is being aired in a forum close to home.

Another front where you can advance your viewpoint on

legislation is, surprisingly, with the executive branch. Although they read occasionally of government officials testifying, few businessmen realize that almost every piece of proposed legislation is sent to appropriate government agencies for comment, and that to an increasing extent legislative proposals actually originate in the executive branch and are introduced in Congress "by request." It is therefore important for you to use the road map of the executive branch provided in following chapters, identifying the agencies likely to be concerned with specific pieces of legislation, then making your ideas known to them. They will have an opportunity to react and to testify before congressional committees. You have an opportunity to shape the reaction and testimony by letting the right people in the executive branch know how a piece of legislation will affect your business, your employees, and your community.

For many reasons, the business executive may find it neither desirable nor practical to deal personally with all the details involved in shepherding a legislative interest on Capitol Hill or a problem with a department or agency. A growing number of major firms maintain Washington staffs to promote and represent the firm's interests in its relationship with the federal government. Others, whose needs do not justify a full-time staff, find their best bet in one of the many private public relations, business consultant, or law firms specializing in performing such services for a number of clients. Some depend on trade associations—more than 1500 have Washington offices to serve their members' interests. Some form of on-the-scene representation by a man who knows the ins and outs of all phases of our government and can undertake daily bird-dogging for you may mean the difference between success and failure in what you hope to accomplish.

Whether you choose to act yourself or have someone act in your behalf, some understanding of how congressional offices and committees are staffed and how they operate will be most helpful. Remembering that you are but one of close to half a million individuals in his district who may call on a representative for help, and that most senators serve several times that many people, you will understand that your congressman cannot personally handle all your requests. He has at his disposal several means of assistance. He can call on executive departments and agencies and the Library of Congress for extensive background studies that would be very expensive, if available at all, from private sources. He may get help from the professional staff members of the various congressional committees. But the main burden of the digging, the leg work, the practical day-to-day operation of his office falls to his personal staff.

Congressional Office Staffs

Their size, organization, makeup, and manner of operation vary widely from office to office. While a typical House member will have a staff of perhaps five, his counterpart in the Senate, with an entire state under his responsibility, may have a dozen or more. House staffers, therefore, tend to be general-utility types, and the businessman need not be too concerned with which one is assigned to his problem. With his larger staff, the senator can give individuals more specialized responsibilities.

Heading his staff, usually with the ability to know what action the senator would take and the authority to act in his behalf in a given situation, is his administrative assistant, or AA in Capitol Hill lingo. Usually a man or woman from his state with a good "feel" for its Washington interests, the AA is generally regarded, and rightly so, as a "third senator" or "assistant senator." The AA, in most situations, is the person closest to the senator, and thus directly reflects his attitudes, inclinations, aims, policies, and methods. The senator must lean heavily upon him for advice, briefing, and in hundreds of other ways. It often falls to the AA to attend meetings, conferences, and social functions that the senator himself is unable to work into his tremendously busy schedule. As a rule of thumb, the administrative assistant is the man to see when you make your initial contact. He will best know whether your problem or case should go directly to the senator, and see that it does, if necessary.

The legislative assistant in a senator's office is almost always a lawyer with considerable legislative and government experience. He is relied upon to keep the senator fully informed on legislative matters affecting his committee assignments and the status and progress of all bills in which the senator has an interest; to keep the senator up to date on the daily business conducted on the floor and to alert him to possible fast-breaking legislative situations that can change hour by hour. It is the legislative assistant's job to promote the senator's legislative purposes, interests, and desires at every turn. His recommendations carry great weight with the senator. He will generally be the best person to see if your problem or interest is strictly legislative in nature.

Many businessmen will find that the senator's caseworker, or agency contact person, is the one who can best process his problems. This person generally has up-to-the-minute knowledge of activities within the myriad of federal departments and agencies and can tell you "whom to see and where," and how to get maximum effect from your efforts. The senator will rely heavily upon his caseworker in agency matters, making a personal telephone call to an agency head, for example, if the caseworker so advises.

The fourth key person in a senator's office is his personal secretary. Her responsibilities will cover a wide range of the senator's official and social appointment scheduling. It usually falls to her to act as a buffer, just as it does to your secretary.

A similar structure is found in the office of a representative, except that there are fewer staff members and each must assume a greater share of responsibility.

The official titles are fewer—one "secretary," the others are classified as "clerks." However, informal titles which correspond to those in Senate offices are usually adopted. The representative's secretary is known as his administrative assistant and will ordinarily fill the shoes of both AA and legislative assistant. In the usual situation, this person is the representative's alter ego. The casework is generally assigned to one or two of the remaining staffers.

Because House staffs are small by comparison to Senate staffs, a more informal "back home" atmosphere prevails. The representative will be found to be, by and large, more readily accessible, down-to-earth, and in closer touch with specific local projects and problems than his Senate counterpart. Members of both House and Senate also maintain smaller staffs in their home districts.

Congressional Committees and Staffs

Each house of Congress will hear your bill in its own separate committee, although certain especially far-ranging and complex subjects, such as atomic energy and the national economy, are handled by joint committees. The organizational structure of congressional committees is determined by two factors: (1) the majority party of each house is given the chairmanship and has more members than the minority; and (2) rank among committee members, from the chairman to the newest member, is determined by seniority, the number of years the member has served on the particular committee. The higher a committee member ranks in seniority, the greater weight his support of or opposition to legislation will have. If you are not acquainted with a top-ranking committee member, ask your friends on Capitol Hill either to introduce you to one or to speak in your behalf to one.

Each committee has a staff of professional, secretarial, and clerical people which, as the chairman directs, does much of the mountainous work that must be done on each item of legislation assigned to it. While most of the staff are appointed by the majority, both the majority- and minority-designated staffers have an obligation to serve the committee and its members of both parties.

Even though committee staffing is generally done on a partisan political basis, it is done with great care to obtain people who are topflight in the fields within which the committee works. For the most part, the professional staff members of the congressional committees have considerable backgrounds of experience and expertise, and they often are extremely influential in shaping legislation, especially when the subject matter is complex or technical.

The key staff person of a congressional committee will generally hold the title of chief counsel or staff director. In some instances he holds both positions. His responsibility is to organize and direct the staff work of the committee, under the supervision of the committee chairman. Since many of the bills under consideration in committee have been sponsored by members not serving on that particular committee, the staffers have frequent occasion to work with a large number of senators and representatives, and within a short time gain a great deal of insight into the interests and operations of nearly every congressman and his staff. Your senator or representative will more than likely be fairly well acquainted with one or more of the staff people working on the item that interests you, and can draw on their expert assistance for you, or arrange for you to meet them, if that appears advisable.

If you are going to do much business on the Hill, you will find the detailed biographical and organization information contained in the *Congressional Directory* (Government Printing Office, Washington, D.C. 20402, $6.80 cloth, $5.05 paper) and the privately compiled *Congressional Staff Directory* (P.O. Box 62, Mt. Vernon, Va. 22121, $15) indispensable. Both publications are revised annually to reflect up-to-the-minute committee memberships, seniority rankings, office and committee staff listings and current organizational makeup of the Congress. A useful companion volume on the executive branch is the *U.S. Government Manual* (Government Printing Office, Washington, D.C. 20402, $4.95).

Hill and "Downtown"

A senator or representative can be extremely helpful to you in dealing with the people "downtown" in the executive departments, agencies, and bureaus. A big part of a congressman's work consists of answering requests for information on programs of the executive branch, expediting local matters pending in one of the agencies, and a hundred similar chores that must be performed to insure speedy and fair treatment for the interests of the people, businesses, and industries of his district or state.

Because the operations of the departments and agencies are under the almost constant scrutiny of Congress through authorizations and appropriations hearings, they are especially anxious to maintain the best possible relationships with members of Congress. One of the best opportunities for them to do just that arises when they can show prompt and careful attention to a matter referred to them by a congressional office.

Every department and agency has a congressional liaison office to handle requests and inquiries from the Hill. A call from a Capitol Hill office regarding your problem is certain to bring fast action in the agency. This is not meant to imply that intercession of a congressional office will bring about a contract award or a favorable ruling or other action in the departments and agencies. But it can be a great help to you by way of assuring that you and your problem are handled with the greatest possible amount of speed and consideration.

Most members of Congress are glad to help their constituents in their relations with the executive departments. If given reasonable advance notice, they are able to arrange appointments, set up conferences, and obtain information for you that would require weeks or months of your own time to accomplish —if you could do it at all. They can alert you to the need for your presence in Washington, if that becomes necessary. In any event, it is advisable to keep your congressman posted on all actions taken in your case, whether by you or by the department involved. When the time comes for his intercession, he will have on hand the background information needed to work with speed and effectiveness.

One of the very first things a new congressman is counseled on by his colleagues is the vital necessity of carefully tending the needs of his state or district and the people he represents. It usually goes something like "not many people back home will ever remember how you voted on this or that bill, but all of them will know what you have done for them and for their communities." The congressman—or at least the one who gets reelected—never loses sight of that admonition. He realizes that a record of service to the needs of his constituents is the most valuable asset a politician has—especially when going before the voters at election time, every six years for senators and every two years for representatives. He wants the longest and best record possible. The results he is able to help you obtain very often will have news and publicity value in his state or district. Certainly he has earned a fair measure of credit, and it will be to your advantage to make sure that he gets it in full measure.

The senator or representative also knows that doing his best for you will earn him your appreciation and good will. That is important to him, for whether you support him politically or not, you are walking evidence of his effectiveness. You will do well to let him know you realize you have profited from his efforts.

Finally, don't ever lose sight of the fact that even though you may put one problem behind you, others are sure to arise in the future. Now that you are acquainted with your congressional offices, you will do well to nurture this contact. An occasional letter, especially one to give credit when due rather than only to serve your own special interests, is certain to pay dividends in the long run.

Key Congressional Committee Personnel

(NOTE: All congressional telephone numbers are area code 202)

SENATE

AERONAUTICAL AND
SPACE SCIENCES

Robert F. Allnutt, Staff Director (225–6477)

Sen. Frank E. Moss of Utah, Chairman

Sen. Barry Goldwater of Arizona, Ranking Minority Member

AGRICULTURE AND FORESTRY

Cotys M. Mouser, Chief Clerk (225–2035)

Sen. Herman E. Talmadge of Georgia, Chairman

Sen. Carl T. Curtis of Nebraska, Ranking Minority Member

APPROPRIATIONS

Thomas J. Scott, Chief Clerk (225–3471)

Sen. John L. McClellan of Arkansas, Chairman

Sen. Milton R. Young of North Dakota, Ranking Minority Member

ARMED SERVICES

T. Edward Braswell, Jr., Chief Counsel & Staff Director (225–3871)

Sen. John C. Stennis of Mississippi, Chairman

Sen. Strom Thurmond of South Carolina, Ranking Minority Member

BANKING, HOUSING, AND
URBAN AFFAIRS

Dudley L. O'Neal, Staff Director & General Counsel (225–7391)

Sen. William Proxmire of Wisconsin, Chairman

Sen. John G. Tower of Texas, Ranking Minority Member

COMMERCE

Frederick J. Lordan, Staff Director (225–5115)

Sen. Warren G. Magnuson of Washington, Chairman

Sen. Norris Cotton of New Hampshire, Ranking Minority Member

DISTRICT OF COLUMBIA

Robert O. Harris, Staff Director (225–4161)

Sen. Thomas F. Eagleton of Missouri, Chairman

Sen. Charles McC. Mathias, Jr., of Maryland, Ranking Minority Member

FINANCE

Tom Vail, Chief Counsel (225–4515)

Sen. Russell B. Long of Louisiana, Chairman

Sen. Wallace F. Bennett of Utah, Ranking Minority Member*

FOREIGN RELATIONS

Carl Marcy, Chief of Staff (225–4651)

Sen. John J. Sparkman of Alabama, Chairman

Sen. George D. Aiken of Vermont, Ranking Minority Member*

GOVERNMENT OPERATIONS

Robert B. Smith, Jr., Chief Counsel & Staff Director (225–4751)

Sen. Sam J. Ervin, Jr., of North Carolina, Chairman

Sen. Charles H. Percy of Illinois, Ranking Minority Member

* Retired January 1975

INTERIOR AND INSULAR AFFAIRS

Jerry T. Verkler, Staff Director (225–4971)

Sen. Henry M. Jackson of Washington, Chairman

Sen. Paul J. Fannin of Arizona, Ranking Minority Member

JUDICIARY

John H. Holloman III, Chief Counsel & Staff Director (225–5225)

Sen. James O. Eastland of Mississippi, Chairman

Sen. Roman L. Hruska of Nebraska, Ranking Minority Member

LABOR AND PUBLIC WELFARE

Stewart E. McClure, Staff Director (225–5375)

Sen. Harrison A. Williams, Jr., of New Jersey, Chairman

Sen. Jacob K. Javits of New York, Ranking Minority Member

POST OFFICE AND
CIVIL SERVICE

David Minton, Staff Director & General Counsel (225–5451)

Sen. Gale W. McGee of Wyoming, Chairman

Sen. Hiram L. Fong of Hawaii, Ranking Minority Member

PUBLIC WORKS

M. Barry Meyer, Chief Counsel & Chief Clerk (225–6176)

Sen. Jennings Randolph of West Virginia, Chairman

Sen. Howard H. Baker, Jr., of Tennessee, Ranking Minority Member

RULES AND ADMINISTRATION

William McWhorter Cochrane, Staff Director (225–6352)

Sen. Howard W. Cannon of Nevada, Chairman

Sen. Marlow W. Cook of Kentucky, Ranking Minority Member

VETERANS' AFFAIRS

Frank J. Brizzi, Staff Director (225–9126)

Sen. Vance Hartke of Indiana, Chairman

Sen. Clifford P. Hansen of Wyoming, Ranking Minority Member

SELECT AND SPECIAL COMMITTEES OF THE SENATE

SELECT COMMITTEE ON NUTRITION AND HUMAN NEEDS

Kenneth Schlossberg, Staff Director (225–7326)

Sen. George McGovern of South Dakota, Chairman

SELECT COMMITTEE ON SMALL BUSINESS

Chester H. Smith, Staff Director & General Counsel (225–5175)

Sen. Alan Bible of Nevada, Chairman

SPECIAL COMMITTEE ON AGING

William E. Oriol, Staff Director (225–5364)

Sen. Frank Church of Idaho, Chairman

HOUSE

AGRICULTURE

Christine S. Gallagher, Chief Clerk (225–2171)

Rep. W. R. Poage of Texas, Chairman

Rep. Charles M. Teague of California, Ranking Minority Member

APPROPRIATIONS

Keith F. Mainland, Clerk & Staff Director (225–2771)

Rep. George H. Mahon of Texas, Chairman

Rep. Elford A. Cederberg of Michigan, Ranking Minority Member

ARMED SERVICES

Frank M. Slatinshek, Chief Counsel (225–4151)

Rep. F. Edward Hebert of Louisiana, Chairman

Rep. William G. Bray of Indiana, Ranking Minority Member

BANKING AND CURRENCY

Paul Nelson, Clerk & Staff Director (225–4247)

Rep. Wright Patman of Texas, Chairman

Rep. William B. Widnall of New Jersey, Ranking Minority Member

DISTRICT OF COLUMBIA

Dorothy E. Quarker, Chief of Staff (225–4457)

Rep. Charles C. Diggs, Jr., of Michigan, Chairman

Rep. Ancher Nelsen of Minnesota, Ranking Minority Member

EDUCATION AND LABOR

Donald M. Baker, Chief Clerk & Associate Counsel (225–4527)

Rep. Carl D. Perkins of Kentucky, Chairman

Rep. Albert H. Quie of Minnesota, Ranking Minority Member

FOREIGN AFFAIRS

Marian A. Czarnecki, Chief of Staff (225–5021)

Rep. Thomas E. Morgan of Pennsylvania, Chairman

Rep. William C. Mailliard of California, Ranking Minority Member

GOVERNMENT OPERATIONS

Herbert Roback, Staff Director (225–5051)

Rep. Chet Holifield of California, Chairman*

Rep. Frank Horton of New York, Ranking Minority Member

HOUSE ADMINISTRATION

John T. Walker, Staff Director (225–2061)

Rep. Wayne L. Hays of Ohio, Chairman

Rep. William L. Dickinson of Alabama, Ranking Minority Member

* Retired January 1975

INTERIOR AND INSULAR AFFAIRS

Sidney L. McFarland, Staff Director & Chief Clerk (225–2761)

Rep. James A. Haley of Florida, Chairman

Rep. John P. Saylor of Pennsylvania, Ranking Minority Member

INTERNAL SECURITY

Donald G. Sanders, Chief Counsel (225–3051)

Rep. Richard H. Ichord of Missouri, Chairman

Rep. John M. Ashbrook of Ohio, Ranking Minority Member

INTERSTATE AND FOREIGN COMMERCE

W. E. Williamson, Clerk (225–2927)

Rep. Harley O. Staggers of West Virginia, Chairman

Rep. Samuel L. Devine of Ohio, Ranking Minority Member

JUDICIARY

Jerome M. Zeifman, General Counsel (225–3951)

Rep. Peter W. Rodino, Jr., of New Jersey, Chairman

Rep. Edward Hutchinson of Michigan, Ranking Minority Member

MERCHANT MARINE AND FISHERIES

Frances P. Still, Chief Clerk (225–4047)

Rep. Leonor Kretzer Sullivan of Missouri, Chairman

Rep. James R. Grover, Jr., of New York, Ranking Minority Member

POST OFFICE AND CIVIL SERVICE

Victor C. Smiroldo, Staff Director & General Counsel (225–4057)

Rep. Thaddeus J. Dulski of New York, Chairman*

Rep. H. R. Gross of Iowa, Ranking Minority Member

PUBLIC WORKS

Richard J. Sullivan, Chief Counsel (225–4472)

Rep. John A. Blatnik of Minnesota, Chairman*

Rep. William H. Harsha of Ohio, Ranking Minority Member

RULES

Laurie C. Battle, Counsel & Staff Director (225–9486)

Rep. Ray J. Madden of Indiana, Chairman

Rep. David T. Martin of Nebraska, Ranking Minority Member

* Retired January 1975

SCIENCE AND ASTRONAUTICS

Charles F. Ducander, Executive Director & Chief Counsel (225–6371)

Rep. Olin E. Teague of Texas, Chairman

Rep. Charles A. Mosher of Ohio, Ranking Minority Member

STANDARDS OF OFFICIAL CONDUCT

John M. Swanner, Staff Director (225–7103)

Rep. Melvin Price of Illinois, Chairman

Rep. James H. Quillen of Tennessee, Ranking Minority Member

VETERANS' AFFAIRS

Oliver E. Meadows, Staff Director (225–3527)

Rep. Wm. Jennings Bryan Dorn of South Carolina, Chairman*

Rep. John P. Hammerschmidt of Arkansas, Ranking Minority Member

WAYS AND MEANS

John M. Martin, Jr., Chief Counsel (225–3625)

Rep. Wilbur D. Mills of Arkansas, Chairman

Rep. Herman T. Schneebeli of Pennsylvania, Ranking Minority Member

* Retired January 1975

SELECT AND SPECIAL COMMITTEE OF THE HOUSE

PERMANENT SELECT COMMITTEE ON SMALL BUSINESS

Howard Greenberg, Staff Director (225–5821)

Rep. Joe L. Evins of Tennessee, Chairman

CONGRESSIONAL JOINT COMMITTEES, COMMISSIONS, AND BOARDS

JOINT COMMITTEE ON
ATOMIC ENERGY

Edward J. Bauser, Executive Director (225–8267)
Rep. Melvin Price of Illinois, Chairman
Sen. John O. Pastore of Rhode Island, Vice Chairman

JOINT COMMITTEE ON
DEFENSE PRODUCTION

Harold J. Warren, Staff Director & Counsel (225–2337)
Sen. John Sparkman of Alabama, Chairman
Rep. Wright Patman of Texas, Vice Chairman

JOINT COMMITTEE ON
INTERNAL REVENUE TAXATION

Laurence N. Woodworth, Chief of Staff (225–3621)
Rep. Wilbur D. Mills of Arkansas, Chairman
Sen. Russell B. Long of Louisiana, Vice Chairman

JOINT ECONOMIC COMMITTEE

John R. Stark, Executive Director (225–5171)
Rep. Wright Patman of Texas, Chairman
Sen. William Proxmire, Vice Chairman

THE EXECUTIVE BRANCH—
FROM THE
WHITE HOUSE DOWN

This book is addressed to two questions: how does the businessman protect his interests in the executive and legislative
branches, with respect to the legislation and administrative rulings that affect him; and secondly, how does the businessman
make intelligent use of the federal services that are available
to him?

Two areas of federal government operation are either excluded or only lightly touched on in this book. The first is
the whole question of the vendor relationship to the federal
government. It will be referred to many times, but this is not a
handbook on how to sell to the federal government, or how to
administer government contracts. That is a highly technical subject that does not come within the scope of this volume.

Secondly, the intricacies of the legal relationships between
the businessman and the major regulatory bodies of government, such as the Interstate Commerce Commission, the Federal Communications Commission, the Securities and Exchange
Commission, and others, are not covered. These relationships
are governed by a large body of law, in the practice of which
many men spend whole lifetimes. Extensive literature exists in

these fields and a great number of fine professionals are available to interpret and apply it.

The bulk of this volume is devoted to exploring, from a businessman's point of view, the executive branch of government, which is made up of eleven departments and dozens of independent agencies, all reporting to the president. The departments (in the order of their establishment but not necessarily of their importance to business) are the Department of State; the Department of the Treasury; the Department of Defense; the Department of Justice; the Department of the Interior; the Department of Agriculture; the Department of Commerce; the Department of Labor; the Department of Health, Education and Welfare; the Department of Housing and Urban Development; and the Department of Transportation. The independent agencies include the Federal Trade Commission, the Small Business Administration, and many others.

Typical Department Structure

The structure of the typical department is a pyramid. At the top is, of course, a secretary, appointed by the President with the advice and consent of the Senate. Under the secretary there is a deputy secretary or undersecretary and often additional undersecretaries for especially important functions that fall within the department. In addition, there are three or more assistant secretaries in each of the government departments. The assistant secretaries have specific areas of responsibility, some in substantive fields and others in such areas as administration, which involves budgeting, personnel, internal management, etc.

The concept of responsibility is much like that in the army—it goes up to the top man, and the whole departmental structure is organized to function in the name of, and through the authority of, the cabinet officer. This also means, in a sense, it functions to protect that cabinet officer. This should always be kept in mind.

Specific operational responsibility in a department usually falls to a bureau or office. This is headed by a chief or a director, sometimes a presidential appointee, sometimes not.

The cabinet officer's legal powers are usually delegated by him to a specific undersecretary, assistant secretary, or bureau or office chief. These delegations are published in departmental orders and are reflected in the department's organization chart.

By and large, it is more effective to deal at the lowest possible level in government. If you have a problem involving hog bristles, the best thing to do is try to go directly to the man most concerned with hog bristles in the Department of Agriculture. If you cannot get your problem solved by the specialist, then you can go to the next higher level and eventually, if necessary, to the cabinet officer.

If, however, you don't know who the right person to go to is, then by all means write to the cabinet officer himself. The department's correspondence control operation will automatically route it to the specific person most concerned.

In dealing with the executive branch of government, two delicate areas of bureaucratic jealousy should be kept in mind.

Within any given department, the career employees at bureau level are likely to be conducting a kind of undeclared guerrilla warfare against the political appointees in the central office. This is particularly true in operations of a technical nature, where the experts tend to resent any interference from persons not specialists in their field. No specific advice can be given the businessman that will cover all such situations. He will have to play it by ear, keeping his radar out for any signals of ruffled egos.

In addition, he must tread carefully in the thicket of overlapping responsibilities between government departments. As will be seen in succeeding chapters, State, Commerce, the Tariff Commission, and the White House interlock for foreign trade matters; Treasury, Federal Reserve, and Federal Deposit Insurance Corporation all get involved in banking questions, and there are many other instances of agencies crisscrossing. The best rule probably is to touch all bases, making sure that every agency concerned is fully informed but not getting drawn into any bureaucratic infighting.

When contemplating a visit to Washington, or when planning to write to Washington, it is often advisable and highly useful to get an introduction to the right agency in government through your congressman or senator. This has two specific uses.

First, the sophisticated background of the congressman or senator will insure that you are directed to the proper person. His office knows how the system works.

Second, fundamental courtesy exists between the executive and legislative branches. The executive does everything possible to accommodate the legislative branch. The people downtown don't want to appear inefficient, uncooperative, unresponsive to a referral from Capitol Hill by a representative or senator, or even by a member of a congressional staff.

A warning, however: One should not use a referral from a representative or senator as any kind of "club" or pressure on people at any level of an executive department! This would be highly resented; it is not needed and will do you very little good.

In many cases the department or agency with which you are concerned has field offices. You will find it less tedious, less expensive, and possibly more effective to initiate an inquiry through a local field office. This has several virtues. It means that you can usually—for a ten-cent phone call—talk to the key person yourself, or even pay him a visit. In some cases the field man will actually come to your office to visit you. It also means that you have an expert in the utilization of government services working on your behalf to get the answer to your question. If the man in the field office doesn't know, the odds are that he knows who does, and this is a mighty helpful asset. Of course, there will be situations in which you are seeking help that is not within the scope of the field office. In such cases, you must go to the seat of responsibility or authority. Most often that is Washington.

It is wise to try to set up an appointment before you go to Washington. Someone will see you in any case, but if you arrive unexpectedly when the right man is testifying before a congressional committee, some foreign teams of negotiators are in town, and several other crises have descended simultaneously, you may be shunted off to a man with only a peripheral interest in, or a limited knowledge of, your particular problem. It's best to try to have an appointment made before you actually go to Washington. This can be done by letter. It can be done by telephone. It can be done by talking to your congressman's office and asking him to set it up for you.

When you are in Washington for any reason, it's usually a good idea to pay your respects to your congressman. This, again, is part of building a fundamental communications program. Even if you don't have any problems with which you need help, it's good to stop in, introduce yourself—make yourself known. Furthermore, as you build relationships in the executive branch, the same thing should be done. If you happen to have some business with an official at the Department of Labor and you also know a man in the Department of Commerce who is interested in your business—the two departments are just across the street from each other—stop over, say hello, and bring the man up to date on how your business is doing, what your current problems are. Find out from him what policies are under discussion in the government that might affect your own operation.

There are some very simple rules of the road, most of which involve normal courtesy and normal business practice, which you shouldn't forget in dealing with a federal agency. First, remember to thank people. If a man helps you, be sure to write him a letter of thanks. This happens much too seldom. If you are one of the few who are that thoughtful, you will be remembered. Another suggestion is to ask questions; probe; find out what is new; ask for advice. Another is to make sure not to threaten. Don't let a man feel that you are trying to push him

around. Don't tell him that "he'll read about this in the newspapers." Don't tell him that the president of your bank is a good
friend of the secretary. Don't tell him that you'll "blow the lid
off of this thing." Don't imply that some congressmen will be
investigating him. Finally, don't use him as only a foul-weather
friend. Make sure to stay in touch with your government's
sources of help and information when you don't need them as
well as when you do.

The White House

To the businessman who wants to know, "How shall I take
my problem to the White House?" the best advice is, "Don't!"

This blunt statement is based not on any lack of sympathy at
1600 Pennsylvania Avenue for the concerns of business, but on
some simple arithmetic.

When the mail bags are emptied at the White House on an
average day, more than five thousand letters spill forth. Divide
this number by sixty-five—the number of staff members engaged
primarily in handling correspondence—and it is easily seen that
most letters must be disposed of by wholesale processes.

The basic technique used to avoid drowning in a white sea of
mail is referral. Sitting on top of the government pyramid, the
White House staff is able to multiply its capacity a thousand-
fold by calling on experts in the appropriate department or
agency to handle public inquiries directed to the President.

Suppose a businessman wishes to register his suggestions
about taxes. If he writes the President, there is an off chance
the letter will reach our fantastically overburdened head of state.
It might get to him as part of a small random sample designed
to keep him in touch with public opinion, or because a White
House staff member detects something in it of special interest
to the President.

What is far more likely, however, is that the letter will, after perhaps a week in the White House paper mill, be sent to the Treasury Department. There an answer will be prepared either for signature by a Treasury official or, in a few cases, as a draft for consideration by the President.

In most cases, therefore, it will save time and be just as effective to write to the government department that handles the particular subject matter. A few exceptions to this general rule can be stated:

1. Where the topic crosses department lines. For example, if a businessman wishes to serve the government in an advisory capacity, and is not certain if he might be most useful in State, Commerce, or Treasury, or perhaps on a presidentially appointed committee, he should volunteer to the White House. His application will be carefully reviewed by a member of the staff specializing in personnel matters. Where the businessman is willing to accept full-time government employment at or just below the head-of-agency level, he should apply to the White House; lower-echelon jobs are handled by the Civil Service Commission and agency personnel offices.

2. Where political considerations may be important. Suppose a new federal installation is being contemplated for an area, but the city where it will be located is an open question. In this case, the businessman who wishes to make his views count should write to his congressman. That gentleman will see that they are brought to the attention of the White House congressional liaison staff, and to the executive department working on the project.

3. Where no satisfaction has been obtained from the department concerned. The White House is then available on an appellate basis. The businessman should report to the President what the department has done on his case, and why he thinks a different course of action is justified. Of course the President, at his discretion, may solicit the views of the department, and then weigh both sides.

4. When a presidential message is desired, as to an associa-

tion convention. Such a request is best made about two months ahead. A proposed draft may be sent, but in any case, complete background on the group should be provided. Ordinarily, only broad public service groups, as opposed to individual companies, rate presidential messages.

In writing to the president, the basic rules for good correspondence become especially important. A letter that is clear and to the point will be gratefully received and more expeditiously handled by the busy people at the White House than one that rambles vaguely over the whole spectrum of public affairs. When it is really necessary to take up several distinct subjects, do it in separate letters. This will speed up the reply by making possible simultaneous handling by different staff specialists or departments.

Of course, the Executive Office of the President is far more than a glorified correspondence section, important as that function may be to a businessman in Seattle seeking to communicate with the chief executive across the width of the United States. It includes several policy-making groups of great significance to businessmen, notably the Council of Economic Advisers and the Office of the Special Representative for Trade Negotiations.

For the most part, these units serve as advisers to the president, and as his liaison and coordinating representatives with government agencies. Only rarely, therefore, will the businessman have occasion to deal with them directly. Since the policy areas in which they operate are of such concern to business, however, he will want to know something about their role. If he has a suggestion of substance in their fields, it is worthwhile to address it to them. They also may provide alternate forums on broad policy questions when an impasse is reached with regular operating agencies.

The Council of Economic Advisers consists of three members, almost invariably drawn from the academic world, who advise the president on major trends in the national economy. They draft the annual Economic Report, which is an authoritative statement of administration views, and public monthly reports which are early indicators of business trends. Titled "Economic Indicators," these are available from the Government Printing Office at $6.50 a year. Theirs is a key voice when decisions are made on such matters as wage and price controls to curb inflation, or the effect on the economy of energy conservation measures. The Treasury and Commerce departments, of course, also participate in such policy discussions, and are somewhat more accessible to businessmen who wish to make their views known.

Council of Economic Advisers,
Executive Office Bldg.,
Washington, D.C. 20506
(202) 395-5034

The President's Special Representative for Trade Negotiations directs United States participation in trade negotiations with other countries. Businessmen with a stake in such matters should first see that he is aware of their situation. This may be done either through testimony by their trade groups at formal hearings, or by direct individual communication. The Commerce Department is in close touch with this White House unit, and may provide another avenue of approach.

Office of the Special Representative for Trade Negotiations
1800 G St. N.W.
Washington, D.C. 20506
(202) 395-3395

For businessmen with a stake in communications matters, the Office of Telecommunications Policy can be significant. It develops proposals for legislation and regulatory policy affecting all segments of the communications industry, including those involving new technologies such as satellites and cable television. It has two advisory bodies drawn from the private sector—the Frequency Management Advisory Council, and the Electromagnetic Radiation Management Advisory Council.

Office of Telecommunications Policy
1800 G St. N.W.
Washington, D.C. 20504
(202) 395-5800

A newly established arm of the Executive Office with potentially enormous impact on all business is the Federal Energy Office. It will allocate and regulate the prices of petroleum products for industrial use, heating, and transportation.

These far-reaching functions will be carried out through both Washington and regional offices. Businessmen wishing to comment on the effects of energy regulations should address communications to:

Executive Secretariat
Federal Energy Administration
Washington, D.C. 20461
(202) 395-3538

Great powers are wielded by the other groups in the Executive Office, but there will be few occasions for the businessman to deal with them. The Office of Management and Budget (OMB) indirectly affects business through its control of government activities and spending. One of its functions is to review questionnaires that government agencies wish to send to business, and to decide whether they are burdensome or duplicate information otherwise available. For help in making such decisions, it has a Business Advisory Council on Federal Reports. An OMB publication that can be useful to businessmen is *Cata-*

log of Federal Domestic Assistance, $7. GPO plus $2.50 for binder.

Office of Management and Budget
Executive Office Bldg.
Washington, D.C. 20503
(202) 395-4790

The Councils

Three bodies, functioning as advisers to the President and coordinators of government policy on matters affecting business, should be known to businessmen. They are the Domestic Council, the Council on Economic Policy, and the Council on International Economic Policy.

Also in the Executive Office is the National Security Council, and under its direction, the Central Intelligence Agency (CIA). Information on foreign trade, along with many other types of data, is grist for the CIA mill.

As far as the immediate staff of the President is concerned, each chief executive organizes that to suit his own style, and changes it to meet his changing needs. Persons with direct access to the President's counselors and special assistants are likely to have minimal need for this book.

To others, we recommend close study of the chapters that follow. They will provide a road map to the departments and agencies where businessmen can find solutions to most of their governmental problems—and often bonuses of help they may not have realized existed.

The
Departments

AGRICULTURE AND ITS
BUSINESS BY-PRODUCTS

The $9.6 billion annual budget of the U.S. Department of Agriculture (USDA) helps businessmen as well as farmers.

In each of the department's five major areas of activity—rural development; conservation, research and education; marketing and consumer services; international affairs and commodity programs; agricultural economics—businessmen can find sources of assistance. Some examples:

- Extensive technical research by USDA laboratories yields many new products and processes with commercial potential.
- The wealth of marketing information compiled by the department is valuable to those who deal not only in farm commodities, but also their end-products, such as food, clothing, and furniture.
- The department aggressively assists business by selling United States agricultural produce overseas.
- Its soil conservation activities produce business for vendors of conservation materials and services, aid developers of income-producing recreational enterprises, and provide money-saving information for builders.
- Its price support programs help not only growers, but also the

businessmen who store, ship, lend money on, and buy price-supported agricultural commodities.
- The department's forest activities are important to the lumber and related industries.
- Through loans and other assistance, it brings electric and telephone service to businesses in rural areas, and helps establish new business and industry.

Rural Development

As urban environmental problems increase, the already rapid growth of nonfarm population in nonmetropolitan areas—19.3 percent during the 1960s compared to 13.3 percent for total U.S. population growth—may accelerate. Congress has given the Department of Agriculture new tasks in rural development, although most of these will be carried out by previously existing agencies, such as the Farmers Home Administration.

Of special interest to businessmen is authorization to make "Rural Enterprise" and "Rural Industrialization Assistance" loans. The former are to help establish small businesses in communities not larger than fifty thousand and to finance their operating expenses. The latter are to help develop industries that will provide employment in such communities.

Other community programs of the Farmers Home Administration involve loans to public agencies and nonprofit corporations which may contract with business for services and supplies aggregating hundreds of millions of dollars. Such loans may be for water and waste disposal systems, flood control dams, irrigation canals, and other necessary community facilities.

Further information can be obtained from one of the agency's 1700 field offices, or: Assistant Administrator, Room 5013 South Agriculture, 14th & Independence, N.W., Washington, D.C. 20250 (202) 447-5243.

Farmers Home Administration also may be a loan source for builders of rental housing in rural areas. In a recent three-year period it financed nearly twelve thousand such units, more than 40 percent of them for occupancy by persons sixty and over.

The building industry may benefit from other rural housing loan programs, all of which, including the rental housing, are limited to towns of up to ten thousand people. They include loans for individual homeownership, repair and rehabilitation, disaster housing, farm labor housing, and conditional commitments to builders to encourage quantity buildings in rural areas.

For information on rural housing, the telephone number is (202) 447-5177, the address the same as above.

A third important category comprises loans to farmers for buying equipment, fertilizer, seed, feed, and other products supplied by business for developing recreation enterprises such as camps, and other purposes.

The source of information on these farmer programs is: Assistant Administrator, 5019 South Agriculture, 14th Street, and Independence Avenue, N.W., Washington, D.C. 20250, (202) 447-4597.

The Rural Electrification Administration (REA) lends money and provides engineering advice and management assistance to private companies, public agencies, and locally owned cooperatives for the purpose of introducing or extending electric or telephone service to rural areas. REA has loaned more than $10 billion, all of which has purchased materials, equipment, and services from business enterprises. The REA-financed electric and telephone systems serve not only farmers and other rural homeowners, but some 425,000 industrial and commercial users of these services as well.

Wholesale purchases of power by REA borrowers yield more than $250 million a year to private electric companies. The market for electrical appliances and equipment in areas served by the 1,092 REA-financed electric systems is estimated at about $1.5 billion a year.

More than 630 independent telephone companies and 240

telephone cooperatives use REA loans to bring modern dial service to more than 2.8 million subscribers; of these, 11 percent are business establishments.

Although organizationally in another area of the department (Conservation–Research–Education), the Extension Service also plays a role in rural development. It works with state and local groups in attracting new industry. For example, the Louisiana Extension Service conducted a statewide survey of vacant buildings suitable for industrial use. Local committees were formed, and brought seven new industries to local areas within a year.

Technical Research

The Agricultural Research Service (ARS) provides service to industry by assisting in adapting research results to commercial production, processing, and utilization of agricultural products.

Although utilization research conducted by USDA at five regional laboratories is motivated primarily by a desire to find new and expanded uses for farm products, outlets for these discoveries are almost entirely through industrial channels:

1. Any person or firm who wishes to use a USDA-developed process may do so by applying to the Secretary of Agriculture for a royalty-free license. About forty public patents have been issued on cotton-ginning developments alone. For lists of available patents, and other materials on research, write Information Division, Agricultural Research Service, Hyattsville, Maryland 20782.

2. The laboratories hold periodic conferences at which technical representatives of industry are invited for discussions of progress in research of special interest to them.

3. The laboratories welcome visits from technical representatives of industry who wish to consult with them and see experimental processes and products under development. The laboratories are located at Philadelphia, Pennsylvania; New Orleans,

Louisiana; Peoria, Illinois; Athens, Georgia; and Albany, California. Some five thousand persons avail themselves of this consulting service each year.

4. Each laboratory has an assistant director whose sole responsibility is acquainting industry personnel with new developments and working with them in plans for commercialization.

5. The laboratories assist industrial plants in the use of ARS-developed processes.

There are many examples of department research serving industry. The process for manufacturing frozen orange-juice concentrate, developed in cooperation with the Florida Citrus Commission, was commercialized quickly, and today about three-fourths of Florida oranges produced are processed into frozen concentrate. More recently, department scientists developed a process for making powdered citrus juices.

Several years ago the frozen food industry requested research help in getting higher quality frozen foods to consumers. The laboratory at Albany, California, responded to this request and developed information on where, how, and how much quality damage occurs in frozen food during processing, storage, handling, and transportation, as well as practical means to avoid such damage. This information was used throughout the industry and is reflected in today's high-quality frozen foods.

Other research developments include durable-press treatments for cotton fabrics for easy-care garments, shrink-proofing treatments that make wool fabrics launderable, starch derivatives used as paper additives for improved wet and dry strength, and anti-spoiling agents from linseed oil that increase concrete highways' resistance to freeze-thaw deterioration.

Current research deals with treatments to make cotton fabrics flame-resistant; new processes for making vegetable protein concentrates; development of new chemicals from starch for paper industries; technology for food processing which minimizes waste formation and reduces environmental pollution; and conversion of animal fats to detergents.

In machinery research and development the department

develops prototype models and welcomes industry representatives for consultations and inspection of experimental equipment.

Much of the *marketing* research work, from early projects on the development of the checkout counter for retail food stores to studies of irradiation as a possible means of prolonging shelf life of fresh fruits and vegetables, has been and continues to be of great value to the food and fiber industries.

Included are research to improve packaging and loading of agricultural products; to improve transportation equipment, methods, and practices; to appraise relative advantages of prepacking at shipping point, during processing, or at wholesale or retail markets; to improve locations, equipment, work methods, and plant layout for various types of marketing facilities; and to recommend more efficient and economical business and accounting procedures. ARS has guided the planning of new wholesale centers and transportation methods for more than thirty-five cities.

Research in *market quality* is directed toward the maintenance, protection, and improvement of food quality by solving chemical, physiological, pathological, and entomological problems often encountered as farm products move through marketing channels. The aim is to get the food to the consumer in better condition while at the same time reducing the heavy spoilage losses that often occur during storage, transit, and distribution.

In recent market quality research, phosphine was found to be an effective fumigant for packaged processed foods, and a tolerance level was established for its use; insect-resistant multiwall paper bags have been developed which kept a milled cereal product free of insect infestation in a commercial shipping test (U.S. to Brazil); peaches and nectarines, stored in controlled atmospheres (1 percent oxygen and 5 percent carbon dioxide), show less decay and ripen slower (normal storage life is doubled); an instrument that uses sound waves to sort fresh fruits and vegetables for ripeness and internal defects was developed.

In *transportation* research ARS developments include a van container with an improved refrigeration system for shipping perishable agricultural products by tractor-trailer on rail flatcars (piggyback), and by ship for overseas shipments. New export markets have been opened as a result of improved transportation techniques.

Recent ARS *soil and water conservation* research includes development of a drainage plow, a machine for installing subsurface drainage or tile drainage. This machine makes it possible to plow a drain tube into the ground without having to excavate a trench. It can plow to a depth of six feet and can handle a plastic drain tube up to six inches in diameter.

Another practical application of ARS research in this field is a rain trap, now being distributed commercially, consisting of a butyl rubber mat and a waterproof storage bag; the trap provides water for livestock.

A third development is a low-cost sealing agent that can be sprayed on concrete walls of irrigation canals to reduce seepage.

Recent *livestock and veterinary* research includes the development of a vaccine to combat Marek's disease, which costs the U.S. poultry industry about $200 million a year; demonstration that cattle can be raised on diets without any protein, permitting the release of millions of tons of traditional protein supplements—soybean, linseed, and cottonseed oil meals—for human and animal use.

Forty years ago a two-year trip by two plant explorers to Asia cost American taxpayers $50,000, but the soybean types they brought back helped establish a new crop now worth more than $2.5 billion a year to growers. The soybean story is dramatic, but not unique. Not a single major food or fiber plant grown in the United States today originated on the North American continent.

Another important research area in the plant sciences is that of finding and developing disease-resistant varieties. The estimated total cost of research by federal, state, and private companies to develop varieties of wheat, corn, and alfalfa resistant to four highly destructive insects was about $9.3 million. The annual savings in reduced losses has been estimated at $308 million.

Foreshadowing a possible business in the space age, four ARS experiments have been carried on an earth satellite. These tests distinguished kinds of vegetation, detected insect infestations, monitored effectiveness of wind-erosion control, and located potential water supplies.

Of interest to the pharmaceutical industry is the ARS collection of nearly seventeen thousand living species and strains of bacteria, molds, and yeasts. From the storehouse at Peoria, Illinois—largest of its kind in the world—scientists develop new and improved processes for production of antibiotics, vitamins, enzymes, etc.

In addition to the department's own research activities, its *Cooperative State Research Service* helps fund extensive programs at state experiment stations and colleges. Information is primarily released through these participating institutions. The Washington contact is Dr. Roy Lovvorn, Room 313-A, Administration Building, 14th & Independence N.W., Washington, D.C. 20250, (202) 447-4423.

For businessmen with special agriculture-related research problems, a visit to the *National Agricultural Library* may be worthwhile. Its collection of more than 1.5 million volumes is the largest of its kind in the United States. It is located fifteen miles northeast of Washington at Beltsville, Maryland 20705, (202) 344-3759.

Take Some Wooden Money

Rights to cut as much as $400 million of national forest timber a year are bought by the United States lumber industry from the Forest Service.

Timber sales are administered by a field organization with

local offices throughout the country. Sales are advertised in newspapers and by direct mail to mills and logging companies, and "show me" trips of the area to be cut are sometimes arranged.

Sales are offered to prospective purchasers on a competitive basis. Sale sizes are designed to meet the needs of dependent purchasers. A small business set-aside program seeks to ensure that small business firms are able to purchase a fair share of the annual sale offerings. Occasionally, long-term timber sales are made to establish a new industry in a particular area.

The Forest Service encourages development of forest-based industries in rural areas. Its booklets, *Forest Industry Opportunities in Rural Development* (AIB-222, free, USDA), *Special Forest Products for Profit* (AIB-278, 45¢, GPO), and *Forests in Rural Areas Development* (PA-494), offer practical, case-history–type information on a variety of businesses that have been successfully launched in recent years. Through the Forest Products Utilization Program, technical advice is provided to loggers and wood processors by state and forest service technologists. Such assistance deals mainly with primary processing (log breakdown), but also covers the range from charcoal-making to manufacture of wooden toys. A free pamphlet entitled *Forest Products Utilization and Marketing Assistance for Woodland Owners, Loggers, and Processors* (PA-752) describes the service in more detail. While it notes that technical assistance for such enterprises can be obtained most readily from state forestry agencies, the Forest Service has specialists available in Juneau, Alaska; San Francisco; Upper Darby, Pennsylvania; Ogden, Utah; Missoula, Montana; Denver; Atlanta; Albuquerque; and Portland, Oregon.

Private capital can develop recreation projects in national forests under special-use permits. Fees for such projects are usually based on a percentage of receipts. Most opportunities are made available through a bidding procedure, with awards made on the basis of service to the public, financial ability, and experience. More than 180 ski resorts have been set up in this way. Some 1,800 concessioners operate hotels, motels, trailer sites, restaurants, stores, and gasoline stations. The nearest USDA Forest Service office will provide help in determining feasibility of recreation projects in national forests and guidance in planning the project if it appears promising.

Special-use permits and easements are issued in the national forests and national grasslands for radio and television transmission sites, utility rights of way, pipelines, etc. Jurisdiction over oil, gas, and mineral developments is split between the Forest Service and Interior's Bureau of Land Management.

In addition to its management of government-owned resources, the Forest Service assists private groups and individuals in the forestry field through its division of State and Private Forestry. It publishes material such as *Tree Planters Notes*, a quarterly periodical, and *Seed and Planting Stock Dealers*, a directory of dealers in seed and planting stock, and the common trees and shrubs they offer.

Research with important industrial applications in the forest products industries comes out of Forest Service facilities, including eight Forest and Range Experiment Stations and the Forest Products Laboratory at Madison, Wisconsin. The experiment stations conduct studies on the full range of forestry activities such as forest fire control, tree genetics, wildlife habitat improvement, range management, forest pest control, strip-mine revegetation, timber stand improvement, watershed protection, and recreation. Research on forest products is conducted at the Forest Products Laboratory as well as at several experiment stations. This research has resulted in improved pulping processes, better saws and sawing practices, more durable and efficient construction systems, and reduction of wood harvesting and processing wastes. Recycling of wood and paper products is being advanced.

Research information may be obtained by writing or visiting the experiment stations or the Forest Products Laboratory. For a pamphlet on forest products research activities, write: Director, Forest Products Laboratory, USDA, Madison, Wisconsin 53705.

Ecology-minded corporations can do some image-building through the Forest Service's Cooperative Outdoor Environmental Program. Hunt-Wesson Co., for example, deposits money with the Forest Service for each of its product labels returned by purchasers. The Forest Service uses the money for planting in National Children's Forests.

Conservation Aids Construction

The technical assistance furnished by the Soil Conservation Service (SCS) is proving to be of increasing assistance to businessmen, especially those involved in some phase of construction activity. Assistance is available locally through over three thousand soil and water conservation districts, which are units of state government receiving aid from federal technical experts.

To date, SCS has published *soil surveys* covering more than one-half of the United States. Proper use of soil surveys and the advice of soil specialists have helped many contractors and engineers to avoid the wet basements, cracked walls, disintegrating roads, malfunctioning septic systems, ragged lawns, and other construction woes that often result when adverse soil properties are not recognized in advance.

One beneficiary was Roy C. Anderson, developer of Long Grove County Club Estates in Long Grove, Illinois. After studying an SCS soil survey map, Mr. Anderson had his architect completely revise the development plans—relocating roads, golf course fairways, and building sites. "Without the soil information," said Mr. Anderson, "it is altogether possible that the future 'dream homes' of some folks might have been turned into nightmares."

Development of *small watershed projects*, under SCS federal leadership, contributes greatly to upstream flood prevention, to providing added municipal and industrial water supplies, and to increasing local opportunities for outdoor recreation. In 1973 small watershed projects created sixty-five hundred new jobs and helped more than three hundred businesses begin or expand.

Added supplies of water for municipal or industrial use are part of ninety-one completed flood-control and small watershed projects that serve more than half a million people. The Mountain Run watershed project in Virginia, for example, adds a billion gallons of water to the municipal water supply of the town of Culpeper. This has attracted a number of new industries, has meant expansion of some industries previously in the town, and has been a factor in helping the town to more than double its growth.

Readily available outdoor recreation facilities make a community a more desirable place in which to live and work, and are a factor in keeping employee morale high. Lake Tobesofkee, in the Tobesofkee Creek Watershed Project near Macon, Georgia, has over 300,000 visitors a year, and is the permanent location of a Boy Scout camp. Opened in 1969, it has stimulated the development of eight sporting goods stores in the area. Moreover, the lake provides over thirty-five hundred acre-feet of water storage for industrial expansion in Bibb County.

River basin surveys and investigations provide an analysis of water and related land resources in an area. Businessmen can use these studies and reports to avoid building in areas where lack of needed resources or serious soil and water problems could cause adverse impacts on business. Over eighty river basin studies have been completed.

Flood hazard analyses identify flood-prone areas and define flood frequencies. They can be used to avoid locating businesses in areas where serious flood damages and related disruptions are likely to occur. Information on these studies can be obtained from state water resource agencies or the state conservationist, Soil Conservation Service, for the particular state.

Water supply forecasts, made primarily on the basis of *snow surveys* arranged by SCS, are used by many businessmen in the western states in preparing seasonal operating plans.

The 123 *Resource Conservation and Development Projects* (RC&D) now underway or being planned have helped to establish or enlarge approximately three hundred industries across America. Technical and financial assistance is provided from many sources, but the federal leadership comes from SCS. Included in the projects is assistance to community conservation improvements such as erosion and sediment control, flood prevention, public water-based recreation, and fish and wildlife habitat development.

An example is the Pence Springs flood prevention measure in the Mountain–Dominion RC&D Project in Summers County, West Virginia. Before 1966, there were no manufacturing jobs in the county. Then a factory was built, but its first two tenants were flooded out of business. Now, due to efforts of the Mountain–Dominion RC&D Project sponsors and others, a dike more than a quarter-mile long surrounds the factory, protecting it from floodwaters of the Greenbrier River. Nearly one hundred local people are at work inside making men's and boys' clothing.

Sponsors of the Little Kanawha RC&D in West Virginia wanted a new seventy-acre lake for flood protection—but ended up with a great deal more. The previous water source was polluted and unreliable. Today, the excellent new water supply, directly or indirectly, has produced the following results: A local company dependent on good water supplies has doubled its original size; another new business dependent upon water will arrive soon and employ 350 more local workers; the small town of Spencer (where six new businesses have located since the project began) will expand its water services to outlying districts; a seventy-unit housing development for elderly and low-income people can now be finished, and a recreation area is planned around the lake.

Marketing and Consumer Services

Nationally uniform standards of quality, developed and issued by USDA's Agricultural Marketing Service (AMS) for all major farm products, are the basis for much of the trade in these products across the nation. They provide the language for trade. And they are basic to the other AMS marketing services —grading and market news. These standards are the tools of the voluntary federal–state grading services which provide official, impartial certification of quality. Official grade certificates are accepted in court as prima facie evidence of quality. The standards are also the basis for federal–state market news reports—the market intelligence that helps producers, wholesalers, and others decide where and when to market or buy products, thus keeping products flowing to the right place at the right time, avoiding unnecessary and costly gluts and shortages.

These services—standards of quality, grading, and market news—are provided for livestock, meats, wool, cotton, grain and related commodities such as dry peas and beans, dairy products, poultry and eggs, tobacco, and both fresh and processed fruits and vegetables.

Services provided by the AMS Livestock Division are typical. They include providing market reporting for livestock, meat, and wool; the grading of meat; formulation of quality standards for livestock, meats, and wool; and the purchasing of meat and livestock products for school lunch use or surplus removal.

Special services for industry include examination of lots of meat from specific shipments to help the buyer, seller, or trucker settle any controversy in connection with the freshness of the product or possible damage suffered in transit. This service is requested mostly by trucking companies.

Another is the meat acceptance service, which involves the selection and stamping of meats and meat products by federal meat graders using specifications set up in cooperation with industry representatives. Private organizations such as hospitals and airlines use this service and find it advantageous.

Marketing orders and agreements enable farmers to develop programs, with help from the Agricultural Marketing Service, to regulate the marketing of their commodities in a more orderly manner. Marketing orders have been established for milk, fruits, vegetables, and certain specialty crops. Marketing regulations are issued by the Secretary of Agriculture in cooperation with producers and handlers. Many of the programs include advertising and promotion.

Agricultural Marketing Service transportation specialists work closely with farmers, shippers, farm organizations, and other federal and state government agencies in negotiating equitable transportation rates and services through carrier bureaus. When necessary, AMS files petitions or complaints and testifies in formal proceedings before state and federal agencies which regulate transportation.

The Packers and Stockyards Act, administered by the Packers and Stockyards Administration, fosters fair and open competition in the marketing of livestock, poultry, and meat. Industry businessmen are protected against those who engage in unfair, deceptive, discriminatory, or monopolistic practices. Livestock dealers, market agencies, poultry handlers, and packers are required to keep full and accurate records, provide prompt and accurate accounting, and file reports with USDA. Public livestock markets are required to provide reasonable services and facilities at rates that are fair and nondiscriminatory. Violators of the act are subject to cease-and-desist orders, suspension of registrations, or civil or criminal court actions which may bar them from doing business.

The Packers and Stockyards Administration also provides assistance to the industry in problem areas, such as helping stockyard operators prevent and control pollution through improved design.

The Federal Seed Act, administered by the Agricultural Marketing Service, regulates the labeling and advertising of agricultural and vegetable seeds in interstate commerce. The act provides minimum standards for imported seed, but has no requirements on exported seed. Through cooperative arrangements with the states, AMS receives suspected violations for investigation and action. Where mislabeling is suspected, seed samples are analyzed in one of four federal seed laboratories, and criminal prosecution or civil action may be brought if violations are found.

Under the Perishable Agricultural Commodities Act, administered by the Agricultural Marketing Service, more than seventeen thousand fruit and vegetable brokers, commission merchants, and dealers are licensed. AMS specialists handle complaints of unfair practices in marketing of fresh and frozen fruits and vegetables, and attempt to arrange informal settlements of disputes. Formal complaints can lead to a reparation award, which—if not paid by the person who caused injury—can result in temporary loss of his license.

"Patent-like" protection is offered under the relatively new (1970) Plant Variety Protection Act to breeders of plants reproduced through seeds. Developers of new varieties of plants such as soybeans, cotton, corn, and ornamental crops can apply to AMS for certificates of protection. AMS examiners determine if the variety actually is novel and entitled to protection. The certificate holder can use the courts to protect his "invention" from being multiplied and sold by others. Information on obtaining protection under the act may be obtained by calling or writing the Plant Variety Protection Office, Grain Division, Agricultural Marketing Service, U.S. Department of Agriculture, 6525 Belcrest Road, Hyattsville, Maryland 20782, (301) 436-8547. A quarterly *Official Journal*—listing applications received, certificates issued, variety descriptions, and related information—is sent free on request.

Has a processor refused to deal with a farmer because he is a member of a producer's association? If so, the farmer can file a complaint with AMS under the Agricultural Fair Practices Act of 1968. It prohibits handlers (except of cotton and tobacco) from coercing, intimidating, or discriminating against farmers because they belong to a producer's association. Farmers whose rights are violated in this respect can get AMS help in asking the federal courts to restrain handlers from such unlawful practices.

Leaflets giving more details on these four regulatory programs are available from the Information Division, Agricultural Marketing Service, U.S. Department of Agriculture, Washington, D.C. 20250.

Purely on a voluntary basis, operators of public warehouses for storage of staples and nonperishables may obtain AMS licenses. More than seventeen hundred warehouses, with a capacity of $7 billion worth of products, are so licensed. The license is a business asset, since it means that receipts issued by the holder for stored products are readily negotiable.

Grain shipped by grade in foreign commerce must be inspected by a state or commercial grain inspector licensed by AMS. An export inspection certificate issued by such an inspector is like money in the bank to the exporter, who gets paid on the basis of this quality certificate.

To assist, as needed, in maintaining an orderly flow of food commodities through regular marketing channels, USDA's Agricultural Marketing Service promotes increased use of those commodities that are temporarily in heavy supply. Communications media and appropriate segments of the food trades, such as retailers and institutional users, are encouraged by AMS to use and direct consumers' attention to those foods which afford especially good consumer value because of greater than usual supplies. When supply situations warrant it, fact sheets on these abundant foods are issued for food industry representatives, and print and broadcast materials are distributed to the communications media.

The National School Lunch Program, which provides food and funds to get lunches served in all the nation's schools, is a growing market for institutional jobbers, wholesalers, and retailers. Annually, more than $1.6 billion worth of food is used in these lunches, with more than 80 percent purchased locally by the schools. School breakfast, milk, and other Child Nutrition Programs broaden the market further. These programs and other institutional uses of department-donated foods offer opportunities for processing contracts, e.g., to make pizza shells from flour and shortening. These contracts are described in *Contracts for Processing Donated Foods—Facts You Want to Know* (FNS-96), available from the Food and Nutrition Service, Washington, D.C. 20250.

Under the Food Stamp Program, eligible low-income families are provided additional food purchasing power through federal food coupons. Research indicates that participating retailers have realized up to 8 percent increases in sales, largely in meats, dairy products, poultry, and fruits and vegetables.

Commodity Exchange Authority

The Commodity Exchange Authority (CEA) administers the Commodity Exchange Act for the prevention and suppression of price manipulation and other unfair practices in trading on commodity exchanges. Trading regulation by the CEA applies to seventeen exchanges licensed under the act, including the Chicago Board of Trade, the grain exchanges at Kansas City and Minneapolis, the mercantile exchanges in Chicago and New York, and the New York cotton and wool futures markets. Trading on these exchanges aggregates about $268 billion annually.

To protect the integrity of prices registered on exchanges and the marketing services they render, the CEA maintains direct surveillance of traders' operations, obtains and analyzes required daily reports from commodity brokers and large traders, and enforces speculative limits applicable to grains, soybeans, cotton, and eggs. In the regulation of commodity brokerage activities, the CEA is responsible for the annual registration of commodity brokers in regulated commodities, conducts audits of brokerage houses to protect the funds of commodity trades, and acts to prevent or suppress cheating and fraud in commodity transactions.

Headquarters telephone is (202) 447-4452. Regional offices are as follows:

OFFICES	MARKETS SUPERVISED	STATES SUPERVISED
Central Region	Chicago Board of Trade	Illinois, Indiana, Michigan, Minnesota, Ohio, Wisconsin
CHICAGO, ILL. 60604 141 W. Jackson Blvd., Rm. A-1 (312) 353–5990 Robert W. Clark, Director (312) 353–5994	Chicago Mercantile Exchange Midamerica Commodity Exchange Minneapolis Grain Exchange	
Suboffice— MINNEAPOLIS, MINN. 55415 510 Grain Exchange Bldg. (612) 725–2025		
Western Region	The Board of Trade of Kansas City, Missouri, Inc.	Alaska, Arizona, Arkansas, California, Colorado, Hawaii, Idaho, Iowa, Kansas, Louisiana, Missouri, Montana, Nebraska, Nevada, New Mexico, North Dakota, Oklahoma, Oregon, South Dakota, Texas, Utah, Washington, Wyoming.
KANSAS CITY, MO. 64112 4800 Main St., Rm. 356 (816) 931–5866 Richard E. Kirchhoff, Director	Merchants' Exchange of St. Louis New Orleans Cotton Exchange Northern California Grain Exchange Pacific Commodities Exchange, Inc. Portland Grain Exchange Seattle Grain Exchange	

OFFICES	MARKETS SUPERVISED	STATES SUPERVISED
Eastern Region	Citrus Associates of the N.Y. Cotton	Alabama, Connecticut, Delaware,
NEW YORK, N. Y. 10006	Exchange, Inc.	Florida, Georgia,
61 Broadway, Rm.	Commodity Exchange, Inc.	Kentucky, Maine,
2101	change, Inc.	Maryland, Massachusetts, Missis-
(212) 264–1028	Memphis Board of	chusetts, Missis-
T. Reed McMinn,	Trade Clearing Association	sippi, New
Director	sociation	Hampshire, New
	New York Cotton	Jersey, New York,
	Exchange	North Carolina,
	New York Mercantile	Pennsylvania,
	Exchange	Rhode Island,
	Wool Associates of	South Carolina,
	the N.Y. Cotton	Tennessee, Ver-
	Exchange, Inc.	mont, Virginia,
		West Virginia.

Animal and Plant Health Inspection

The Animal and Plant Health Inspection Service (APHIS) combines programs to protect and improve animal and plant health for the benefit of man and his environment and to help protect the wholesomeness of meat and poultry products for human consumption.

Meat and poultry inspection is provided at about 5,500 establishments throughout the country. Federal inspectors also check foreign inspection systems and establishments producing meat and poultry products for export to the United States.

The Plant Protection and Quarantine Programs staff conducts cooperative federal–state projects to control or eradicate plant pests and diseases. PP&Q inspectors administer international and interstate regulations that prohibit or restrict the entry of foreign pests and plants, plant products, animal products and by-products, and other materials that may harbor pests.

Veterinary Services staff carries out cooperative programs with the states to control and eradicate animal diseases. Veterinary Services inspectors enforce interstate shipping regulations for livestock; enforce import regulations for livestock, birds, and certain zoo animals; and provide health certification for animals being exported.

Veterinary Services programs license or register dealers in laboratory animals and in wholesale pet trade; research institutions using animals; and circuses, zoos, or other exhibitors of nonfarm animals. Veterinary Services also enforces regulations under federal law that assure that all animal vaccines and other veterinary biologicals sold in interstate commerce are safe, pure, potent, and effective.

Price Supports

The Agricultural Stabilization and Conservation Service (ASCS) and the Commodity Credit Corporation (CCC) cooperate with many businesses in carrying out the department's programs for supporting commodity prices.

The principal methods of providing support are loans to and purchases from producers. The commodities serve as collateral for the loan, and on maturity the producer may deliver or forfeit the commodities to satisfy his obligation without further payment. CCC also makes direct purchases from processors as well as producers, depending on the commodity involved. Set-aside payments are provided for in farm legislation on feed grains, wheat, and cotton. Because of high demand for U.S. farm products, however, the set-aside provision was suspended for the 1974 crop year as farmers were encouraged to produce all they could for market sales.

In support operations, normal trade facilities are used to the maximum extent practicable—cooperatives and financial institutions in lending activities, commercial facilities for storage.

Information on CCC-owned commodities available for sale is

contained in a Monthly Sales List issued by CCC on the last working day of each month and effective for the following month. This list, which varies from month to month as CCC's inventory changes, is designed to aid regular commercial channels. It specifies the kinds of commodities available, the terms and conditions under which the commodities are offered, and the numbers of the different sales announcements. Requests to receive the list regularly should be addressed to the Director, Grain Division, ASCS, USDA, Washington, D.C. 20250.

These large-scale dealings with business are conducted primarily in the two ASCS commodity field offices in Prairie Village, Kansas, and Minneapolis. The commodity offices use commercial storage facilities and the services of domestic carriers, banks and other lending agencies, purchase and sales agents, processors, handlers, producer and cooperative associations, exporters, and other elements of the trade.

The ASCS Prairie Village Commodity Office is concerned with corn, soybeans, wheat, oats, barley, cotton (upland and extra long staple), cottonseed, cottonseed oil, rye, grain sorghums, dry edible beans, flaxseed, rice, tung oil, and castor oil. Address: Brymar Building, 75th and Boots Street, Prairie Village, Kansas 66208, (816) 361-6401. George L. Eastling is director.

The Prairie Village office maintains branch merchandising offices in Minneapolis—Room 310, Grain Exchange Building, Minneapolis, Minnesota 55415, (612) 725-2051; Chicago—Room 106, 226 West Jackson Boulevard, Chicago, Illinois 60604, (312) 353-6581; Portland—921 S.W. Washington Street, Portland, Oregon 97205, (503) 221-2715; and Houston—2320 La Branch Street, Houston, Texas 72004, (713) 226-4206.

The Houston office serves as a coordinator on USDA export shipments through the gulf and South Atlantic ports. This office also maintains liaison with port authorities, customs offices, steamship companies, and other governmental and private organizations as necessary on commodity movements.

The branch offices represent the Prairie Village Commodity Office in developing and maintaining liaison with the trade, ASCS state offices, and others in their respective areas. They make domestic and export sales and allocate inbound shipments against open sales or storage commitments. These branch offices also provide advice to the merchandising and shipping trade, as well as to other government offices, by researching and reporting on market conditions, price quotations, and port activities.

The Minneapolis Commodity Office is responsible (domestic and export use) for the storage, handling, and disposition of more than sixty processed commodities, including dairy products (butter, cheese, and milk), and other fresh and processed commodities such as dry edible beans and milled rice, various oils, canned fruits and vegetables, and poultry and meat. Address: 6400 France Avenue South, Minneapolis, Minnesota 55435, (612) 725-3201. Donald L. Gillis is director.

Information on purchasing or processing of milled rice, rolled wheat, bulgur, rolled oats, fats and oils, and dairy products not owned by CCC is available from the Minneapolis Commodity Office.

The activities of the commodity offices are coordinated in Washington, D.C., under the overall policy guidance of the ASCS administrator who is also executive vice president of CCC. He is Kenneth E. Frick, Room 206-W, USDA Administration Building, Washington, D.C. 20250, (202) 447-3467.

Exports

With total U.S. agricultural exports in the neighborhood of $13 billion in 1972–73 and $19 billion in 1973–74, programs of the Export Marketing Service (EMS) last year assisted with nearly 25 percent of that huge amount. EMS commercial programs accounted for two-thirds of its total contribution; Food for Peace (Public Law 480) the balance.

On the commercial side, EMS administers the CCC Export

Credit Sales Program and the CCC Barter Program. The former finances exports of agricultural commodities for periods of up to three years. Interest is charged at rates announced each month. The Barter Program, which has been temporarily suspended, involves contracts with U.S. firms to export agricultural commodities to generate funds for the procurement of goods and services needed abroad by U.S. government agencies, chiefly Department of Defense and AID. For information about these two programs: Assistant Sales Manager (Commercial Credit and Barter), Export Marketing Service, USDA, Washington, D.C. 20250, (202) 447-6301. Separate pamphlets are available on each program.

The Food for Peace programs (Public Law 480) offer U.S. businessmen opportunities to sell agricultural commodities abroad through agreements negotiated with foreign governments under long-term credit. Here's how it works:

EMS authorizes a country to buy under the program. Copies of the purchase authorizations, which tell which country is buying what, and where bid information can be obtained, are distributed by EMS to firms on commodity mailing lists. To get on the list, write Program Operations Division, EMS, USDA, Washington, D.C. 20250. Detailed information on purchase authorizations issued each day is available by telephone after 3 P.M. Call (202) 447-6211. USDA also issues press releases announcing issuance of purchase authorizations.

The department encourages all those qualified, including small businessmen, to take an active part in this program. To qualify, submit a financial statement, a list of affiliated companies and their chief executive officers, and a résumé of experience in agricultural exporting.

The Foreign Agricultural Service works with business groups at home and abroad to develop overseas markets. For example, it helped four Pacific Northwest states to organize a regional exporting group, and combined with a Midwest state group to stage a successful food fair in Tokyo. It worked with the citrus industry on a marketing campaign that pushed fresh grapefruit exports to Japan to more than $18 million a year. The service publishes a useful annual directory of organizations, available free. Ask for *Food and Agricultural Export Directory*.

Federal Crop Insurance Corporation

In a recent year the Federal Crop Insurance Corporation provided $856,133,000 of insurance protection to farmers for $42,129,000 of premium, from which $25,239,000 of indemnities were paid to farmers who suffered crop losses due to causes beyond their control.

Federal Crop Insurance has value not only for insured farmers. Agri-businessmen and agencies lending to farmers can be protected on money owed them through the collateral assignment provision of the FCIC policies, under which indemnities can be assigned to creditors. The entire business community thus profits from the benefits of the emergency assistance provided by FCIC when severe crop losses occur.

Additional information may be obtained through the offices of the Manager and Deputy Manager of the Corporation, Rooms 4094–96, South Building, USDA, Washington, D.C. 20250, (202) 447-6795 and 447-6797.

Economics and Statistics

Here are some of the uses to which businessmen put the agricultural statistics and analyses issued by the department's Economic Research Service (ERS) and the Statistical Reporting Service (SRS):

- Processors, dealers, and handlers of agricultural products use the reports in planning the establishment of their plants; determining the source and volume of their raw products; the size of their operation; and in marketing their products.

- Railroads, trucking companies, and other transport services use the material to determine the number of cars and trucks needed to move the agricultural products in particular areas. The statistical data on production and time of harvest enable these carriers to distribute their equipment where it is most needed. While this is especially important in areas with perishable products, such as fruits and vegetables, it is also vital to proper movement of livestock and grains.
- Industrial organizations, manufacturers, jobbers, merchants, and mail-order houses put these reports to good use. They are used in planning production, sales, inventories, and advertising programs—to provide the customer with the goods he needs when he needs them.
- Banks, insurance, and credit organizations use the data in calculating the risks in financing farm production and storage, and in marketing. They also use the reports to help in the management of farm properties under their control. The insurance companies use the reports in insuring farmers against crop failures, livestock losses, and so on.
- Operators of warehouses and other storage facilities use the reports in planning the storage of crops and livestock products. Storage holding reports are important tools to the businessman in appraising the total market situation. These holdings can have both a long- and short-term influence in the market, because the commodities stored can be moved quickly into the channels of trade, or held for varying periods.

The thousands of businessmen who furnish production supplies to farmers are heavy users of Department of Agriculture economic and statistical reports. Vendors of such items as machinery, fertilizer, pesticides, and petroleum products can make more informed business decisions with reports on changes in numbers and size of farms, farm machinery use, and credit requirements.

Department of Agriculture economic and statistical information is used also by those who transport, store, and process farm products, who buy and sell at wholesale and retail levels, and who ship to foreign markets. Among the many reports period-ically issued, the following may be of special interest:

Each month, ERS publishes the *Farm Index,* a popular maga-zine describing current research ($3.50 a year from GPO); the *Agricultural Outlook Digest,* summarizing last-minute situa-tion and outlook information; *Foreign Agricultural Trade of the United States*; and *Checklist of Reports,* citing recently pub-lished reports.

At the beginning of each year, ERS issues *Periodic Reports of Agricultural Economics and Statistics*, listing release dates for about 80 situation and outlook reports and some 550 reports relating to crops and livestock. Another popular annual release is the *Handbook of Agricultural Charts,* issued each fall (65¢, GPO).

For economic publications, or information on specific prob-lems or questions, write or phone Division of Information, Eco-nomic Research Service, U.S. Department of Agriculture, Wash-ington, D.C. 20250, (202) 447-7837.

SRS publishes the monthly *Agricultural Situation,* providing current news and articles for producers ($2.40 annually from GPO). *Crop Reporting Board Reporter,* published each year by SRS, provides release dates and summaries for all SRS releases.

For statistical publications, write the Division of Information, Statistical Reporting Service, U.S. Department of Agriculture, Washington, D.C. 20250, (202) 447-5455.

Cooperatives—A Big Business

Some seventy-eight hundred purchasing and marketing coop-eratives do a volume of business exceeding $19 billion a year. USDA's Farmer Cooperative Service (FCS) offers many research, technical assistance, and educational services to help them function more efficiently.

Types of activity to which the agency directs efforts are: (1)

Improving the efficiency of cooperative marketing and business systems in the performance of the interrelated functions in the marketing and distributing of farm products; (2) improving individual cooperative firm operations so they better meet the needs of farmer-members, whether for marketing services or for purchasing supplies; (3) conducting member and public education programs to maintain members' involvement and control of their cooperatives as they grow in size and sophistication; (4) assisting new groups of farmers who have an interest in using cooperatives to enhance their income, whether these farmers have limited resources or operate in the mainstream of commercial agriculture.

FCS contact points are: research (202) 447-8936; technical assistance (202) 447-8940; publications (202) 447-6486.

Publications

For a comprehensive list of Department of Agriculture publications, request USDA List No. 11.

U.S. Department of Agriculture
14th & Independence S.W.
Washington, D.C. 20250
(202) 447-2791

COMMERCE:
THE BUSINESSMAN'S HOME
IN GOVERNMENT

For businessmen ranging from the storekeeper trying to decide whether to set up a suburban branch to the export manager looking for overseas distributors for auto repair equipment, an amazing assortment of aids is available from the Department of Commerce in Washington and its forty-two field offices.

Although specifically set up to foster the nation's economic growth, the department's facilities are known and used by only a minority of businessmen. The number who profit from its services is growing, however. Use of census data, for example, is estimated to have increased tenfold in the last ten years.

The department offers help to business in five major fields: economic information, promotion of foreign and domestic commerce and tourism, trade adjustment assistance, science and technology, and ocean shipping.

More broadly, it seeks to act as ombudsman for business, and in 1971 created an office with that very name (now known as Office of Business Assistance). It is officially offered as "the one central place in the federal government where businessmen and others [can] address their requests for information and service, as well as to voice their complaints, criticisms and suggestions."

In handling some five hundred cases a month, this office is able to contact senior officials of fifteen federal agencies who have been designated as liaison to get action on businessmen's problems.

Economic Information

As businesses apply market research techniques to a widening spectrum of operations, the basic economic data available from the Census Bureau, the analyses by the Bureau of Economic Analysis, and the industry studies by the Bureau of Competitive Assessment and Business Policy become increasingly important tools for executives. The American Marketing Association cites these uses of census data: economic or sales forecasting; analysis of market potentials; analysis of distribution; layout of sales territories; analysis of sales performance; location of plants, warehouses, and stores; and determination of samples in market studies.

Actual cases include the Chicago company that used census statistics in developing sales quotas for its one thousand franchised hardware retailers, and the businessman who obtained a special county-by-county tabulation of farms producing hay to help him determine whether to invest in the manufacture of one-man haybalers.

Most people are aware of the big Census of Population and Housing taken every ten years, and many know of the Census of Business, Manufactures, Mineral Industries, and Agriculture taken every five years. Few realize that these are supplemented by a variety of current surveys, taken as often as monthly, on retail sales, housing starts, etc. Nor is it well known that census figures can be obtained not only "ready-made" in publications sold by the Government Printing Office, but also "tailored to order" in tabulations especially prepared by the Census Bureau under a contract arrangement with a business. If a check with a

Commerce Field Office reveals that the desired information is not available in published form, inquiry should be made to the Census Bureau, Suitland, Maryland, about the cost of a special tabulation.

Census results have been made more accessible to businessmen through bureau recognition of some 170 privately operated Summary Tape Processing Centers.

Census questionnaires are regularly reviewed in an effort to improve the data's usefulness to business. Businessmen's suggestions, made individually or through trade associations, are welcomed, and often result in constructive changes.

The Bureau of Economic Analysis makes many analytical studies of value to the thoughtful businessman, on subjects such as inventories, corporate profits, availability of funds, and other factors affecting business investment decisions. It also publishes the important monthly *Survey of Current Business,* containing twenty-five hundred statistical series on specific lines of business, and special articles reporting on surveys of businessmen's expectations and other topics of significance to business. The *Survey of Current Business* is available from the Government Printing Office at a subscription rate of $20 a year.

Another source of economic information at Commerce is the Bureau of Competitive Assessment and Business Policy. Its staff of industry specialists produces *U.S. Industrial Outlook,* giving trends and forecasts for more than two hundred industries. It is available from the Government Printing Office for $6.50. The Bureau issues reports on opportunities for particular industries, such as *Data Communications Market: Information Sources* and *Franchising Opportunities Handbook.*

The bureau performs several services other than the dispensing of economic information. It protects business interests that may be involved in the actions of other government agencies. When the Defense Department, for example, plans to put surplus goods up for sale, the bureau will advise it whether release of the proposed quantity would upset the market for new production. The bureau, therefore, is often a good place for the businessman to go when he has a problem with any government agency, or with legislation.

It conducts conferences for businessmen in Washington and other cities on such practical topics as industrial modernization in the light of changes in the tax laws. At these conferences, businessmen have the opportunity to question top government officials, and present the views of the business community to them. It also organizes the National Defense Executive Reserve, composed of businessmen who are willing to make their special skills available to government in an emergency, and to take part in periodic exercises for keeping abreast of mobilization problems. It plays an important advisory role in the federal government's critical materials program, and through its administration of a priorities system occasionally can help a businessman who is having trouble obtaining an item, like cadmium, he needs to fulfill a defense contract.

Promoting Commerce

The central source of government information and promotional services for American businessmen interested in exports, imports, and foreign investment is the Bureau of International Commerce (BIC). If more American entrepreneurs knew the sweeping array of aids it can provide, they might export more than the present 4 percent of the United States gross national product. The businessman starting from scratch in the export field can purchase (for a nominal sum) a "trade list" of distributors in other countries handling his type of product. Should he be unable to locate a suitable representative through such a list, for a small additional cost he may order a special "trade contact" survey, which BIC arranges to have conducted by a State Department commercial officer in the appropriate country. Once he has identified a foreign firm as a prospective trading partner, he can buy BIC's "World Trade Directory" report on the firm. BIC publications will provide him a wealth of basic data, by country, on market conditions, import regulations, etc., which he can supplement every week through the magazine, *Commerce Today* ($33 a year from the GPO). In the course of a year, this periodical publishes more than sixty-five hundred specific leads on trade and investment opportunities.

A powerful trio of overseas sales aids are trade centers, trade fairs, and trade missions. The fifteen permanent United States trade centers (London, Frankfurt, Milan, Mexico City, Tokyo, Paris, Sydney, Stockholm, Singapore, Buenos Aires, Beirut, Vienna, Osaka, Seoul, and Taipei) stage exhibits of products with special appeal in their areas. The first week the London Trade Center was open, United States exhibitors wrote up $1 million in orders, and eighteen exhibitors concluded arrangements for British representatives to handle their lines. In a recent year, United States firms using these centers made sales exceeding $400 million and lined up more than one thousand agents and distributors. Trade fairs, once primarily a vehicle for selling the "American way of life," now are being located on a "hard-sell" basis, where the best potential markets are. United States companies chalked up more than $3 million in new sales at a single fair in Tokyo. Trade missions—groups of businessmen under Department of Commerce leadership (or industry-organized with department assistance) who spend several weeks abroad with no compensation beyond transportation and a per diem for subsistence—will present any company's business proposals. Upon their return, they conduct meetings to report to American business on trade opportunities uncovered during their trips. Information on how to participate in trade missions, trade fairs, or trade centers may be obtained by writing the Bureau of International Commerce, Washington, D.C. 20230, or through the nearest Department of Commerce district office (see list at end of chapter). These offices, and the Regional Export Expansion Councils of volunteer businessmen for which they provide an executive secretariat, conduct hundreds of meetings a year to encourage more entries in the export field and to share know-how. The district offices also arrange consultations for businessmen with Foreign Service commercial officers who are on home leave. The district offices are the starting point for companies seeking presidential "E" awards in recognition of successful export expansion programs.

Businessmen interested in attracting foreign capital to their enterprise or their community can get help from the Office of International Finance and Investment in BIC. It acts as a two-way clearing-house, also assisting when United States capital seeks foreign opportunities, particularly in developing countries where such investment would expedite achievement of United States foreign-aid goals.

On the regulatory side of foreign trade, Commerce's Bureau of East-West Trade issues export licenses where required for shipments to the Soviet bloc and to China, and seeks to assist businessmen develop the newly opened avenues of East-West trade. Products of a clearly nonmilitary nature can be shipped under a general license covering a list of named commodities, while makers of other goods must apply for a special license. The nearest Commerce field office should be consulted for guidance on this sensitive subject.

A board in Commerce is responsible for establishment of Foreign Trade Zones—one of the newer ones is at McAllen, Texas —where overseas materials or parts may be imported without tariff and used in the manufacture of items for sale outside the United States.

The United States Travel Service (USTS) offers attractive opportunities for hotel operators, transportation companies, and others in the tourist field to win foreign customers. Through overseas offices, advertising and promotion campaigns (ask the Visitor Services Division about matching grants for these), it seeks to bring more tourists to the United States. While it may not favor an individual concern, it is always glad to consider suggestions for cooperative efforts which may bring more visitors to an area and thereby benefit its entire tourist industry. Its "Busivisit" program encourages U.S. companies with international interests to offer incentives to overseas personnel to visit America. USTS does not have field offices; it should be addressed in Washington.

U.S. trade show and convention organizers who want their activities publicized in a directory abroad should contact the Special Programs Manager, Marketing Division, before August 15 of each year.

An Office of Minority Business Enterprise seeks to give members of minority groups an opportunity to own a fair share of America's business, through such means as:

- Financing one-stop centers in twenty-seven cities to provide information and counseling.
- A joint government-business program to promote $100 million of deposits in minority banks.
- Attempting to place minority-owned concessions in federal installations across the country.
- Developing a roster of minority-owned professional consulting services and encouraging government to use them.
- Preparing a special catalog of federal assistance programs for minority businesses.

The Economic Development Administration and seven Regional Action Planning Commissions had been scheduled by the administration for phasing out of existence, but Congress gave them an additional lease on life.

EDA seeks to assist local, state, and regional efforts to create new industry and jobs in areas of economic distress. Its programs include business loans, public works, technical assistance, planning assistance, and research.

The regional commissions are a mechanism for joint state–federal decision-making on economic development problems extending beyond state lines. They are as follows: Coastal Plains (Georgia, North Carolina, South Carolina); Four Corners (Arizona, Colorado, New Mexico, Utah); New England (Connecticut, Maine, Massachusetts, New Hampshire, Rhode Island, Vermont); Ozarks (Arkansas, Kansas, Missouri, Oklahoma);

Upper Great Lakes (Michigan, Minnesota, Wisconsin); Old Trails West (Montana, Nebraska, North Dakota, South Dakota); and Pacific Northwest (Idaho, Oregon, Washington).

Trade Adjustment Assistance

A Bureau of Resources and Trade Assistance is the principal point of contact in Commerce for businessmen affected by import competition. Its services are threefold:

1. As a prelude to possible government action, it makes studies of market penetration by imports. Steel, nonrubber footwear, and consumer electronic products are examples of industries whose difficulties have been analyzed.

2. It certifies for government loans companies which must adjust to competition from increased imports caused by U.S. trade concessions. The biggest beneficiary to date is Fourco Glass Co. of Clarksburg, West Virginia, with a $7 million loan.

3. Its Office of Textiles works closely with Department of State and other agencies on bilateral cotton textile agreements, and monitors imports of wool and man-made fiber textile products.

Science and Technology

With one of the largest civilian scientific organizations in government, the Commerce Department strives to put science and technology to work for American business. It underlined this effort by establishing a post of Assistant Secretary for Science and Technology, who provides leadership and coordination for the National Bureau of Standards, the Patent Office, the Office of Telecommunications, and the National Technical Information Service. In addition, the National Oceanic and Atmospheric Administration offers important services to business in the fields of weather and the sea.

As its name implies, the National Bureau of Standards (NBS) specializes in precise measurement, without which mass production would be impossible. It develops standards in such frontier areas as cryogenics (the phenomena of extreme cold, for which many industrial uses are being found), while continuing to provide an authoritative reference point for more common types of measurement. It conducted more than 138,000 calibrations for industry and government in a recent year, and provided more than 66,000 samples of standard materials to laboratories.

Commodity standards, promulgated by Commerce when agreed upon by the industry concerned, permit many production and sales economies. An example of the more than five hundred such standards in effect is that for bedding. Thanks to its definition of double-bed size as fifty-four inches, it is possible for manufacturers, dealers, and consumers to be sure that any double mattress will fit any double bed.

NBS facilities helpful to business include a full-size "house" to explore such problems as heat loss through walls, roofs, and foundations.

The National Technical Information Service (NTIS) puts at the disposal of business the results of the billions of dollars a year the federal government spends on research, plus much translated information on foreign work. This it does by selling reports—some 2,500,000 a year—at extremely modest prices. A 50-cent report has been known to save a company $50,000 in research costs, plus the value of the time saved. Reports may be examined at twelve regional centers as well as purchased, either through the forty-three Commerce field offices or directly from NTIS, Department of Commerce, Washington, D.C. For a fee, NTIS will make a computerized search of post-1964 reports and furnish a printout of abstracts. Call (703) 321-8523 for details.

The Patent Office is at least as valuable to businessmen as it is to inventors. A patent does give protection to its owner, but it also publishes to the alert businessman a piece of important information about the state of the art in his field. By checking an appropriate segment of the nation's more than three million patents, he (or more conveniently, a professional patent searcher) may find a device which is the answer to a production problem he faces, and therefore worth paying royalties for, or he may determine where present knowledge in the field ends and room exists for profitable research and development. The weekly *Patent Official Gazette* (available at $89 a year from the GPO) may help him locate exciting new products he can arrange to manufacture or distribute. The federal government owns thousands of patents which it will license royalty-free. Some are listed every Wednesday in the Federal Register (see Index). The Patent Office is also the place for businesses to register trademarks they are using. It publishes an edition of the *Gazette* dealing only with trademarks for $17 a year. Two booklets, *General Information Concerning Patents* and *General Information Concerning Trademarks,* are available at 30 cents each through Commerce field offices or the GPO.

The National Oceanic and Atmospheric Administration (NOAA), as its name implies, covers a far-reaching territory, much of it offering new frontiers for business development.

NOAA's Office of Sea Grant, for example, is financing research on processes which would first extract protein concentrate from shellfish and then use the shells to produce chitin, a cellulose-like substance useful in papermaking, pharmaceuticals, paint, and other industries. It guaranteed a market for a Seattle pilot plant by purchasing its output of chitin and distributing it to researchers throughout the country.

Airlines, shipping companies, fishing enterprises, and other businesses depend on the National Ocean Survey as the source of marine and air navigation charts, which it develops, prints, and sells. Less known to business, but potentially very valuable, is the survey's seismographic and oceanographic research. Its sea-going scientists probe the oceans for conditions which may affect commercial fishing grounds, disposal of nuclear waste products, and new sources of mineral wealth.

The retailer planning a sale, the builder scheduling his work, and many others in business make constant use of National Weather Service forecasts. Within reasonable limits imposed by availability of time, the nearest Weather Service station will provide not only current forecasts but also some historical information on weather trends in the area which may be useful to businessmen planning their programs. New units in selected cities issue air stagnation advisories when pollution-producing meteorological conditions may call for curbs on industrial activity and vehicular traffic.

Under the 1972 National Coastal Zone Management Act, NOAA helps the states control development of coastal lands. For a period of three years it is authorized to make grants so that zoning of coastal areas can be planned on a statewide rather than community-by-community basis. Thereafter it is authorized to give the states grants for implementing those plans, on a basis of $2 of federal money for each state dollar.

Ocean Shipping

The Maritime Administration is vital to the U.S. maritime industry in two major ways:

1. Through construction-differential subsidies, amounting to approximately $100 million a year, it assists in building or modernizing privately owned merchant ships.

2. Through operating-differential subsidies of about $250 million a year, approval of tax-deferred construction reserves, ship mortgage insurance, marketing information, and government cargo preference, the agency enables the American merchant marine to remain competitive.

For all the activities of the Commerce Department, district offices provide the businessman a close-to-home source of advice and information. Whether he wants to know if beehives may be shipped to Trinidad, or how to write up an export license application for cable going "to the middle of the Atlantic Ocean, not consigned to anyone," a district office man will know the answer or where to get it. Businessmen can purchase Department of Commerce and related publications through the district offices, and may subscribe to *Commerce Business Daily* ($63.50 a year), which lists government invitations to bid, surplus sales, and contract awards, and to *Business Service Checklist* ($5.50), a weekly guide to Commerce publications.

Department of Commerce
14th St. & Constitution Ave. N.W.
Washington, D.C. 20230
(202) 783-9200

As you enter the main entrance on 14th Street, you will find a glassed-in office just to the left of the elevators. Here you will be directed to the appropriate unit in the department. To the right is a GPO bookstore.

District Offices

U.S. Courthouse—Rm. 316
Albuquerque, N.M. 87101
William E. Dwyer, Director
(505) 843–2386

412 Hill Bldg.
632 6th Ave.
Anchorage, Alaska 99501
Everett W. Buness, Director
(907) 272–6531

Suite 523
1401 Peachtree St., N.E.
Atlanta, Ga. 30309
David S. Williamson, Director
(404) 526–6000

415 U.S. Customhouse
Gay and Lombard Sts.
Baltimore, Md. 21202
Carroll E. Hopkins, Director
(301) 962–3560

Suite 200-201
908 S. 20th St.
Birmingham, Ala. 35205
Gayle C. Shelton, Jr., Director
(205) 325–3327

10th Floor
441 Stuart St.
Boston, Mass. 02116
Richard F. Treadway, Director
(617) 223–2312

910 Federal Bldg.
111 W. Huron St.
Buffalo, N.Y. 14202
Robert F. Magee, Director
(716) 842–3208

Federal Bldg.
Suite 631
334 Meeting St.
Charleston, S.C. 29403
Paul Quattlebaum, Jr.,
    Director
(803) 577–4171

3000 New Federal Office Bldg.
500 Quarrier St.
Charleston, W. Va. 25301
J. Raymond DePaulo,
    Director
(304) 343–6181, Ext. 375

6022 O'Mahoney Federal
    Center
2120 Capitol Ave.
Cheyenne, Wyo. 82001
Joseph D. Davis, Director
(307) 778–2220, Ext. 2151

1406 Mid Continental Plaza
    Bldg.
55 E. Monroe St.
Chicago, Ill. 60603
Gerald M. Marks, Director
(312) 353–4400

8028 Federal Office Bldg.
550 Main St.
Cincinnati, Ohio 45202
Thomas E. Ferguson, Director
(513) 684–2944

Rm. 600
666 Euclid Ave.
Cleveland, Ohio 44114
Charles B. Stebbins, Director
(216) 522–4750

Rm. 3E7
1100 Commerce St.
Dallas, Tex. 75202
C. Carmon Stiles, Director
(214) 749–3287

Rm. 161
New Customhouse
19th and Stout Sts.
Denver, Colo. 80202
John G. McMurtry, Director
(303) 837–3246

609 Federal Bldg.
210 Walnut St.
Des Moines, Iowa 50309
(515) 284–4222

445 Federal Bldg.
Detroit, Mich. 48226
John Byington, Acting
    Director
(313) 226–6088

258 Federal Bldg.
West Market St.
P.O. Box 1950
Greensboro, N.C. 27402
Joel B. New, Director
(919) 275–9111

Rm. 610-B
Federal Office Bldg.
450 Main St.
Hartford, Conn. 06103
Richard C. Kilbourn, Director
(203) 244–3530

286 Alexander Young Bldg.
1015 Bishop St.
Honolulu, Hawaii 96813
John S. Davies, Director
(808) 546–8694

1017 Old Federal Bldg.
201 Fannin St.
Houston, Tex. 77002
Edward T. Fecteau, Jr.,
    Director
(713) 226–4231

Suite 129
4080 Woodcock Dr.
Jacksonville, Fla. 32207
John Marshall III, Acting
    Director
(904) 791–2796

Rm. 1840
601 E. 12th St.
Kansas City, Mo. 64106
George H. Payne, Director
(816) 374–3141

11201 Federal Bldg.
11000 Wilshire Blvd.
Los Angeles, Calif. 90024
Stanley K. Crook, Director
(213) 824–7591

Rm. 710
147 Jefferson Ave.
Memphis, Tenn. 38103
Bradford H. Rice, Director
(901) 534–3214

Rm. 821
City National Bank Bldg.
25 W. Flagler St.
Miami, Fla. 33130
Roger J. LaRoche, Director
(305) 350–5267

Straus Bldg.
238 W. Wisconsin Ave.
Milwaukee, Wis. 53203
David F. Howe, Director
(414) 224–3473

306 Federal Bldg.
110 S. 4th St.
Minneapolis, Minn. 55401
Glenn A. Matson, Director
(612) 725–2133

Suite 533
24 Commerce St.
Newark, N.J. 07102
Thomas R. Skidmore, Acting
    Director
(201) 645–6214

909 Federal Office Bldg., S.
610 South St.
New Orleans, La. 70130
Edwin A. Leland, Jr., Director
(504) 527–6546

41st Floor
Federal Office Bldg.
26 Federal Plaza, Foley
    Square
New York, N.Y. 10007
Arthur C. Rutzen, Director
(212) 264–0634

Jefferson Bldg.
1015 Chestnut St.
Philadelphia, Pa. 19107
Patrick P. McCabe, Acting
    Director
(215) 597–2850

508 Greater Arizona Savings
    Bldg.
112 N. Central
Phoenix, Ariz. 85004
Donald W. Fry, Director
(602) 261–3285

431 Federal Bldg.
1000 Liberty Ave.
Pittsburgh, Pa. 15222
Lewis E. Conman, Director
(412) 644–2850

521 Pittock Block
921 S.W. Washington St.
Portland, Ore. 97205
J. D. Chapman, Director
(503) 221–3001

2028 Federal Bldg.
300 Booth St.
Reno, Nev. 89502
Joseph J. Jeremy, Director
(702) 784–5203

8010 Federal Bldg.
400 N. 8th St.
Richmond, Va. 23240
Weldon W. Tuck, Director
(703) 782–2246

2511 Federal Bldg.
1520 Market St.
St. Louis, Mo. 63103
Donald R. Loso, Director
(314) 622–4243

1201 Federal Bldg.
125 S. State St.
Salt Lake City, Utah 84111
Ray L. White, Director
(801) 524–5116

Federal Bldg.
Box 36013
450 Golden Gate Ave.
San Francisco, Calif. 94102
Philip M. Creighton, Director
(415) 556–5864

Rm. 100
Post Office Bldg.
San Juan, P.R. 00902
Enrique Vilella, Director
(809) 723–4640

235 U.S. Courthouse & Post
   Office Bldg.
125-29 Bull St.
Savannah, Ga. 31402
James W. McIntire, Director
(912) 232–4321

Rm. 706
Lake Union Bldg.
1700 Westlake Ave. N.
Seattle, Wash. 98109
Judson S. Wonderly, Director
(206) 442–5615

DEFENSE:
OUR BIGGEST BUSINESS

It is well established that the government is business' biggest customer, and almost equally well known that among government agencies the Department of Defense (DOD) is by far the biggest buyer, accounting for well over half the federal procurement budget. Inevitably, these facts have a significant impact on the economy quite apart from their meaning to the businessman who wants to sell his products to the government.

The Defense Department is a massive operation, but the basic principles followed in selling to it are the same applied in dealing with the commercial business field: identify the customer's needs and buying policies, and locate where the buying is done.

Solutions to most of the businessman's difficulties in getting through the procurement maze lie within the Defense Supply Agency. The DSA was created to buy supplies and services common to all three military services. The DSA operates through a network of purchasing centers specializing in various types of products—petroleum, clothing, electronic supplies, and so forth.

To sell to the DSA, it is necessary to determine the appropriate supply center for the particular product and deal with that center directly. In order to be placed on the bidder's list, request a bidder's mailing list application from the supply center. A list of these centers is given at the end of the chapter. Also, there is a Small Business and Economic Utilization Specialist at each of these supply centers whose job it is to help small business participate in DSA procurement. Specific questions concerning procedure or policy should be directed to one of these specialists at the appropriate supply center.

Many items are not procured under the DSA "single manager" concept. In this instance it is necessary to determine the appropriate military procurement offices within each service. The booklet, *Selling to the Military,* available from the GPO for 90 cents, lists the major purchasing offices for the three services as well as listing the DSA purchasing centers. In addition, a DSA and General Services Administration (GSA) commodities list with class codes is included in the newest edition (fall, 1973) of this handbook.

Another helpful source is *Commerce Business Daily,* which publishes proposed procurements by DOD and other government agencies, and large contract awards which may lead to subcontracting opportunities. A sample copy of the *Daily* is available for inspection at each of the field offices of the Small Business Administration, the field offices of the Department of Commerce, and many local chambers of commerce. An annual subscription is sold for $63.50 a year by the Superintendent of Documents, Government Printing Office, Washington, D.C. 20402.

The purchasing procedure for the Defense Department takes many shapes, depending on the nature of the item, whether a major defense system or small subsistence items. The armed forces buy significant quantities of their supplies under a formal advertising, or competitive procurement, procedure. Having learned of an invitation to bid through a bidder's mailing list, the trade press, *Commerce Business Daily,* or some other source, the businessman submits a sealed bid by the specified time. The contracting officer analyzes the bids and makes the award to the lowest bidder who has the facilities, technical capability, and financial resources to meet the terms of the specifications.

Negotiated purchases are made mainly for food, for contracts under $2,500, and for special situations. For subsistence items, Notices of Intent to Purchase (NIPs) and "sight buying" procedures are used. Offers may be submitted by telephone to the nearest DSA Subsistence Regional Headquarters.

Entire procurements, or parts of procurements, may be set aside exclusively for competition among small business firms. "Set-asides" also are negotiated with firms in certified eligible and/or labor surplus areas. The Small Business and Economic Utilization Specialist at each DSA Buying Center will help the businessman participate in these procurements.

Another opportunity for participating in Department of Defense business other than by contracting directly is by subcontracting with firms which have existing contracts. DOD contracts of $500,000 or more, with substantial subcontracting possibilities, require that the contractor maintain a Defense Small Business Subcontracting and Labor Surplus Area Program. Such contractors designate a Small Business Liaison Officer who administers the subcontracting program. The *Commerce Business Daily* is useful in identifying firms that offer subcontracting opportunities.

Forward-looking manufacturers who may not be interested in peacetime contracts with the armed services may want to explore the DSA Industrial Mobilization Program. This involves arrangements with several thousand manufacturers who agree that on declaration of an emergency they will immediately take certain actions planned in advance to expedite production for military needs. Inquiries concerning this program should be directed to any supply center or the Defense Contract Administration Service Office, Headquarters, DSA, Cameron Station, Alexandria, Virginia 22314.

For any further information concerning general policy for procurement or DOD procedure, the businessman may write to Directorate for Small Business and Economic Utilization Policy, Office of the Assistant Secretary of Defense, (Installations and Logistics), Room 3D777, Pentagon, Washington, D.C. 20301, (202) 697-1481.

Since the military is such a big buyer, the specifications it lays down have a powerful effect in the marketplace. The department of Defense has declared that it places considerable importance on industry comments and participation in the development of its specifications, but many businessmen are unaware of this stand and how they can make their voices heard. The DOD strives to give full consideration to industry practices and, where practicable and desirable, to seek assistance in standardization from industry itself. It is essential, too, that industry be aware, at an early stage, of the changing requirements of the armed forces. In this way it is possible for the DOD to offer businessmen the opportunity to evaluate the proposed changes in the light of technical soundness; foreseeable costs or procurement delays; need for retooling; new processes or techniques required; training of the labor forces; and the effect upon full and free competition.

Copies of current specifications and standards for all Defense Department purchases are available for private industry from the Naval Publications and Forms Center without charge. Requests should be sent to the Commanding Officer (Code 512), Naval Publications and Forms Center, 5801 Tabor Avenue, Philadelphia, Pennsylvania 19120, (215) 697-2179. The particular specifications desired should be identified by number and title. General suggestions and comments on the specifications and standards program should be submitted to the Naval Publications and Forms Center. Industry suggestions about individual military specifications should be mailed to one of the agencies named as "custodians" on the last page of the particular specification.

The type of contracts available from the Department of Defense is consistent with the characteristics of the program or item. For instance, in procurement of major defense systems where substantial development effort or risk is involved, cost-plus type prime and subcontracts are preferred. The fixed-price type contract is standard for most procurements, however. "Letter contracts," under which work may start before a price is agreed upon, are minimized.

Economic Adjustment Committee

Businessmen in communities heavily dependent on defense installations or contracts can fall on sudden hard times when the installation is closed or the contract terminated. To ease such blows, the President of the United States established within the Defense Department the Economic Adjustment Committee (EAC). The job of this committee is to work with community leaders of impacted areas to undertake a vigorous effort to diversify the community's economy by prudent and quick utilization of the surplus work force and any surplus military property in a manner that enhances the overall development effort of the entire community. The EAC, assisting only those communities that request assistance, endeavors to provide the professional, technical, and financial assistance needed to develop an action program that will help the community help itself. Often the EAC, with the help of other government units, develops ingenious solutions for the problems involved.

An example of an effective transition occurred when DOD announced the closing of an active air force base. The news meant 600 civilian and 1,450 military jobs would be lost to the area's economy. The EAC team was invited to survey the situation. Working with community leaders, a recovery program was outlined to take every possible advantage of existing base facilities. Little more than a year later, three exciting new programs were underway. The first was the establishment of a vocational–technical community college campus. The campus occupied about half the entire base area and utilized the former base hospital, the former motor pool, the old ammunition storage area, and the military dormitories. The second new program established a center for the mentally retarded and handicapped. The third program created a public airport utilizing the base's landing strip and flight line facilities. About half the land set aside for this final phase of development will be used by nonaviation business to help support the airport operation. Between education and industry, 1,175 potential new jobs were created within the year and the area's unemployment rate dropped to 3½ percent.

The EAC will also participate in charting a forward-looking course toward economic stability for communities. It will stay with the job until the community's program is well underway—helping to enlist assistance from appropriate federal sources. The extent of the EAC involvement depends on the effect of the defense realignment.

Further information may be obtained from the Chairman, Inter-Agency Economic Adjustment Committee, Office of the Secretary of Defense, Attention: Director for Economic Adjustment, Room 3E787, Pentagon, Washington, D.C. 20301.

Defense Supply Agency Service Centers

Defense Documentation Center (DDC), Cameron Station, 5010 Duke Street, (Bldg. 5), Alexandria, Virginia 22314, (202) 274-6864, acquires, stores, announces, and provides secondary distribution of all types of formally recorded research, development, test, and evaluation results of the military departments and all other DOD components. Unclassified reports having no distribution limitations are announced in the Department of Commerce publication *Government Reports Announcements.* Access to classified and controlled documents is restricted to users who have been registered for classified service. Information concerning publications may be obtained from DDC Headquarters.

Defense Logistics Services Center (DLSC), Battle Creek Federal Center, Battle Creek, Michigan 49016, (616) 962-6511, provides a variety of logistics data, item identification, and related supply-management intelligence services. DLSC is responsible for the cataloging program of the entire federal government. Private industry has access to DLSC services, the most helpful being stock number and item identification for procurement procedures.

DSA Major Buying Offices

Defense Construction Supply Center, 3990 East Broad Street, Columbus, Ohio 43215, (614) 236-3541, purchases items ranging from construction and highway maintenance equipment to diesel engines, automotive supplies and repair parts, and water purification and sewage treatment equipment. A subdivision of this supply center specializing in lumber is the Wood Products Office, DCSC, P.O. Box 2926, Portland, Oregon 97208, (503) 777-4441, ext. 315.

Defense Electronics Supply Center, 1507 Wilmington Pike, Dayton, Ohio 45401, (513) 252-5231, buys electrical equipment and promotes standardization of the different armed services' requirements in order to reduce an estimated one million separate items listed for procurement.

Defense Fuel Supply Center, Cameron Station, 5010 Duke Street (Bldg. 8), Alexandria, Virginia 22314, (202) 274-7428, obtains various petroleum-based chemicals and fuel oils.

Defense General Supply Center, Bellwood, Petersburg Pike, Richmond, Virginia 23219, (804) 275-3617 or 3287, fills the requirements for the military services for food service equipment, clothing repair equipment, hand tools, photographic equipment, and other items of a general category.

Defense Industrial Supply Center, 700 Robbins Avenue, Philadelphia, Pennsylvania 19111, (215) 697-2747, purchases chain, rope, electrical wire, fastening devices, and miscellaneous hardware for the armed forces.

Defense Personnel Support Center (DPSC), 2800 South

20th Street, Philadelphia, Pennsylvania 19101, (215) 271-2321, buys men's and women's clothing, textile items including tents, flags and footwear, and medical and dental supplies and equipment. In addition the DPSC purchases food items for the military. Large quantities are bought through nationwide competitive bids while less-than-car-lot quantities are procured locally by the individual regional headquarters. These regional headquarters are: Chicago Subsistence Regional Headquarters, DPSC, 536 South Clark Street, Chicago, Illinois 60605, (312) 353-4986; New York Subsistence Regional Headquarters, DPSC, 60 Hudson Street, New York, New York 10013, (212) 264-8927; New Orleans Subsistence Regional Headquarters, DPSC, 4400 Dauphine Street, New Orleans, Louisiana 70140, (504) 947-5571, ext. 468; Oakland Subsistence Regional Headquarters, DPSC, 2155 Webster Street, Alameda, California 94505, (415) 869-4030.

Military Traffic Management and Terminal Service, a service of the Army not under DSA, procures commercial transportation services for movement of world-wide military freight and passenger traffic on land and water. Inquiries about transportation procurement should be directed to the Director of Passenger Traffic, (202) 756-1706; the Director of Inland Traffic, (202) 756-1094; the Director of International Traffic, (202) 756-1610; or the Director of Personal Property, (202) 756-1140. All of these offices are located in the Headquarters, Military Traffic Management and Terminal Service, Nassif Building, Washington, D.C. 20315.

Businessmen interested in bidding for personal property that has become surplus to the needs of the military can get on a centralized mailing list for sales conducted by the ten Defense Surplus Sales Offices. Application to be placed on this list is obtained from DOD Surplus Sales, P.O. Box 1370, Battle Creek, Michigan 49016. The Defense Surplus Sales Offices are located as follows:

P.O. Box 8019
Philadelphia, Pa. 19101

P.O. Box 660
Newport, R.I. 02840
(In addition, a Sales Office for
   all Military Vessels)

P.O. Box 646
Forest Park, Ga. 30050

P.O. Box 31261
Jacksonville, Fla. 32230

Stanwick Building
3661 East Virginia Beach
   Blvd.
Norfolk, Va. 23502

P.O. Box 13110
Columbus, Ohio 43213

P.O. Box 6297
Fort Worth, Tex. 76115

P.O. Box 58
Defense Depot Ogden Station
Ogden, Utah 88401

P.O. Box 23402
Main Office Station
Oakland, Calif. 94623

Fleet Station
San Diego, Calif. 92132
(In addition, a Sales Office for
   all Military Aircraft)

The Department of Defense
The Pentagon
Washington, D.C. 20301
(202) 697-5131

HEALTH, EDUCATION,
AND WELFARE (HEW)

Performing functions that a generation ago were not even dreamed of for the federal government, and at a cost ($94 billion a year) that exceeds the Defense Department budget, HEW reaches actively and importantly into the operations of every business in the country.

The role of its Social Security Administration in the operations of American business is obvious. Less apparent, but likely to be just as significant, is the relationship of the Food and Drug Administration (FDA) and the five other agencies of HEW's Public Health Service (PHS) to the business community. Businessmen also have a stake in the activities of the department's other major units—the Office of Human Development, the Office of Education, the National Institute of Education, and the Social and Rehabilitation Service.

Food and Drug Administration (FDA)

The FDA's main concern continues to be enforcement of the Federal Food, Drug, and Cosmetic Act of 1938, including the amendments strengthening controls over food additives, color additives, drug effectiveness, and factory registration. The act is designed to insure the purity, safety, and truthful labeling of foods, drugs, cosmetics, and therapeutic devices shipped in interstate commerce, or imported. Its basic impact is on three major industries: foods, drugs, and cosmetics.

In checking foods, FDA inspectors visit food-growing areas, factories, warehouses, and stores, and collect market samples for laboratory analysis. FDA scientists must approve all new drugs shipped in interstate commerce, usually on the basis of test data submitted by the manufacturer. And they study products of the $2.5-billion-a-year beauty business for possible toxic effects.

But the thrust of FDA can and does extend to other important businesses, such as packaging. Under the food additives amendment, manufacturers of paper, paperboard, and other packaging materials must be sure that no ingredient in their product could cause a hazard to the public health by entering the food it encases. This 1958 addition to the law caused paper makers to reexamine their methods; for instance, the use of chemical agents whose safety could not be established was discontinued.

Many businesses cooperate with FDA in working out mutually satisfactory arrangements for compliance with what could be troublesome requirements of the law. Working with FDA, the National Canners Association and label manufacturers, for example, long ago developed a formula for "conspicuousness" of certain required labeling information.

Acting to deal with serious specific problems in the canning industry, the National Canners Association later proposed a strong regulation calling for registration of commercial food canners, mandatory code marking, and highly detailed production controls for processing of hermetically sealed low-acid foods.

One provision of the proposal was that supervisors of retort (cooking) operations and container sealing be required to attend an approved school and be certified on the basis of written examinations as qualified to assure the safety of processing operations and the integrity of containers.

Based on pilot school results, courses are being planned at university food technology centers in important canning areas. Industry personnel concerned with cooking and can closure operations will be required to attend. The training will also be provided to FDA food plant inspectors.

In this program FDA and the canning industry are cooperating to deal directly with the potential hazards of microbial food contamination. Retort operations involve heat processing to destroy microorganisms such as botulinus which are common to the environment and are capable of producing deadly toxins. In addition to microorganisms which can cause harm to humans, there are many others which are not harmful to human health if consumed, but can spoil food if not destroyed.

The legal basis for the program is the FDA Good Manufacturing Practice Regulations for Foods. These general food sanitation requirements are being supplemented with specific codes of sanitation practice for the different food industries. The canning industry proposals are being incorporated into this overall system.

On the other hand, the FDA can be extremely tough on those who buck it. This is particularly true in the drug area since the Kefauver–Harris drug amendments of 1962 armed it with additional powers, including compliance with "good manufacturing practices" in prescription drugs. The FDA commissioner said in a speech that the provision "will require drastic changes in the practice of those pharmaceutical firms whose scientific controls are substandard. If they do not adopt reasonable controls they will go out of business."

Other teeth in the law require all drug firms to register annually, and be inspected every two years; be staffed with adequately trained technical and professional personnel; and prove effectiveness, as well as safety, of new drugs before marketing them.

Some 4,000 prescription drugs, reviewed before 1962 for safety only, thereafter were reviewed for effectiveness under an FDA contract with the National Academy of Sciences/National Research Council. With this program virtually completed, FDA turned its attention to the more than 100,000 over-the-counter drugs. It is doing this on a class-by-class basis, having panels of nongovernment experts develop monographs establishing conditions under which these drugs may be marketed.

What happens if the FDA finds a business is not complying? First it may ask the courts to authorize seizure of the allegedly adulterated or misbranded merchandise for removal from market channels. Then, after a hearing, it may decide to recommend prosecution by the Department of Justice. This may result in fines or imprisonment. The publicity surrounding any such action, of course, is a weapon in itself.

FDA is also bringing about far-reaching changes in food labeling, stressing more information on nutritional content.

Under the Fair Packaging and Labeling Act, FDA deals with foods, drugs, and cosmetics, while other products are handled by the Federal Trade Commission. FDA has issued regulations governing "cents-off," economy sizes, introductory offers, and other labeling promotions. The food industry has revised thousands of labels as a result, but many noncomplying commodities were found by state agencies acting under contract with FDA.

Food continues under FDA jurisdiction if it is served aboard an interstate train, airline, bus, or ship. FDA enforces regulations to prevent the transmission of communicable diseases, through inspection of travel facilities such as galleys on airplanes, through development of guidelines for use by industry, and through promotional methods such as awards to companies for good sanitation practice.

In addition to its direct jurisdiction over interstate and foreign commerce, FDA also works with industry and with state and local agencies on recommended codes for activities which may not be wholly of a federal character. Some examples are:

a poultry ordinance offered for local adoption, in order to avoid a multiplicity of regulations which could become a trade barrier; an ordinance in the growing field of food and beverage vending machines; an arrangement under which states certify to FDA that their interstate milk shippers are in compliance with a Public Health Service code. The FDA also cooperates with the food service industry in developing personnel training programs for sanitation purposes, and giving its endorsement to approved state programs for shellfish industry sanitation in both harvesting and shucking.

Improvements in technology make continuing cooperation imperative. For example, a new technique of pasteurizing milk by steam injection has been developed. FDA has devised testing procedures to evaluate the performance of the new equipment.

FDA's work on radiation protection has an impact on several industries, notably the makers of X-ray machines. It promulgated a standard requiring improved controls for beam limitation in diagnostic equipment and components manufactured after August 15, 1973. Studies also are under way of possible health effects of ultrahigh frequency sound and low levels of microwave radiation. In addition, FDA is drafting safety performance standards for laser products and nonmedical cabinet X-ray systems used in research and industry.

For more information about FDA, contact John Walden, (301) 443-4177.

Occupational Health

Occupational health hazards have become a major concern of the federal government since 1970. While the Department of Labor enforces the law in this field, the principal agency for research, education, and training is HEW's National Institute for Occupation Safety and Health (NIOSH). Its main research laboratories in Cincinnati, Ohio, study not only the effects of hazardous substances used in the work place, but the motivational and behavioral factors involved, including noise. Short courses are given at Cincinnati to train occupational safety and health specialists. For more information, contact NIOSH Office of Public Information, Post Office Building, Cincinnati, Ohio 45202.

A Bureau of Community and Environmental Management (BCEM) has two functions with some relationship to business. It provides matching grants for urban rat control projects, important since rats cost the United States up to a billion dollars annually through contaminating food, causing fires by gnawing through electrical insulation, and other destruction. A second activity is lead-poisoning control, in which the bureau has the active cooperation of the National Paint and Coatings Association. BCEM address is 255 E. Paces Ferry Road N.E., Atlanta, Georgia 30305, (404) 633-6747. BCEM and NIOSH both are functions of HEW's Center for Disease Control.

National Institutes of Health

The National Institutes of Health are directly important to many suppliers of medical items and services because the institutes spend more than $254 million a year for everything from chemicals to X-ray film, and indirectly to all business because their research may serve to reduce the tremendous economic toll of illness. Each year, Americans suffer more than 396 million acute illnesses or injuries requiring medical attention or imposing at least one day of restricted activity.

Among the institutes, the National Cancer Institute will be a focal point in the years immediately ahead. Part of its projected half-billion-dollar-a-year program will become more heavily involved with the occupation-related exposures to cancer-causing agents, experienced, for example, by asbestos workers, uranium miners, and smelter refinery workers. And of significance to the tobacco industry will be contemplated projects to provide health education among targeted groups on the possible hazards of smoking.

Other specialized institutes deal with such chronic conditions as arthritis, allergy, and heart disease. Since half the population has at least one chronic condition, the research progress of these institutes will tend to reduce absenteeism and increase productivity.

A newly formed Alcohol, Drug Abuse, and Mental Health Administration (ADAMHA) will be spending approximately $650 million a year to combat these three problems that affect so many workers. More than 5 percent of the nation's work force are estimated to be alcoholics. ADAMHA provides consultation and assistance to employers in developing rehabilitation programs, which usually show a success rate of better than 50 percent.

Two special categories of workers—merchant seamen and migrant labor—are among the beneficiaries of the Health Service Administration (HSA). HSA funds ninety-four family health clinics that provide some services to 355,000 migrant workers and their families each year.

Under the Health Maintenance Organization Act which became law late in 1973, HEW will pay out $325 million by July 1, 1978 to new or existing organizations offering prepaid group health plans. These so-called HMOs, whether profit-making or nonprofit, will be eligible for grants, contracts, loans, or loan guarantees. Private groups are especially encouraged to start serving rural and inner-city populations.

Social Security Administration

Every employer knows that under the Social Security Act he must file quarterly earning reports on his employees and pay taxes that include his own contribution plus an equal amount deducted from their wages.* The rate is 5.85 percent for each, on earnings up to $12,000 in 1974. The contribution rate will rise gradually in the future to keep the social security program self-supporting. The annual maximum earnings subject to contributions will increase automatically in the future as general earning levels rise. The same Form 941 used for social security returns also serves to report income tax withheld. The employer must, however, provide employees with written statements of earnings; these are due by January 31 following the year in which the wages were paid, or if employment terminates before year-end, within thirty days after the last payment. The Treasury W-2 form is usually used for this purpose.

The employer's record-keeping requirements do not end here. He must maintain records showing amounts and dates of wage payments; names, addresses, social security numbers, and occupations of employees; their periods of employment; and his own employer identification number (obtained by filing Form SS-4 either with the social security district office or the local Internal Revenue Service office). In addition, he must keep for at least four years duplicate copies of the quarterly and annual social security returns. More detailed information can be obtained in Circular E, *Employer's Tax Guide*, available from local Internal Revenue Service offices.

In turn, the employer may obtain from the Social Security Administration information he originally supplied, such as the social security number of any of his employees (if he submits a written request identifying the employee or visits a district office where he is known); and a copy or a summary of a coverage or wage decision relating to one of his employees. No other information will be furnished without written consent of the employee concerned.

Self-employed people, including professionals, who have net earnings of $400 or more in a year are also covered under social security and must pay social security contributions on those

---

* Railroads are under a separate program administered by the Railroad Retirement Board, an independent government agency.

earnings. Since only one source is paying a tax, the rate is less than the combined employee–employer contribution. The rate is 8 percent of self-employment income, up to $12,000 in 1974. As with the employee–employer contribution, this rate will rise gradually in the future; the annual maximum earnings subject to contributions will increase automatically in the future. Reports and payments are made as part of the federal income tax return. Detailed information can be found in the Internal Revenue pamphlets, *Your Federal Income Tax* and *Tax Guide for Small Business*, sold by the Superintendent of Documents and local Internal Revenue Service offices for 75 cents each. Businessmen interested in a comprehensive manual on the social security system should order the *Social Security Handbook* from the Social Security Administration, Baltimore, Maryland 21235.

Medicare

A portion of the social security contributions by employers, employees, and self-employed people finances the hospital insurance known as Medicare. Many private health insurance companies, the Social Security Administration notes, "point out that their policies for people 65 and over are designed only to supplement Medicare. They recommend that their policyholders sign up for medical insurance under Medicare to get full protection. Even if you have other insurance, it may not pay for some medical services that are covered by Medicare, such as treatment at your doctor's office or his calls at your home. If you have other health insurance, you may want to get in touch with your insurance agent or the office where you pay health insurance premiums for specific information on this point."

In a single recent year, Medicare has paid out more than $7 billion in hospital care, physicians' services, and other health services to about twenty million people.

Social and Rehabilitation Service (SRS)

Primarily through grants to the states, SRS assists programs which enable employers to hire hundreds of thousands of disabled or disadvantaged persons. The vocational rehabilitation program now qualifies more than 300,000 physically and/or mentally handicapped persons per year for gainful employment. Employers may obtain detailed information from state vocational rehabilitation agencies, or from SRS's Rehabilitation Services Administration.

SRS also is involved in the Work Incentive (WIN) Program with the U.S. Department of Labor. SRS's Community Services Administration helps the states provide child care and other supportive services to persons participating in training or work under the WIN program. Private employers of WIN participants are eligible for a tax credit equal to 20 percent of the individual's wages for the first year, provided that at least two years of employment are completed. The WIN program is discussed further in the chapter on the Labor Department.

Many providers of Medicaid services, such as nursing homes, are subject to standards developed by SRS's Medical Services Administration.

Aging

The more than twenty-one million Americans over sixty-five constitute a large specialized market for U.S. business. The Administration on Aging, one of several HEW agencies grouped under a recently established Assistant Secretary for Human Development, helps fund state and local programs which may offer market opportunities. Among projects financed in its more than $195-million-a-year program are the provision of nutritionally sound, low-cost meals, and of transportation services geared to the needs of older persons. The agency also is a source of statistical information potentially valuable to business. Ask for its series of booklets, *Facts and Figures on Older Americans*.

The Human Development agencies also reach to the other end of the age spectrum. Companies that provide day care services for employees' children may be interested in one or more in the series of eight handbooks on day care practices published by the Office of Child Development. Number 7, dealing with administration of day care programs, including guides for management, is free.

Education

Federal education programs are a cornucopia that requires an 891-page catalog to describe. (Available at $3.25 from GPO; ask for Stock Number 1780-01095.) Many of these programs are administered by HEW's Office of Education (OE), National Institute of Education (NIE), and Fund for the Improvement of Postsecondary Education. The three agencies spend more than $5 billion annually. Most of this is allocated to state departments of education, the seventeen thousand local school systems, and to colleges and universities. These recipients make the actual spending decisions.

A major thrust of the Office of Education with widespread implications for business has been its "Career Education" concept. This gives students at all levels opportunities to explore the world of work, climaxing in the high school years with actual job experience by cooperative arrangements with business and industry. It is much broader than traditional vocational education in that even students in the lower elementary grades get exposure to a spectrum of occupational "clusters," such as transportation or health. A number of states, and some large-city school systems like Dallas and San Diego, have begun to install the concept, which is endorsed by the U.S. Chamber of Commerce.

OE works directly with the business community in several specific ways. As an example, OE's Division of Manpower Development and Training (DMDT) funds programs that teach automotive mechanics how to repair emission control devices. Businessmen who cannot find employees with such specialized skills can arrange with DMDT for setting up needed skills training programs.

In another instance, OE awarded a contract to the Portland Cement Association, the National Ready Mixed Association, and the American Concrete Institute to develop and evaluate a two-year concrete technology curriculum. The results of this cooperative effort have been field-tested and refined at six educational institutions across the country. Similar cooperative efforts between business and education are resulting in the development and updating of curriculums in office occupations, transportation, construction, health industries, and many other fields.

OE has created the post of Federal Coordinator for Industry–Education–Labor, as recommended by the Education Committee of the National Association of Manufacturers. The OE Federal Coordinator has named I–E–L coordinators in each of the fifty states and in many cases the state coordinators have named local level coordinators. Names of state coordinators may be obtained by writing to: State Coordinator, I–E–L, State Department of Education (State Capital), or to Commissioner of Education, 400 Maryland Avenue S.W., Washington, D.C. 20202.

The National Institute of Education was established in 1972 to improve American education through the conduct of research and development activities. With a budget in excess of $110 million, it plans to encourage proposals initiated in the research community, including studies of technology and productivity. It also will take over OE's career education program and the education vouchers program formerly under the Office of Economic Opportunity. Contractors will provide some support to NIE staff. For more information about NIE, contact Director,

National Institute of Education, 1200 9th Street S.W., Washington, D.C. 20208.

Publications of all HEW components are listed in a cumulative catalog, issued annually. For copies, write Thomas B. Joyce, HEW Office of Public Affairs, Washington, D.C. 20201.

Regional Offices

Since HEW operations are being increasingly decentralized, the department's regional offices are important contact points. Regional directors with their addresses and phone numbers are as follows:

Robert Fulton
John F. Kennedy Federal Bldg.
Government Center
Boston, Mass. 02203
(617) 223-6831

Bernice L. Bernstein
Federal Bldg.
26 Federal Plaza
New York, N.Y. 10007
(212) 264-4600

Gorham L. Black, Jr.
3535 Market St.
Philadelphia, Pa. 19101
(215) 597-0488

Frank J. Groschelle
Peachtree-Seventh Bldg.
50 7th St., N.E. (Rm. 149)
Atlanta, Ga. 30323
(404) 526-5817

Richard E. Friedman
300 S. Wacker Dr.
Chicago, Ill. 60607
(312) 353-5160

Stuart H. Clarke
1114 Commerce St.
Dallas, Tex. 75202
(214) 749-3396

Max Milo Mills
Federal Office Bldg.
601 E. 12th St.
Kansas City, Mo. 64106
(816) 374-3436

Rulon R. Garfield
Federal Office Bldg.
Rm. 11037, 1961 Stout St.
Denver, Colo. 80202
(303) 837-3373

Fernando E. C. DeBaca
Federal Office Bldg.
50 Fulton St.
San Francisco, Calif. 94102
(415) 556–6746

Bernard E. Kelly
Arcade Bldg.
1321 Second Ave.
Seattle, Wash. 98101
(206) 583–0420

Department of Health, Education, and Welfare
330 Independence Ave. S.W.
Washington, D.C. 20201
(202) 245-6296

HOUSING AND URBAN
DEVELOPMENT (HUD)

As anyone connected with the building business knows, federal housing programs have been undergoing a major overhaul. Many, especially those in the community development area such as urban renewal and model cities, have been terminated or suspended. Others, particularly those which subsidize the building of new low-income housing, are continuing on a limited basis while the administration seeks legislation for a new approach that stresses direct cash assistance to the home-seeker.

Recognizing that in areas where housing is short a cash assistance program might serve only to put pressure on rents, HUD also calls for some new construction. The approach here, according to the Secretary of HUD, is to say to the developer when he is putting together plans for a project: "If you will take a certain number of units in this project that you are building to satisfy the regular market, we will pay the difference between the rent that can be afforded by lower-income families and what you could get in the marketplace."

Meanwhile, some of HUD's meat-and-potatoes programs such as FHA mortgage insurance for unsubsidized housing continue full strength, and other operations less-known but significant to business, such as crime insurance and interstate land sales registration, are growing.

Mortgage Insurance

Mortgage insurance may cover a great variety of construction: private residences, rental housing, cooperatives, condominiums, mobile homes, nursing homes and intermediate care facilities, nonprofit hospitals, group practice medical facilities, land development, mobile home parks. Generally, applications are submitted through the mortgage lender. In the case of multifamily rental projects, the applicant first submits a request for feasibility determination to HUD.

Two programs of nonsubsidized mortgage insurance for rental housing have continued in operation. Section 207 provides insurance on private mortgages up to $20 million for projects containing eight or more units of rental housing for middle-income families.

Section 221 (d)(4) covers mortgages up to $12.5 million on projects of five or more rental units for families of lower-middle income. They may be rehabilitated as well as new construction.

In both programs, FHA regulates rents and rates of return. Mortgages may run forty years, and at the time of writing the maximum interest rate is 9½ percent. FHA charges an application fee of $1.50 per thousand of mortgage amount, which is deductible from the $3 per thousand fee on commitment amount. In addition, there is a $5 per thousand inspection fee, and an insurance premium of ½ of 1 percent of the mortgage amount. The mortgagee may make a service charge up to 2 percent.

FHA also insures mortgages up to $25 million for purchase of raw land and development of improved building sites or development of new communities. Repayment periods, except for mortgages covering new communities or sewer and water systems, may not exceed ten years. Application is made to FHA-approved lending institutions.

All FHA programs were affected in 1973 by the shortage of mortgage money. Late in 1973 the President took two steps to ease the tight mortgage situation. He directed HUD's Government National Mortgage Association (GNMA) to commit itself to buy up to $3 billion of residential mortgages carrying interest rates somewhat lower than the market rates. Nearly $2 billion will be in FHA or VA unsubsidized multifamily or single-family mortgages, and $1 billion for subsidized multifamily mortgages. Under a so-called "tandem plan," GNMA then sells the mortgages at market prices, absorbing any differential from its purchase price. Early in 1974, this plan was expanded to a possible total of $6.6 billion in mortgages.

At the same time, he directed the Federal Home Loan Bank Board to launch a "forward commitments" program, under which it promises to loan up to $2.5 billion to savings and loan associations to cover any mortgage commitments they make now.

GNMA's normal mode of operation is to guarantee timely payment on two types of mortgage-backed securities. The "pass-through" type is long term, maturing in step with the underlying mortgages. These are sold in issues of not less than $2 million each, mainly by mortgage banking institutions. In addition, "bond type" securities are issued by the Federal National Mortgage Association and the Federal Home Loan Mortgage Corporation. GNMA mortgage-backed securities are freely assignable, and an active secondary market has been established for them by major security dealers.

Two new types of securities in the GNMA program are:

Construction loan certificates, backed by FHA-insured advances on multifamily housing, hospitals, and nursing homes. On completion, these are exchanged for regular pass-through securities.

Mobile-home loan certificates, for pools in the minimum amount of $500,000.

Some HUD statistics will help put the government's housing role in perspective. Of some 3 million housing units produced or rehabilitated in the nation during 1972, HUD programs, including FHA, accounted for 486,000, or about 16 percent.

HUD impact on construction extends beyond financing. It sets minimum quality and environmental standards for property built with its assistance. These fill three volumes of mandatory standards and one of acceptable practices. HUD-developed noise standards are being used to evaluate sites for insured housing.

HUD also influences housing management. Before a multi-family project can be finally endorsed for insurance, a management plan must be drawn up according to a HUD guide, which includes a requirement for establishing realistic operating cost estimates. This is more a matter of self-protection than government interference, since HUD now finds itself the owner of more than 26,000 multifamily properties.

HUD also has established a National Center for Housing Management, which trains owners, managers, and other personnel in both private and public housing. It has the goal of becoming self-supporting at an early date.

Crime, Riot, and Flood Insurance

Among the newer HUD programs which deserve to be better known by business is Federal Crime Insurance. HUD's Federal Insurance Administration (FIA) makes such insurance available where it cannot be obtained at affordable rates through normal markets or state programs. Though HUD sets the provisions, application is made through local insurance agents and brokers. It is now sold in twelve states and the District of Columbia.

A related program provides urban property protection against losses from riots. Businessmen obtain this coverage from insurance companies, which in turn get reinsurance for excess losses from HUD. HUD limits such reinsurance to companies that cooperate with state insurance authorities in developing plans to assure property owners fair access to insurance requirements. Some four hundred companies in twenty-five states, the District of Columbia, and Puerto Rico are involved.

A third type of insurance is offered to protect businessmen and others against flood losses in areas prone to such disasters. On *existing* properties in areas so identified, the owner pays a subsidized rate to the insurance company, and FIA pays the difference between that and the normal premium. If an owner goes ahead and builds or substantially improves properties in an area after it has been identified as flood-prone, he must pay the full premium rate. FIA provides the insurance industry with reinsurance against heavy losses. The FIA Administrator feels that the number of people who have purchased protection is inadequate, and has asked state insurance commissioners to require licensed companies to notify all applicants and policy-holders of the availability of federal flood insurance. Businessmen may obtain up to $200,000 of coverage.

Interstate Land Sales

Either as a developer or purchaser of land, the businessman would do well to know about the full disclosure requirements administered by HUD's Office of Interstate Land Sales Registration (OILSR). Anyone who sells or leases, by use of the mails or any other means of interstate commerce, lots in a subdivision of fifty or more must file a statement with OILSR and must furnish pertinent extracts from that statement to purchasers at least forty-eight hours before the signing of an agreement. Otherwise, the purchaser has forty-eight hours after signing to void the sale. Approximately 4,800 developments have registered; three criminal convictions have been obtained, and administrative actions taken against 207 developers, including suspension of their right to sell land.

In a recent year, HUD placed 673 contracts with private industry for a total of more than $120 million, in support of its research and development programs and other activities. Businessmen interested in HUD contracts should get in touch with its office of General Services, or one of the ten Regional Office General Services Divisions in the list of field offices at end of this chapter.

For publications or other information, contact:
Program Information Center
Department of Housing and Urban Development
451 Seventh St. S.W.
Washington, D.C. 20410
(202) 755-6420.

Field Offices

REGION I

Regional Administrator—
  James J. Barry
Rm. 800, John F. Kennedy
  Federal Bldg.
Boston, Mass. 02203
(617) 223-4066

AREA OFFICES
999 Asylum Ave.
Hartford, Conn. 06105
(203) 244-3638
Area Director—Lawrence L.
  Thompson

Bulfinch Bldg.
15 New Chardon St.
Boston, Mass. 02114
(617) 223-4111
Area Director—M. Daniel
  Richardson, Jr.

Davidson Bldg.
1230 Elm St.
Manchester, N.H. 03101
(603) 669-7681
Area Director—Creeley S.
  Buchanan

INSURING OFFICES
Federal Bldg. and Post Office
202 Harlow St.
P.O. Box 1357
Bangor, Maine 04401
(207) 942-8271
Director—Wayne M. Johnson

330 Post Office Annex
Providence, R.I. 02903

(401) 528-4351
Director—Charles J. McCabe

Federal Bldg.
Elmwood Ave.
P.O. Box 989
Burlington, Vt. 05401
(802) 862-6501
Director—Leslie E. Snow

REGION II

Regional Administrator—
    S. William Green
26 Federal Plaza, Rm. 3541
New York, N.Y. 10007
(212) 264-8068

Grant Bldg.
560 Main St.
Buffalo, N.Y. 14202
(716) 842-3510
Area Director—Frank D.
    Cerabone

AREA OFFICES
The Parkade Bldg.
519 Federal St.
Camden, N.J. 08103
(609) 963-2541
Area Director—Philip G.
    Sadler

120 Church St.
New York, N.Y. 10007
(212) 264-2870
Area   Director—Joseph   D.
    Monticciolo (Acting)

COMMONWEALTH AREA OFFICE
255 Ponce de Leon Avenue
Hato Rey, Puerto Rico
Mailing Address:
    G Post Office Box 3869
    San   Juan,   Puerto   Rico
        00936

Gateway 1 Bldg.
Raymond Plaza
Newark, N.J. 07102
(201) 645-3010
Area   Director—James   P.
    Sweeney

(809) 765-0404
Area Administrator—José E.
    Febres Silva (Acting)

INSURING OFFICES
Westgate North
30 Russell Rd.
Albany, N.Y. 12206
(518) 472-3567
Director—Robert J. Wolf
    (Acting)

175 Fulton Ave.
Hempstead, N.Y. 11550
(516) 485-5000
Director—Michael Leen
    (Acting)

REGION III

Regional Administrator—
    Theodore R. Robb
Curtis Bldg.
625 Walnut St.
Philadelphia, Pa. 19106
(215) 597-2560

AREA OFFICES
Universal North Bldg.
1875 Connecticut Ave. N.W.
Washington, D.C. 20009
(202) 382-4855
Area   Director—Harry   W.
    Staller (Acting)

Two Hopkins Pl.
Mercantile   Bank   and   Trust
    Bldg.
Baltimore, Md. 21201
(301) 962-2121
Area Director—Allen T. Clapp

Curtis Bldg.
625 Walnut St.
Philadelphia, Pa. 19106
(215) 597-2665
Area   Director—Joseph   A.
    LaSala (Acting)

Two Allegheny Ctr.
Pittsburgh, Pa. 15212
(412) 644-2802
Area Director—Charles J.
    Lieberth

701 E. Franklin St.
Richmond, Va. 23219
(804) 782-2721
Area   Director—Carroll   A.
    Mason

INSURING OFFICES
Farmers Bank Bldg., 14th Fl.
919 Market St.
Wilmington, Del. 19801
(302) 571-6330
Director—Henry McC. Win-
    chester, Jr.

New Federal Bldg.
500 Quarrier St.
P.O. Box 2948
Charleston, W. Va. 25330
(304) 343-6181
Director—H. William Rogers

SPECIAL RECOVERY OFFICE
Lackawanna County Bldg.
Spruce and Adams Ave.

Scranton, Pa. 18503
(717) 344-7393
Director—James D. Corbin

REGION IV

Regional Administrator—
E. Lamar Seals
Peachtree-Seventh Bldg.
50 7th St., N.E.
Atlanta, Ga. 30323
(404) 526-5585

Children's Hospital Founda-
tion Bldg.
601 S. Floyd St.
P.O. Box 1044
Louisville, Ky. 40201
(502) 582-5251
Area Director—Virgil G.
Kinnaird

AREA OFFICES
Daniel Bldg.
15 S. 20th St.
Birmingham, Ala. 35233
(205) 325-3264
Area Director—Jon Will Pitts

101-C Third Fl., Jackson Mall
300 Woodrow Wilson
Ave., W.
Jackson, Miss. 39213
(601) 366-2634
Area Director—James S.
Roland

Peninsular Pl.
661 Riverside Ave.
Jacksonville, Fla. 32204
(904) 791-2626
Area Director—Forrest W.
Howell

2309 W. Cone Blvd.
Northwest Pl.
Greensboro, N.C. 27408
(919) 275-9111
Area Director—Richard B.
Barnwell

Peachtree Center Bldg.
230 Peachtree St., N.W.
Atlanta, Ga. 30303
(404) 526-4576
Area Director—William A.
Hartman, Jr. (Acting)

1801 Main St.
Jefferson Sq.
Columbia, S.C. 29202
(803) 765-5591
Area Director—Clifton G.
Brown

One Northshore Bldg.
1111 Northshore Dr.
Knoxville, Tenn. 37919
(615) 584-8527
Area Director—Carroll G.
    Oakes

INSURING OFFICES
3001 Ponce de Leon Blvd.
Coral Gables, Fla. 33134
(305) 445-2561
Director—Louis T. Baine
    (Acting)

4224-28 Henderson Blvd.
P.O. Box 18165

Tampa, Fla. 33609
(813) 228-2501
Director—K. Wayne Swiger

28th Fl., 100 N. Main St.
Memphis, Tenn. 38103
(901) 534-3141
Director—Glynn G. Raby, Jr.
    (Acting)

1717 West End Bldg.
Nashville, Tenn. 37203
(615) 749-5521
Director—George N. Gragson

REGION V

Regional Administrator—
    George J. Vavoulis
300 S. Wacker Dr.
Chicago, Ill. 60606
(312) 353-5680

AREA OFFICES
17 N. Dearborn St.
Chicago, Ill. 60602
(312) 353-7660
Area Director—John L.
    Waner

Willowbrook 5 Bldg.
4720 Kingsway Dr.
Indianapolis, Ind. 46205
(317) 633-7188
Area Director—Choice Ed-
    wards (Acting)

5th Fl., First National Bldg.
660 Woodward Ave.
Detroit, Mich. 48226
(313) 226-7900
Area Director—John E. Kane
    (Acting)

Griggs-Midway Bldg.
1821 University Ave.
St. Paul, Minn. 55104
(612) 725-4701
Area Director—Thomas T.
    Feeney

60 E. Main St.
Columbus, Ohio 43215
(614) 469-7345
Area Director—Elmer C. Bin-
    ford (Acting)

744 N. 4th St.
Milwaukee, Wisc. 53203
(414) 224–3223
Area Director—Richard A. Kaiser (Acting)

INSURING OFFICES
Lincoln Tower Pl.
524 S. 2nd St., Rm. 600
Springfield, Ill. 62704
(217) 525–4414
Director—Boyd O. Barton

Northbrook Bldg. No. 11
2922 Fuller Ave., N.E.
Grand Rapids, Mich. 49505

(616) 456–2225
Director—Alfred Raven

Federal Office Bldg.
550 Main St., Rm. 9009
Cincinnati, Ohio 45202
(513) 684–2884
Director—Charles Collins II (Acting)

Federal Bldg.
1240 E. 9th St.
Cleveland, Ohio 44199
(216) 522–4065
Director—Charles P. Lucas

REGION VI

Regional Administrator—
  Richard L. Morgan
Rm. 14B35, New Dallas Federal Bldg.
1100 Commerce St.
Dallas, Tex. 75202
(214) 749–7401

AREA OFFICES
Rm. 1490, Union National Pl.
Little Rock, Ark. 72201
(501) 378–5401
Area Director—Thomas E. Barber

Plaza Tower
1001 Howard Ave.

New Orleans, La. 70113
(504) 527–2063
Area Director—Thomas J. Armstrong

301 N. Hudson St.
Oklahoma City, Okla. 73102
(405) 231–4181
Area Director—Robert H. Breeden

2001 Bryan Tower, 4th Fl.
Dallas, Tex. 75202
(214) 749–1601
Area Director—Manuel Sanchez III

Kallison Bldg.
410 S. Main Ave.
P.O. Box 9163
San Antonio, Tex. 78285
(512) 225-5511
Area Director—Finnis E. Jolly

INSURING OFFICES
514 Ricou-Brewster Bldg.
425 Milam St.
Shreveport, La. 71101
(318) 425-1241
Director—Rudy Langford

625 Truman St., N.E.
Albuquerque, N.M. 87110
(505) 766-3251
Director—Luther G.
    Branham

1708 Utica Sq.
P.O. Box 4054
Tulsa, Okla. 74152

(918) 581-7435
Director—Robert H. Gardner

819 Taylor St.
Rm. 13A01, Federal Bldg.
Fort Worth, Tex. 76102
(817) 334-3233
Director—Richard M.
    Hazlewood

Two Greenway Pl. E., Suite
    200
Houston, Tex. 77046
(713) 226-4335
Director—William A. Painter

Courthouse and Federal Office
    Bldg.
1205 Texas Ave.
P.O. Box 1647
Lubbock, Tex. 79408
(806) 747-3711
Director—Don D. Earney

REGION VII

Regional Administrator—
    Elmer E. Smith
Federal Office Bldg., Rm. 300
911 Walnut St.
Kansas City, Mo. 64106
(816) 374-2661

AREA OFFICES
Two Gateway Ctr.
4th and State Sts.

Kansas City, Kan. 66101
(816) 374-4355
Area Director—William R.
    Southerland

210 N. 12th St.
St. Louis, Mo. 63101
(314) 622-4760
Area Director—Elmo O.
    Turner

Univac Bldg.
7100 W. Ctr. Rd.
Omaha, Neb. 68106
(402) 221–9301
Area Director—Guy J. Birch

INSURING OFFICES
210 Walnut St.
Rm. 259, Federal Bldg.

Des Moines, Iowa 50309
(515) 284–4512
Director—Nate Ruben

700 Kansas Ave.
Topeka, Kan. 66603
(913) 234–8241
Director—Jim Haff (Acting)

REGION VIII

Regional Administrator—
    Robert C. Rosenheim
Federal Bldg.
1961 Stout St.
Denver, Colo. 80202
(303) 837–4881

INSURING OFFICES
4th Fl., Title Bldg.
909 17th St.
Denver, Colo. 80202
(303) 837–2441
Director—Joseph G. Wagner

616 Helena Ave.
Helena, Mont. 59601
(406) 442–3237
Director—Orvin B. Fjare

Federal Bldg.
653 2nd Ave. N.
P.O. Box 2483
Fargo, N.D. 58102

(701) 237–5136
Director—Duane R. Liffrig

119 Federal Bldg. U.S.
    Courthouse
400 S. Phillips Ave.
Sioux Falls, S.D. 57102
(605) 336–2980
Director—Rodger L.
    Rosenwald

125 S. State St.
P.O. Box 11009
Salt Lake City, Utah 84111
(801) 524–5237
Director—L. C. Romney

Federal Office Bldg.
100 E. B St.
P.O. Box 580
Casper, Wyo. 82601
(307) 265–5550
Director—Marshall F. Elliott
    (Acting)

REGION IX

Regional Administrator—
Robert H. Baida
450 Golden Gate Ave.
P.O. Box 36003
San Francisco, Calif. 94102
(415) 556–4752

AREA OFFICES
2500 Wilshire Blvd.
Los Angeles, Calif. 90057
(213) 688–5973
Area   Director—Roland   E.
Camfield (Acting)

1 Embarcadero Ctr.
Suite 1600
San Francisco, Calif. 94111
(415) 556–2238
Area   Director—James   H.
Price

INSURING OFFICES
244 W. Osborn Rd.
P.O. Box 13468
Phoenix, Ariz. 85002
(602) 261–4441
Director—Merritt R. Smith

801 I St.
P.O. Box 1978

Sacramento, Calif. 95809
(916) 449–3471
Director—Richard D.
Chamberlain

110 W. C St.
P.O. Box 2648
San Diego, Calif. 92112
(714) 293–5310
Director—Albert E. Johnson

1440 E. 1st St.
Santa Ana, Calif. 92701
(714) 836–2451
Director—Robert L. Simpson

1000 Bishop St., 10th Fl.
P.O. Box 3377
Honolulu, Hawaii 96813
(808) 546–2136
Director—Alvin K. H. Pang

1050 Bible Way
P.O. Box 4700
Reno, Nev. 89505
(702) 784–5356
Director—Morley W.
Griswold

REGION X

Regional Administrator—
Oscar P. Pederson
Arcade Pl. Bldg.

1321 2nd Ave.
Seattle, Wash. 98101
(206) 442–5415

AREA OFFICES
520 S.W. 6th Ave.
Portland, Ore. 97204
(503) 221-2558
Area Director—Russell H.
  Dawson

Arcade Pl. Bldg.
1321 2nd Ave.
Seattle, Wash. 98101
(206) 442-7456
Area Director—Marshall D.
  Majors

INSURING OFFICES
334 W. 5th Ave.

Anchorage, Alaska 99501
(907) 272-5561, ext. 791
Director—James Tveit
  (Acting)

331 Idaho St.
P.O. Box 32
Boise, Idaho 83707
(208) 342-2711
Director—Charles L.
  Holley, Jr.

W. 920 Riverside Ave.
Spokane, Wash. 99201
(509) 456-4571
Director—E. Daryl Mabee

INTERIOR: RESEARCH
AND RESOURCES

If the average businessman ever thinks of the Department of the Interior, it is probably not as an agency with a bearing on his business, but as the custodian of national parks and monuments he might like to visit on his vacation.

Yet, within this sprawling department—it has more than a dozen bureaus and two thousand field offices—is a storehouse of information, and opportunity, for the businessman who knows what to look for and where to find it. Unlike the Department of Commerce or the Small Business Administration, which regard their mission in life as helping the businessman, Interior is primarily concerned with conservation of the nation's natural resources. Consistent with this goal, it is perfectly willing to be of service to business, but for the most part, the businessman will have to take the initiative. If he does, he will find such widely diverse activities of potential interest to business as:

- Experiments in conversion of salt water to fresh;
- Production of low-cost power for homes and industry;
- Research grants for development of clean coal;
- Help to employers for on-the-job training of Indian people;

- Tax incentives to attract industry to United States island territories.

The scope of the department can best be grasped in terms of its four operating areas:

Energy and Minerals. Work in this area is carried out by the Geological Survey, the Bureau of Mines, the Mining Enforcement and Safety Administration, the Office of Oil and Gas, the four regional Power Administrations (Alaska, Bonneville [Northwestern], Southeastern, Southwestern) and Offices of Research and Development, Energy Conservation, and Energy Data and Analysis.

Land and Water Resources. Here we find the Bureau of Land Management, the Bureau of Reclamation, Office of Land Use and Water Planning, Office of Saline Water, and Office of Water Resources Research.

Fish and Wildlife and Parks. A Bureau of Sports Fisheries and Wildlife is the arm of the government for wildlife resources, important, the Secretary of Interior says, "because animals reflect subtle changes in the environment that serve as early warnings." The Bureau of Outdoor Recreation helps states acquire land for recreational purposes, and has already made more than $800 million in such grants. The National Park Service operates 162 national parks and seashores and maintains hundreds of historical sites.

Indian Affairs. The Bureau of Indian Affairs provides educational, economic, and technical aid to 488,000 reservation-dwelling Indian people.

The Office of Territorial Affairs is concerned with some 200,000 people in the U.S. territories of Guam, American Samoa, and the Virgin Islands, and it also administers the Micronesian Islands under a trusteeship arrangement with the United Nations.

Each of the areas of Interior is worth a more detailed examination. The businessman who dips into this grab bag is likely to come up with something of value.

Finding and Using Minerals

A significant example of joint impact on business by several operating areas of Interior is the action on the oil companies' application for a right-of-way permit to cross federal lands in building a trans-Alaska pipeline. The first step Interior took was to launch a massive environmental impact study of the pipeline proposal.

Geological Survey prepared strip maps of the proposed corridor, orthophoto maps of the oilfield development around Prudhoe Bay, and identified problems of construction of a hot-oil pipeline in the permanently frozen layers beneath the surface.

The Bureau of Sports Fisheries and Wildlife studied potential effects on the migratory habits of caribou, and how fish spawning habits and life cycles might be changed by alterations in terrain.

The Bureau of Land Management organized public hearings in Washington and Anchorage.

The Bureau of Indian Affairs contracted for a study analyzing the economic and cultural effect of the pipeline on the native population.

Interior made 136 geologic maps in a recent year; the goal of complete geologic mapping of the United States is still only a goal. Nevertheless, the help that Interior can give in finding new mineral resources is of increasing economic importance as our mineral hunger grows—twice during the last three decades we have doubled the money value of mineral production as we consumed more minerals than those used by all the people in previous history. Interior helps uncover minerals in three ways.

Geologic mapping and direct exploration. For example, the department's Geological Survey discovered new deposits of beryllium ore in the Lost River area of Alaska. Beryllium, a scarce metal worth approximately $70 a pound, is important to the government, as well as to industry, because of its potential uses in supersonic planes, space craft, missiles, and nuclear reactors. Geological Survey mapping and geochemical exploration programs have resulted in important discoveries of coal, copper, gold, molybdenum, and zinc in recent years.

Implications of research. Mesquite leaves and twigs have been found to accumulate zinc, lead, barium, strontium, copper, and molybdenum. Thus, analyses of ash from mesquite might provide geochemical clues to hidden ore bodies.

Financial assistance to exploration. The Geological Survey's Office of Minerals Exploration will contract to pay up to three-fourths the cost of exploring for thirty-six different minerals. To get such help, you do not have to be an experienced miner yourself, though you will be responsible for getting competent people to supervise the exploration. What you do have to show is ownership, lease, or other sufficient interest in the property to be explored; that funds are not available from private sources on reasonable terms; and that you would not ordinarily undertake the exploration solely at your own expense. If the exploration is successful, you will have to repay the government's contribution by a 5 percent royalty on production; if nothing is produced, there is no obligation to repay. More detailed information on this program may be obtained either from Washington (a question-and-answer booklet, *Exploration Assistance*, is available without charge from Office of Minerals Exploration, United States Department of the Interior, Washington, D.C. 20242) or from field offices in Spokane, Washington (W. 920 Riverside Avenue), Menlo Park, California (345 Middlefield Road), Denver, Colorado (Building 26, Federal Center), and Knoxville, Tennessee (301 West Cumberland Avenue).

In the course of its geologic researches, Interior sometimes comes up with by-products useful to businesses completely unrelated to minerals. Thus, new maps in the San Francisco, Denver, Knoxville, and Connecticut valley areas have proved useful to real-estate developers in avoiding potential natural hazards. Planners of any major construction project can use information about surface and subsurface conditions when available from a Geological Survey map.

These maps include not only the geologic type mentioned earlier, but also topographic—the survey completes some sixteen hundred of the latter kind each year. For most areas of the nation, such maps are available at 75 cents each. It also offers contact prints of aerial photographs at $1.25 to $1.75 a print (or enlargements at additional cost). The survey's Map Information Office will direct the businessman to reliable sources of materials not produced by the department.

Interior does not stop with mapping, exploration, or financial help for the discovery of minerals. It conducts an extensive research program looking toward new and improved uses of minerals, the results of which potentially affect every businessman. For example, large reserves of nonmagnetic taconites have been bypassed by mining companies as a domestic source of iron ore for lack of an acceptable process to concentrate them. The Bureau of Mines has conducted a vigorous technological development program to make flotation of nonmagnetic taconites an economically feasible process. In 1972, after several years of cooperative effort with the bureau, the Cleveland-Cliffs Iron Co. announced plans to allocate $190 million for its Tilden project using the bureau-developed selective flotation process for concentration of the iron ore.

A new process for removing sulfur dioxide from waste gases of base-metal smelters has been developed by the Bureau of Mines. It reduces the sulfur dioxide to elemental sulfur, which can be stored with a minimum of land pollution and without air and water pollution. A pilot plant at a western copper smelter effectively captured more than 90 percent of the sulfur from the smelter gas. The process has attracted favorable comment from the smelting, electric utility, chemical, and oil industries.

In the Bureau of Mines, a major research effort is now focused on the construction of a new type of recycling plant that will reclaim metals, minerals, and combustibles from unburned refuse. Successful development should go a long way toward relieving solid waste problems and toward slowing the drain on natural resources.

Important progress in the recovery of gold has been achieved through a bureau-developed process that capitalizes on the ability of activated carbon to selectively absorb gold. A cooperative pilot plant test of the process at the Homestake Mining Co., in Lead, South Dakota, was successful. As a result, the company has built a new 2,350 ton-per-day carbon-in-pulp plant to replace its old slime plant, and the efficiency of its gold processing operation has increased.

The Bureau of Mines has developed a new high-temperature soft-soldering system based on zinc, which promises to fill the need for solders with temperature capabilities intermediate between lead-tin solders and the brazing alloys. Between the temperatures of 140° C. and 500° C., there have been no industrially accepted solders for copper, copper alloys, and low-carbon steel. The new high-strength solder systems for this intermediate temperature region can be significant in the electronic, home appliance, and heat exchange industries.

When it comes to helium, the bureau wears three hats— seller, buyer, and researcher. Until recently, it was the only commercial supplier in the free world; it remains the largest producer. Now it also buys helium recovered from natural gas by private industry. Methods it has developed have brought the price of helium down from $2,500 a cubic foot at the turn of the century to less than $40 a thousand cubic feet today. It is also contributing to the rapid discovery of new uses. Originally prized as a nonflammable substance for inflating lighter-than-air craft, helium is now used in arc welding, anaesthesia, quality-control testing, and cryogenics (low-temperature research). Tomorrow, liquid helium may permit a metallic coil, weighing less than a pound, to generate a protective magnetic shield around spaceships passing through the Van Allen radiation belt.

Both the Bureau of Mines and the Office of Coal Research (OCR) are developing processes to convert coal into low-sulfur or sulfur-free gas.

Under a cost-sharing program with the American Gas Association, OCR is advancing a variety of coal-to-pipeline gas processes through three pilot plants. Industry is expected to assume primary responsibility as the processes enter the demonstration phase, which would involve reduced federal funding.

The Interior Department, through the Bureau of Mines and the Office of Oil and Gas, plays a powerful role in the affairs of the petroleum and natural gas industry, which in turn affects many other industries. Its voice is important in decisions of an interagency committee on allowable imports, on which the price and availability of oil products used by industry may hinge.

Research projects continually come up with methods of increasing oil recovery and utilization, and with such unlikely bonuses as the identification of detrimental substances in petroleum which can be screened for possible carcinogenic characteristics.

Businessmen needing information on oil and gas matters will find available to them, in the Department's Central Library, four thousand volumes on petroleum, one of the most complete collections on the subject open to the public.

Water and Power

The water and power activities of the Interior Department are of particular importance to the West, but their business significance is by no means limited to that area. As President Kennedy said on the twenty-fifth anniversary of the Bonneville Power Administration, "The economic growth of the Pacific Northwest has created a bigger market for Detroit cars and Pittsburgh steel and Boston shoes and Atlanta textiles."

The department seeks to put water to work for a variety of purposes, all of which may benefit the businessman directly or indirectly. The multipurpose approach involves irrigation, power generation, municipal and industrial water supply, flood control, and recreation.

Here's what to look for where a water resources project is established. Leaving aside the opportunities for construction contractors (a not easily overlooked item of some $400 million a year), the building of a dam often results in the establishment of a whole new town, creating openings for all types of enterprises. Such was the case of Page, Arizona, born of the Glen Canyon Dam. More than one hundred commercial buildings have been erected to meet the needs of nine thousand residents and thousands of tourists who visit the dam.

Next, we find that irrigation water tends to encourage diversified farming with higher income and greater business prosperity for the whole area. In 1973, the total value of crops grown on the 8.8 million acres of federally irrigated land was well over $2.7 billion. This not only made better consumers of the more than half a million people on these farms, but also created job opportunities in the area for twice that many people, each of whom had twice as much income as the typical agricultural worker. Hence, irrigation project areas are likely to be good locations for retail and service enterprises. Write the Bureau of Reclamation, Department of the Interior, Washington, D.C. 20240 for more information.

Accumulation of water naturally leads to generation of power, and the department annually markets more than $439 million of electricity, generated at 112 large and small federally operated power plants. The availability of this power often is an incentive to locating new industry. In the Northwest, for example, the Bonneville Power Administration's industrial rate—one of the lowest in the nation—has brought into being a large-scale electro-process industry in light metals, chemicals, and abrasives.

The nation's electric power needs double every decade, and in certain areas, at certain times, industry faces a threat of power shortage. Working in cooperation with private utilities, Interior is taking some bold steps to minimize the threat. Pooling is one such step. A pioneering agreement involving seventy-eight government and private plants in the Pacific Northwest produces an extra million or more kilowatts of power that would be wasted if each utility operated its hydroplants independently.

Still another new method of wringing the utmost energy out of a drop of water is "pumped-back storage." Energy which can be acquired cheaply at periods of low demand is used to pump water to high elevations, there to be released for generation of hydroelectricity at hours of peak consumption.

Finally, the atom is being used. Steam created by the heat from the Atomic Energy Commission's reactor at Hanford, Washington, is used in the generating of 800,000 kilowatts. New industries have been attracted by this source of inexpensive energy, produced in this plant and distributed by Interior's Bonneville Power Administration.

In the course of building its huge water and power projects, Interior conducts research on methods and materials which yields information of value to the entire construction industry. More than 250 laboratory reports a year are issued, covering such varied subjects as weed control, protective coatings, foundation sites, weathering, and concrete mix design.

Thus far, in mentioning water, we have meant only fresh water. But in some areas, with a growing industry and a growing population, more fresh water is needed than is available. Interior's experiments with the conversion of salt and brackish water to fresh is helping to solve this problem.

In ten years, the cost of conversion has been reduced from $5 a thousand gallons to as little as $1, which in some areas is economically attractive. In the Virgin Islands, for example, drinking water had to be brought in by barge at a cost of more than $3 a thousand gallons. Now a saline water plant is producing about 300,000 gallons daily for $1.63 a thousand.

Businessmen facing problems of water supply that might be solved by installation of such equipment can get more information about it from the Office of Saline Water, Department of the Interior, Washington, D.C. 20240.

Other information on water of potential importance to businessmen is available from the Geological Survey, which collects data on the chemical characteristics of natural waters at some 750 points, makes daily checks on the flow of streams at more than 7,400 points, and publishes reports on ground water levels and artesian pressures.

Land and People

Interior's Bureau of Land Management is leasing agent for mineral rights to public land under its own jurisdiction or that of other federal agencies. It also leases mineral rights to privately owned land where mineral rights were reserved to the federal government. Occasionally, the bureau sells, for business or other use, tracts of land that are surplus to government needs.

Some idea of how big a landlord this one branch of government is can be gained from the fact that 700 million acres of federal lands are eligible for leasing. Royalties from leasing oil, gas, and other minerals on public lands contributed nearly half a billion dollars to the federal Treasury in fiscal 1973. The department also is moving toward leasing of oil shale and geothermal land. Some 8.3 million acres of public land contain oil shale. Interior sees a potential for private industry's producing 900,000 barrels of shale oil a day by the mid-1980s. Known geothermal areas totaling about 1 million acres have been proposed for leasing by competitive bidding. Millions more acres prospectively valuable for geothermal development would be available for noncompetitive leasing if proposed regulations are adopted. In addition, the bureau administers some of the most valuable Douglas fir forests in the world, selling more than a billion board-feet of lumber a year.

For more details, consult the state directors of the Bureau of Land Management in Juneau, Alaska; Phoenix, Arizona; Sacramento, California; Denver, Colorado; Boise, Idaho; Billings, Montana; Reno, Nevada; Santa Fe, New Mexico; Portland, Oregon; Salt Lake City, Utah; or Cheyenne, Wyoming. If more convenient, write Bureau of Land Management, Department of the Interior, Washington, D.C. 20240.

The National Parks are the focus for a substantial service

business to meet the needs of the people who made some ninety million visits in a recent year. Opportunities to obtain concessions are dwindling, because of a policy of trying to preserve the wilderness. But the constantly increasing use of the National Parks means increasing opportunities for restaurants, service stations, and other enterprises in the areas surrounding the parks. And within the parks, the service is exploring the possibility of using various forms of mass transit—from shuttle bus to aerial cable cars, tramways, and mini-railroads—as alternatives to private cars. Here, too, private enterprise may find a role. A booklet, *Information Pertaining to the Granting of Concessions in Areas of the National Park System,* may be obtained without charge from the Director, National Park Service, Department of the Interior, Washington, D.C. 20240.

Economic development is getting new emphasis in the Bureau of Indian Affairs, with potential benefits to businessmen as well as to the American Indian. The Bureau is actively encouraging Indian people throughout the country to engage in their own commercial, industrial, and tourist activities. To date, 238 industrial and commercial enterprises have been established on or near Indian reservations in twenty-three states including Alaska. Among these are a diamond processing plant at Chandler, Arizona, started by Harry Winston, Inc., internationally famous diamond merchants of New York City; and Fairchild Semi-conductor Division, established on the Navajo Reservation at Shiprock, New Mexico, to produce solid-state electronic components. More than 90 percent of the employees at Fairchild are Indian people. Fabri-Cut Inc., at Pryor, Oklahoma, manufacturer of bedspreads, started in 1973 with 140 employees of whom 98 are Indian people. The Red Lake Sawmill, a tribal enterprise in Redby, Minnesota, is undergoing plant expansion that will double its capacity, adding four million board-feet of lumber to its output.

The Bureau of Indian Affairs not only can provide information about plant sites and related services, but also offers financial assistance for on-the-job training of Indian employees. For more details, write the Bureau of Indian Affairs, Department of the Interior, Washington, D.C. 20240.

Territories

The businessman who wants to eat his profit cake, and have his dreams too, would do well to get acquainted with Interior's Office of Territorial Affairs. It can tell him about opportunities in such romantic places as American Samoa, Guam, the Virgin Islands, and the Trust Territory of the Pacific Islands.

Samoa, once accessible only by boat to Pago Pago, now has a $4.5-million jet airstrip which puts it within four hours' flight of Hawaii. Hotels and other tourist facilities are a natural outgrowth of this development; a watch processing plant, a clothing factory, and other light industries are being established.

Guam has experienced a boom in investment and business activity following the lifting of a rule imposed in 1941 that required even United States citizens entering the island to get a naval security clearance. Some 147,000 tourists, many of them Japanese, visited the island in 1972. Over twenty hotels are in operation, and by 1974 Guam is expected to have 2,900 hotel rooms. The Commissioner, Department of Commerce, Agana, Guam, can provide details on business opportunities.

Industry as well as tourism is growing rapidly in the Virgin Islands, because of the attractive tariff and tax situation. The Virgin Islands are not a free port as commonly defined, but their exports to the United States are duty-free if they are of native origin, or if they contain foreign materials valued at half, or less, of their total value. In other words, you can set up a watch assembly plant in the Virgin Islands at which you assemble Swiss watch parts; if the parts are valued at less than half the value of the watch, you can bring it into the United States duty-free. This has, in fact, been done by producers of jewelry and woolens as well as watchmakers. Since 1954, more than twenty new enterprises have been established in the Virgin

Islands, to fabricate foreign materials into products exported to the United States. They employ about six hundred persons with an annual payroll exceeding $1.1 million.

Normally, there is a 6 percent duty on foreign goods brought into the Virgin Islands. The above-mentioned law is an exception to the 6 percent rule. Another exception, of special interest to prospective retailers, is the $200 exemption enjoyed by tourists. That is, $200 worth of foreign goods purchased in the Virgin Islands can be brought into the United States by American tourists duty-free; the same goods purchased in, say, Trinidad, would be duty-free only up to the $100 level.

The Virgin Islands has an Industrial Incentive Program, which permits the Virgin Islands Tax Exemption Board to grant a ten-year exemption from property taxes and fees to establish or expand a manufacturing industry and certain other specified enterprises (including tourist hotels; housing and other real-estate developments; television broadcasting; water transport; aerial cable car tramway). The holder of a Virgin Islands tax exemption certificate also may be granted a rebate of 75 percent of income taxes and 90 percent of the 6 percent customs duties collected in the Virgin Islands. For exporters of inexpensive goods, on which the United States tariff is not especially high, the local tax exemption may be of more importance than duty-free status in the United States market. The man to write for more details is the Commissioner of Commerce, St. Thomas, Virgin Islands.

Guam likewise has a tax exemption law, and there are no duties of any sort. As in the Virgin Islands, goods shipped from Guam to the United States may enter free of United States duties if the goods are of native origin or contain foreign materials valued at not more than 50 percent of their total value.

American Samoa has a tax exemption law of its own, similar to that of the Virgin Islands. Write the governor at Pago Pago, Tutuila, American Samoa, for details. It also has the 50 percent feature on fabricated goods; items containing not more than 50 percent foreign materials (by value) can be brought into the

United States from Samoa duty-free. There is *no* property tax, but property ownership is clouded because the land is held communally by tribes or clans. No duties are levied on imports into American Samoa. Excise taxes are levied on liquor, tobacco, automobiles, etc., at port of entry. Samoa also has its own income tax law.

Through a high commissioner, the Interior Department administers the Trust Territory of the Pacific Islands, with headquarters at Saipan in the Marianas. Tourist development is starting in the Trust Territory and in 1972 surpassed the copra (dried coconut) industry as a source of income. Details on economic development may be obtained from Director, Resources and Development, Trust Territory of the Pacific Government, Saipan, Mariana Islands 96950.

Fish and Wildlife

Even sports fishing, also a concern of Interior, has its business side. Fishing and hunting, the companion responsibilities of Interior's Bureau of Sports Fisheries and Wildlife, put some $3 billion a year into the coffers of businesses serving American anglers and hunters. The bureau offers a variety of aids to the conservation of wildlife which is the basis for this business and sport. As one instance, it will provide, without charge, hatchery-raised fish to ponds constructed on individual farms. For another, it has developed a method of chemically treating seeds so that rodents will not eat them. This has enabled tree farmers of the Pacific Northwest to save up to $18 an acre by direct seeding, with southern watermelon growers also benefiting from the discovery.

Because of concern about the effect of heavy metals, plasticizers used in industrial processes, and pesticides on fish and wildlife, the Bureau of Sports Fisheries and Wildlife is stepping up research on their impact. Businesses emitting or producing these items could be significantly influenced by the results.

How to Find Out More

No attempt will be made here to list the two thousand field offices operated in all sections of the country. But a good way to start getting information about Interior's service to businesses without going to Washington is through one of the department's eight Field Special Assistants, who represent the entire department in their regions. Their locations are as follows:

JFK Federal Bldg., Rm. 2003K, Boston, Mass. 02203

536 S. Clark St., Chicago Ill. 60605

517 Gold Ave. S.W., Rm. 4030, Albuquerque, N.M. 87101

1002 N.E. Holladay St., P.O. Box 3612, Portland, Ore. 97208

148 Cain St., N.E., Atlanta, Ga. 30303

Bldg. 67, Rm. 688, Federal Center, Denver, Colo. 80225

450 Golden Gate Ave., P.O. Box 36098, San Francisco, Calif. 94102.

All the above addresses should be preceded by the words "U.S. Department of the Interior."

In Washington, the department headquarters is:
C St. between 18th & 19th Sts. N.W.
Washington, D.C. 20240
(202) 343-1100

DEPARTMENT OF JUSTICE:
FRIEND OR FOE?

Ask the average businessman for his immediate reaction to the Department of Justice, and he'd say "trouble—something I want to stay as far away from as possible."

To a degree, he'd be justified. A certain number of businessmen meet the Department of Justice only on the receiving end of its prosecutions for alleged antitrust violations, tax evasion, or fraud. But it is also true, and less known, that businessmen can and do turn to the department for help. In fact, a surprising number of its prosecutions are a result of complaints by businessmen that they have been or are likely to be hurt by the actions of other businessmen. This is especially true in the antitrust field.

Complaints of antitrust violations received from businessmen cover every conceivable commodity—from concrete pipes and corrugated boxes to rock salt, waste paper, drugs, milk, and meat. Big businesses as well as small are among the complainants. There is no specific format for complaints. All that need be done is to state the facts in a letter to the Antitrust Division, Department of Justice, Washington, D.C. 20530.

Price-Fixing

About half of the antitrust cases filed in 1972 involved price-fixing; the balance were mostly merger and monopoly charges. A former attorney general conceded that some areas of the antitrust laws are complex and subject to honest differences of view, but took an uncompromising attitude toward businessmen who engage in price-fixing:

> A conspiracy to fix prices or rig bids is simply economic racketeering and the persons involved should be subject to as severe punishment as the courts deem appropriate. When possible, I believe that we should not only take action against the corporations or companies involved, but against the individuals who have participated in these frauds. I am against granting immunity to the individuals, with the result that the cases end with their companies paying a fine. I think those responsible should be held responsible.

He based his position not only on moral grounds, but also on the economic destructivenesss of price-fixing. "In almost every instance when we have successfully completed a price-fixing case, competition has been restored; prices to the consumer have dropped; and the competitors who were not involved in the conspiracy have received a new lease on life and can begin to do business again."

An assistant attorney general in charge of the Antitrust Division invited businessmen who have "evidence or reasonable ground for suspicion of a price-fixing conspiracy among sellers to report the facts to the Department of Justice. Any such report will be treated confidentially, if so requested, and will be fully investigated." The same official also stated, however, that there always are more complaints than it is possible to investigate fully and more potential antitrust cases than it is possible to prosecute.

Price-fixing cases involve items that have widespread application to business. For example, one consent judgment obtained by the department enjoined three banks from agreeing upon common service charges. As a result of this case, the Comptroller of the Currency issued a directive to all national banks emphasizing the illegality of such agreements and announcing that his bank examiners would investigate and take appropriate action if any were discovered. This might tend to reduce one cost of doing business. In a recent year, the division brought thirty-one civil and fourteen criminal actions on price-fixing.

Mergers

Before 1950, the law prohibited the acquisition by one corporation of the shares of another corporation where the effect might be to lessen competition between the two. Now the law prohibits acquisition of shares or assets where it may lessen competition in any line of commerce in any section of the country.

Under the new law, the number of merger cases has increased, but they remain few compared to the total number of mergers which take place without opposition. In a recent eight-month period, 757 mergers or acquisitions were recorded by the Federal Trade Commission. During a recent year, Justice filed only nineteen antimerger cases, nine involving banks.

"Many mergers," a former attorney general pointed out, "promote vigorous competition just as some mergers have the opposite effect." The Supreme Court spoke to the same effect in a 1962 decision which notes that mergers between two small companies may enable the resulting combination to compete more effectively with larger companies in the industry.

Other Antitrust Pitfalls

All combinations to restrain competition or achieve monopoly are prohibited under the antitrust laws. Some practices, like price-fixing, are conclusively presumed to be illegal. The

Supreme Court has made similar findings about agreements among competitors for allocation of customers or territories or pooling of profits. The Antitrust Division frequently challenges reciprocity—a company's use of large-scale purchasing power to promote sales. Other acts must be individually examined. With price differentials, for example, the question is whether they make only due allowance for differences in cost of manufacture, sale, or delivery, or if they constitute illegal discrimination.

Justice brought thirteen civil suits and one criminal action on monopoly charges in a recent year. In addition to actual suits, the Antitrust Division may issue civil investigative demands when it suspects unlawful conduct. Such a demand is similar to a subpoena and requires a firm to produce relevant documents for investigation and copying. The division issues upwards of 125 such demands a year. When it goes to court, the division usually is the victor. In a recent year, it won fifty-one cases, lost two, and dismissed one.

Is it possible for a businessman or his lawyer to go to the Department of Justice Antitrust Division and obtain advance clearance of proposed mergers or prospective business activities? Within certain limitations, the answer is yes. Under the business review procedure, a request for a business review letter is submitted in writing to the assistant attorney general in charge of the Antitrust Division. The requesting parties are considered to be under an affirmative obligation to submit complete information on the proposed business conduct. This information may be supplemented with additional investigation by Justice personnel. After a review of the request, a letter will be sent to the parties which may: (a) state the division's present enforcement intentions with respect to the proposed conduct; (b) decline to pass on the request because of insufficient information or other reasons; or (c) take such other position or action as is considered appropriate. When a business review letter states that the division does not presently intend to bring suit against the proposed conduct, the letter includes the proviso that the division reserves the right to take action in the future if other evidence or subsequent developments warrant it. Businessmen should be aware that their request, the information they supply to support it, and the division's response will be placed in a public file, unless they succeed in showing that disclosure would have a detrimental effect on their operations. During a recent year, the division received eighteen requests for business review letters.

Possibly an answer may be found without requesting a business review letter by consulting the free Department of Justice publication, *Merger Guidelines*.

Taxes

The Tax Division of Justice, according to a former assistant attorney general, strives "to avoid subjecting taxpayers to the burden of litigation without real justification." The figures seem to bear him out. With sixty-one million taxpayers, the Tax Division averages only ten thousand cases a year.

In most tax cases, the Department of Justice is in the strange position of being the defendant. Businessmen or other citizens pay taxes about which they disagree, then sue the government to recover. They recover in less than 25 percent of the cases.

To keep cases out of the already jammed courts, the department takes the initiative in hastening compromise wherever possible. It accepts approximately 80 percent of settlement offers.

The basic source of tax advice in the government is, of course, the Internal Revenue Service. A former assistant attorney general makes the interesting point to businessmen and other taxpayers that they have a duty to avail themselves of such advice. He says:

> Too often, I am afraid, individuals prefer not to inquire about the answers to tax questions which they do not know, but suspect may be unfavorable to their pocketbooks. There seems to be, for some people, a vague kind of comfort in not being 100 percent positive that they are violating the law.

It is not a crime to fail to pay a tax out of genuine ignorance that it is owed. But tax obligations are well publicized, and we believe that cases of genuine ignorance are rare. Aside from the fact that we do regard as criminal a failure to pay taxes out of a reckless and conscious indifference to what the law may be, it is a citizen's plain duty to inquire in any case where the question occurs to him.

Fraud

The reputable businessman has little reason to fear prosecution by the Department of Justice for his activities, unless they fall into some of the gray areas of administrative regulation, such as those arising under the Food, Drug, and Cosmetic Act. And he may have occasion to look to the department for corrective action against unethical business practices of which he is the victim.

Drug companies that have invested large sums in developing and marketing products under their brand names, for example, can only take satisfaction from the prosecution of other firms that blithely distribute such products as their own.

Similarly, the companies that supplied $100,000 worth of furniture and appliances on credit to a firm that disposed of the merchandise without paying them must have a sympathetic interest in the prosecution of that firm for conspiracy and bankruptcy fraud.

Surely, too, legitimate land developers rejoice in the campaign against those who use the mails to sell nearly worthless desert land as lush homesites at inflated prices, often to couples preparing for retirement on modest life savings.

Special Situations

Several other aspects of the work of the Department of Justice have an important bearing on the business community.

On the water pollution front, the department filed 191 criminal cases and 54 requests for injunctions in a recent year. "Many of these cases," the attorney general said, "have been against very large companies, resulting in great reduction in dumping of waste." They have also resulted in large expenditures by the firms involved; a pulp-processing plant was ordered to construct a waste-treatment facility at a cost of about $22 million.

A firm holding a defense contract will have its employees cleared by the FBI if they deal with classified material (though the bureau does not provide a security clearance service for private business as such). The FBI invites business cooperation in reporting alleged crimes in interstate commerce, and attempted Soviet technological espionage.

The Civil Rights Division deals with several statutes concerned with employment and housing having special significance for businessmen. It has been instrumental in obtaining Supreme Court rulings against employment tests that discriminate against Blacks and mothers of preschool-age children. It also has moved against large real estate developers on racial discrimination in apartment rentals and home sales.

The Community Relations Service is involved in economic development as part of its effort to conciliate conflicts based on race or nationality. It does not have funds of its own for development, but it has, for example, helped a Chicano group obtain a $350,000 bank loan to purchase a sporting goods store.

Should a businessman wish to bring a foreign scientist or other specialist into the United States, he may file a visa petition with Justice's Immigration and Naturalization Service, assuming, of course, that there is an opening in the quota for the country concerned. The petition would assert that the person sought is "highly skilled, urgently needed, and a benefit to the United States." Once the petition is cleared by Immigration, it also must be approved by the State Department through its consul in the appropriate country.

Federal Prison Industries buys more than $20 million in

goods a year, on the basis of responses to its published invitations to bid. Its output is sold only to government agencies, thus minimizing any tendency to unfair competition with private business. It seeks to train inmates in skills that will be marketable when they are released, emphasizing such occupations as automatic data processing and automotive repairs.

Department of Justice
10th & Constitution N.W.
Washington, D.C. 20530
(202) 737-8200

LABOR: YOUR
DEPARTMENT TOO

Although it is commonly said that the Labor Department represents the interests of labor in government, almost everything that it does for labor also serves business.

This will be more apparent as we look at some of the department's major areas of activity—apprenticeship and training; employment service; unemployment insurance; industrial safety; and collection of labor statistics, whose varied coverage includes employment, unemployment, wages, and prices.

Many of these programs were born during the New Deal; others go back even before the establishment of a separate Labor Department in 1913; and some, such as the requirement for public disclosure of union finances, originated as recently as 1959. This department, like all others, acquires new functions or reshapes old ones in response to changing public demands. Thus the Manpower Administration was set up in 1963. The businessman with a problem in the labor field has as much right as a labor union official to turn to the Labor Department for information and service, and the department encourages him to do so.

In an era when properly qualified employees are often difficult to find, the Labor Department complex of training and placement programs is perhaps its most important service from the businessman's standpoint. The word "complex" is used advisedly—training and placement activities are carried out by an assortment of bureaus and offices, at both federal and state levels.

Employment Service

The place where the businessman is most likely to find employment service help is at one of the twenty-four hundred public employment offices operated by state employment services. These state services are affiliated with the United States Employment Service (USES), a part of the Labor Department's Manpower Administration. That agency is responsible for providing guidance to state agencies, and for carrying out responsibilities of the federal government, with respect to the employment service, unemployment insurance, and job training.

The basic function of public employment offices is to match workers and jobs. In fiscal year 1972 they made more than 3.8 million nonfarm placements. They offer other personnel services which can be of considerable importance to small and medium-sized businesses that do not have extensive personnel departments. A get-acquainted visit at the local office or an invitation to the state employment service to send a representative may reveal possibilities of assistance and advice in addition to those touched on in this chapter.

When an employer wants to use the USES affiliates to find workers, as more than 900,000 do each year, a telephone call is sufficient to get the process started. (There's no charge, of course, to employer or employee.) The interviewer will write up an "employer order," which should give as complete a picture as possible of the job to be filled. Therefore, the more information the employer gives, the more likely he is to get a person who will satisfy his requirements.

The interviewer will classify the job order by occupational title and code number and then choose from his files the cards of applicants similarly classified. He will review their records, interview personally those who seem qualified, then refer the best candidates to the employer for final selection.

If workers with the required skills are not available locally, the office can work out arrangements for the employer to draw on applicants registered with affiliated offices in other cities. This may involve a representative of the employer going to one or more cities to conduct interviews, but the candidates will at least have been located and prescreened, saving the employer time and expense. (USES affiliates have information on the availability of labor in all parts of the nation, helpful in choosing locations for new plants.)

The Manpower Administration has committed itself to computerization of the employment service through the use of Job Banks. The system brings people and jobs together. Basically, it provides in a labor market area a computer-assisted system of listing and updating job orders on a daily basis and distributes them to local state employment service offices and other manpower units throughout the area. As of mid-1973, statewide Job Bank systems blanketed thirty-three States and the District of Columbia. The thirty-four systems involve a total of 1,413 local employment service offices.

Here is an actual case of public employment service help to an employer faced with a problem of recruiting skilled workers. A small machinery company in Nevada was awarded a defense contract for tooling aircraft and missile jigs and fixtures. To fulfill the contract, the firm needed to more than triple its employment, the heaviest requirement being for machinists, tool and die makers, and other skilled workers who were in short supply. The order was circulated to all public employment offices in the state, and when recruitment possibilities there were exhausted, to offices in California and other nearby states. The company agreed to pay for newspaper advertising which asked applicants to contact local offices of the state employment service, and to accept collect long-distance calls in order to interview by telephone previously screened applicants. As a result of these efforts, ninety workers were hired, eighty-five of them in highly skilled jobs, and the company was able to complete its contract on schedule.

In the course of forty years of operation, the USES has developed a testing program for applicants before offering them to business and industry. Eight out of ten public employment offices now have facilities to give proficiency tests for typists and stenographers, or aptitude tests that measure capacity for learning new skills in a wide variety of occupations.

Tests are available for many types of jobs, but not all. In the latter cases, it may be possible for the employer, through his state employment service, to have the USES develop a battery of tests for his recruiting needs.

An availability test solved the problem for a manufacturer of electrical products, who wanted to correct the wide variations in productivity and quality records of workers in his mounting operation. Local Employment Service people and a test technician from the central office of the state agency investigated. They recommended that facilities be installed in the local Employment Service Office to give selection tests for mounting work, and that future hiring in this occupation be done with the help of the tests. After the adoption of this recommendation, mounting became the company's most efficient operation.

Turnover

Turnover and absenteeism are problems with which the USES and state services often can help employers. Causes, and some of the cures, are described in the USES publication, *Suggestions for Control of Turnover and Absenteeism*, available for 30 cents from the GPO.

One situation where the public employment service played a helpful role occurred at a Wisconsin company. It was experiencing very high turnover in a department where women were performing precision machine and inspection work on small parts. When the Wisconsin State Employment Service was asked to help, it recommended use of the USES aptitude test for Bomb Fuse Parts Assembler in selecting future employees, and made other suggestions involving use of occupational analysis techniques. The company agreed, and 320 women took the recommended tests. About 200 demonstrated aptitude, and 150 were hired. Not only did turnover in the department drop markedly, but training time was reduced from two or three weeks to a few days.

Unemployment Insurance

Most employers have a stake in the federal–state unemployment insurance system. They support this program by paying a 0.58 percent tax to the federal government on the first $4,200 of each employee's wages and by paying a state unemployment compensation tax on payrolls. The state taxes are used solely for payment of unemployment compensation benefits. The federal tax provides funds which are appropriated by the Congress to cover administrative costs of state and federal agencies for both employment services and unemployment insurance. By providing insured workers with partial compensation for wages lost during involuntary unemployment, the insurance program acts as an economic stabilizer of business in the community, state, and nation.

Training

Information and assistance in setting up training programs or obtaining trainees from existing programs can be obtained from any of the state employment services or the Labor Department's Manpower Administration. This administration oversees different types of training activities under the Manpower Development and Training Act and The Economic Opportunity Act, the latter including Job Corps. Some of these programs are administered nationally, others regionally, and still others by state and local governments. The Office of Research and Development is responsible for demonstration and experimental training projects. With the Department of Health, Education, and Welfare, the Department of Labor operates the Work Incentive (WIN) programs to help welfare recipients get jobs. Private employers can claim a tax credit of 20 percent of the first year's wages for employing a WIN participant. Manpower Administration staff in the Labor Department's ten regional offices may be called upon for assistance. (See list of offices at end of chapter.)

Employers also may call on the Bureau of Apprenticeship and Training (BAT) field staff in every state to work with them and with labor in setting up apprenticeship and allied programs to meet their specific training needs. Where programs are already under way, the bureau's specialists can be a source of technical advisory service, when needed. To promote voluntary cooperation, joint apprenticeship committees have been set up by management and labor.

For more information about manpower programs, contact Jack Hashian, Room 2104 Main Labor, Washington, D.C. (202) 961-2822.

Employment Standards

The federal minimum wage law, known as the Fair Labor Standards Act, has been in effect since 1938.

As of May 1974 the law requires a minimum wage of $2 an hour for all covered workers; overtime at time and a half for all hours after forty in a week; and a general minimum working age of sixteen, with work permitted at fourteen in a few occupations, and banned until eighteen in occupations the secretary of labor declares hazardous. Employers also must keep certain records prescribed by the secretary.

Inadvertently or otherwise, many employers run into trouble with this law. Those requiring technical assistance in complying with its provisions should not hesitate to call the nearest of approximately 350 Wage and Hour Division offices, listed in most telephone directories under U.S. Government, Department of Labor.

Staffed with approximately nine hundred Compliance Officers, the Wage and Hour Division is empowered by the Fair Labor Standards Act to investigate establishments for compliance, routinely or on the basis of specific complaints.

As a result of these investigations in fiscal year 1973, employers agreed to restore more than $9.5 million in unpaid minimum wages and more than $24 million in unpaid overtime to their employees.

Whenever back wages are not paid voluntarily, the secretary of labor may, at the written request of an employee, bring suit, or the employee may do so on his own. In addition, the secretary is authorized to seek a court injunction restraining the employer from withholding payments of minimum wage or overtime compensation.

The Equal Pay Act, added in 1963 as an amendment to the Fair Labor Standards Act, prohibits employers with workers subject to the act's minimum wage provision from discriminating on the basis of sex in the payment of wages. Since this amendment took effect in 1964, Wage-Hour has found more than $65.5 million due almost 142,600 workers, nearly all of them women, and has filed more than five hundred suits to obtain compliance.

Wages higher than those provided in the Fair Labor Standards Act can be required under the Walsh–Healey Public Contracts Act, which applies to employers handling government contracts of more than $10,000, and in certain cases, to secondary suppliers of the prime contractor. The secretary of labor determines the "prevailing" minimum wage of the industry, which then becomes a floor in government supply contracts. Before making a final determination, the secretary of labor makes public a tentative finding, to which interested parties may file exceptions.

If an employer owes money to employees as a result of violations of the Public Contracts Act, the government may withhold such amount from anything due him under the contract, or it may sue for the amount and distribute it to the employees.

Employment standards involve not only wages and hours, but workmen's compensation. Employers of workers covered by certain federal laws providing death and injury benefits must deal with the Labor Department's Office of Workmen's Compensation Programs. The workers, more than two million, include longshoremen and other harbor workers in private maritime employment on navigable waters of the United States; workers engaged in exploring for and developing natural resources on the outer continental shelf; those employed by government contractors on public works outside the United States; and all persons in private employment in the District of Columbia.

The employer of such workers must pay benefits for job-related injury or death, and as security that he will do so, must either take out liability insurance with a carrier authorized by the office or satisfy its requirements for qualifying as a self-insurer.

The office administers these laws through district offices, located in port cities for convenience to maritime operations.

For more information on employment standards, contact Robert Cuccia, Room 5135 Main Labor, (202) 961-5044.

Labor Facts and Figures

The Bureau of Labor Statistics (BLS) is best known for its consumer and wholesale price indexes and monthly figures on employment and unemployment. For the alert businessman, however, it is the source of a great deal of other information that can be applied in his operation.

If he wants a single source that provides an overall view of labor and labor statistics, then he should use the *Monthly Labor Review* ($9 a year, GPO). The *Monthly Labor Review* provides authoritative articles on employment, wages, prices, productivity, unit labor costs, and related fields; regular departments; significant labor decisions and developments in industrial relations; and thirty-four tables of current labor statistics. In addition, *Employment and Earnings* ($10 a year, GPO) furnishes employment and unemployment data in depth, and the *Handbook of Labor Statistics, 1972,* Bulletin 1735 ($5.25, GPO), contains BLS historical series. An invaluable publication, and one which is basic to the use of BLS data, is *BLS Handbook of Methods*, Bulletin 1711 ($2, GPO), which describes the creation and purpose of each major data collection program, how the results may be used, and states the limitations to be remembered when one is using the data.

Should he be interested in occupations, the *Occupational Outlook Handbook, 1972–73 Edition,* Bulletin 1700 ($6.25, GPO), contains job descriptions and employment outlook information for white-collar, blue-collar, and service occupations. The *Area Wage Survey* series (cost varies), which is available for ninty-six areas, provides the wages for office clerical, professional and technical, maintenance and powerplant, and custodial and material-moving occupations, while the *National Survey of Professional, Administrative, Technical and Clerical Pay, March 1972,* Bulletin 1764 ($1.25, GPO), covers white-collar pay exclusively.

The employer who wants a solid background of information for union negotiations can consult the bureau's file of current union contracts in Washington, or order reproductions at 25 cents a page. He can obtain its published analysis of union agreements in individual industries and of agreement provisions on specific subjects, such as vacations, sick leave, and rest periods.

If data on employee productivity are needed in connection with wage adjustments, improving plant operation, or for any other purpose, the bureau publishes annual indexes of output per man-hour. These include indexes for the entire private economy, for the manufacturing and nonmanufacturing sectors, and for all employees in some twenty industries.

Price information, which can be important in marketing plans and in collective bargaining—some union contracts call for wage adjustments keyed to changes in the BLS Consumer Price Index—is another useful product of the Labor Department. It includes monthly reports on wholesale prices for individual commodities; retail price indexes for categories such as food and clothing; and consumer price indexes for large cities.

Employers interested in doing business abroad will find guidance in the international labor comparisons published in the *Monthly Labor Review* and the *Handbook of Labor Statistics*. Another useful item is the "U.S. Export Price Index" in a free periodic press release.

All employers are concerned with the safety and health of their employees. For many years the bureau has collected and published national data on work-injury frequency and severity rates, estimates of average days of disability per injury, and percent of disabling injuries resulting in death, permanent impairment, and temporary total disability for workers in American industry.

Currently the bureau has in the works projections of the economy in 1985, a directory of minority data sources, and either a data book or chartbook on minorities.

For more information about labor statistics, the Washington contact is Herbert Morton, Room 2029, GAO Building, 441 G Street N.W., Washington, D.C. 20212, (202) 961-2327.

Occupational Safety and Health

The Occupational Safety and Health Administration (OSHA), in the Department of Labor, is the federal government's major agent for assuring safety and health in the workplaces of the nation. OSHA administers the Occupational Safety and Health Act of 1970, the most comprehensive legislation ever enacted to protect America's workers from on-the-job hazards to their safety and health. The act covers sixty million employees in five million establishments, with separate provisions for safety and health programs for the nearly three million federal government employees. OSHA engages in the following activities:

1. Setting standards: With full public participation, OSHA develops and issues standards in all phases of occupational safety and health. Most OSHA standards are horizontal, applying to hazards in all types of establishments. Some are vertical and apply to particular industries, such as longshoring, construction, and agriculture. Standards cover everything from personal protective equipment to limits on exposure to hazardous substances. OSHA also works closely with the National Institute for Occupational Safety and Health of the Department of Health, Education, and Welfare in developing and researching new standards.

2. Enforcement: OSHA administers a nationwide two-part compliance program: first, employers are urged to comply with standards voluntarily, even before an OSHA inspection; second, OSHA's trained compliance officers, working out of a network of eighty-four field offices, inspect workplaces to assure employer compliance with standards. In fiscal year 1973, OSHA conducted more than 47,000 inspections in establishments employing nearly six million workers. OSHA alleged 153,000 violations of standards in 28,000 citations to employers, resulting in proposed penalties totaling more than $4.4 million.

When enforcement actions of OSHA are contested by employers, employees, or employee representatives, they are adjudicated by an independent agency, the Occupational Safety and Health Review Commission. Review Commission judges stationed in nine field offices hear and decide cases, subject to review by the three members of the Review Commission upon motion of any one of the three. Commission offices are at 1825 K Street, N.W., Washington, D.C. 20006, (202) 382-6214.

3. Education, training, and information: To encourage voluntary compliance, OSHA promotes awareness of good safety and health practices through publicizing and clarifying the standards, offering technical assistance and consulting services, and offering educational and training programs. OSHA prepares and distributes to the public general and technical publications on job safety and health, and offers subscriptions to its official monthly magazine, *Job Safety & Health* ($4.50 annually from GPO).

4. Working with the states: The act encourages the states to assume responsibility for their own job safety and health programs. To gain jurisdiction, the states must develop programs "at least as effective as" OSHA's. Of the fifty-six jurisdictions covered by the act, forty-six have submitted plans for their programs. By June 30, 1973, OSHA had approved fourteen state plans. OSHA does not relinquish authority over job safety and health programs in a state for at least three years, and then only if the state has completed all developmental steps and its actual operations are in conformity with OSHA criteria.

5. Collection of statistics: In cooperation with the Bureau of Labor Statistics, OSHA is gathering data to provide the first reliable national profile on job-related deaths, injuries, and illnesses. The first figures, covering a six-month period, show 3.1 million job-related injuries and 4,300 deaths.

6. Other responsibilities: OSHA also administers standards issued under the Walsh–Healey, Service Contract, Construction Safety, National Foundation of the Arts and Humanities, and

Vocational Rehabilitation acts. Any of these standards may be superseded by standards issued under the Occupational Safety and Health Act.

Inquiries concerning OSHA activities should be addressed to Bill Dwyer, Special Assistant for Public Affairs, (202) 961-5111; Samuel M. Sharkey, Director, Office of Information Services, (202) 961-3914; or Malcolm Barr, Chief, Media Services Division, (202) 961-3914; U.S. Department of Labor, Occupational Safety and Health Administration, Washington, D.C. 20210.

Reporting Requirements

Since 1959, when the Labor-Management Reporting and Disclosure Act was passed, employers have been required to report to the Labor Department payments made to labor relations consultants and union officers and employees, just as unions were required to report on their finances. More than 1,450 reports have been filed by employers.

Disclosure of information about the provisions and financial operations of employee welfare and pension plans is also required under the Welfare and Pension Plans Disclosure Act. In a recent year, more than 7,500 new plans, 20,290 amendments, and 69,160 annual reports were received by the Labor Department. This formidable volume of paper work for plan administrators was called for as a way of protecting the more than $15 billion a year paid into these plans by employers and employees.

Publications of interest are *Union Financial Statistics 1960–1970, Welfare and Pension Plan Statistics 1971, Characteristics of 178,670 Plans on File January 1, 1973,* and *The 100 Largest Retirement Plans 1960–1971.*

Information about both of these laws may be obtained from the Labor-Management Services Administration, Office of La-

bor-Management and Welfare-Pension Reports, 8757 Georgia
Avenue, Silver Spring, Maryland 20910, (301) 427-7158.

Department of Labor
Constitution Ave. & 14th St. N.W.
Washington, D.C. 20210
(202) 393-2420

Regional Information Offices

The U.S. Department of Labor operates through ten regional
offices located in major cities across the country. The regional
information officers in those offices will be glad to help. Their
names, addresses, and telephone numbers are listed below, as
are the states in the respective regions:

William I. Allgood
Rm. 317
1371 Peachtree St. N.E.
Atlanta, Ga. 30309
(404) 526–5495

Alabama, Florida, Georgia,
Mississippi, North Carolina,
South Carolina, Tennessee,
Kentucky

Leo W. Allman
Federal Building & U.S. Courthouse
Rm. 7C42
1100 Commerce St.
Dallas, Tex. 75202
(214) 749–2308

Arkansas, Louisiana, New
Mexico, Oklahoma, Texas

Ernest Hood
Arcade Plaza
Rm. 2034
1321 Second Ave.
Seattle, Wash. 98101
(206) 442–7620

Alaska, Idaho, Washington,
Oregon

Neal A. Johnson
Federal Office Bldg.
Rm. 1904
911 Walnut St.
Kansas City, Mo. 64106
(816) 374–5481

Iowa, Kansas, Missouri, Nebraska

Joe B. Kirkbride
14280 Gateway Bldg.
3535 Market St.
Philadelphia, Pa. 19104
(215) 597–1139

Delaware, District of Columbia, Maryland, Pennsylvania, Virginia, West Virginia

Paul F. Neal
Rm. E-308
JFK Federal Bldg.
Boston, Mass. 02203
(617) 223–6767

Massachusetts, Connecticut, Rhode Island, Maine, New Hampshire, Vermont

Ernest E. Sanchez
Rm. 16408
Federal Bldg.
1961 Stout St.
Denver, Colo. 80202
(303) 837–4234

Colorado, Montana, North Dakota, South Dakota, Utah, Wyoming

Tor Torland
Rm. 10007
Federal Bldg.
450 Golden Gate
San Francisco, Calif. 94102
(415) 556–3423

Arizona, California, Hawaii, Nevada

Edward I. Weintraub
Rm. 3510
1515 Broadway
New York, N.Y. 10036
(212) 971–5477

New Jersey, New York, Puerto Rico, Virgin Islands

Lillian Calhoun
12th Floor
300 S. Wacker Drive
Chicago, Ill. 60606
(312) 353-6976

Illinois, Indiana, Michigan,
Minnesota, Ohio, Wisconsin

DEPARTMENT OF STATE:
SALESMEN–DIPLOMATS

Filling our daily headlines with its international political activities, the Department of State's increasingly close relationship with American business in both domestic and foreign commerce is sometimes overlooked. In addition to its traditional role as coordinator for all government departments in matters concerning foreign economic policy, the State Department has a number of special offices and programs to promote the government's campaign to increase American exports; it fields some 450 economic and commercial officers in missions abroad, which claim such achievements as an agreement for sale to Japan of more than $1 billion in coal over a ten-year period; and it is the home of the Agency for International Development (AID) program, an important source of overseas opportunities for American business.

"The fundamental objective of our foreign policy," former Secretary of State Rogers told the U.S. Chamber of Commerce, "is to assure the international conditions of competition and cooperation which can keep our economy strong."

He told the chamber that he had written every American ambassador reemphasizing "my conviction that export promotion is not just the responsibility of the specialists but of everybody in the mission, from the ambassador on down. . . . I have directed . . . our assistant secretary of state for economic affairs . . . to give high priority to export promotion and to our ties with American business . . . our commercial services to American business can play a relatively more important role in helping you in those areas of the world where you don't have established contacts and marketing services."

Interchange of ideas with the business community takes place at an annual National Foreign Policy Conference for Business Executives, and at consultations arranged when ambassadors and other senior officials are in the United States.

There are several avenues through which the businessman might seek the assistance of the State Department, including the field offices of the Commerce Department. A good first step for a businessman seeking assistance on trade promotional matters, such as overseas business connections or inquiries on products and markets, is to contact the nearest Department of Commerce field office, or if this is not practical, to write to the Department of Commerce in Washington. In a great number of cases, he need go no further. Commerce has extensive information on overseas firms and products, and market opportunities; it serves as storekeeper and analyst for the information State collects overseas.

But if the businessman wishes to go straight to the source, he may contact any of State's commercial attachés overseas, or the Department in Washington. Businessmen calling at foreign posts are, of course, provided with on-the-spot information and assistance. (A pocket-size list of "Key Officers of Foreign Service Posts—Guide for Businessmen" is available from Superintendent of Documents, U.S. Government Printing Office, Washington, D.C. 20402, for 35 cents. It includes not only the economic/commercial officers, but others who might be helpful to businessmen, such as the labor, agricultural, and scientific attachés.) Direct mail inquiries are answered as well. Before either writing or going overseas, however, businessmen are well advised to check with the Department of Commerce to determine if the information is already available here at home, and if not, to work with Commerce in providing the overseas posts the right type of background so that the officers can act intelligently on their request.

With both State and Commerce concerned with our overseas trade promotional activities, a joint arrangement has been worked out to utilize each department's facilities most efficiently. The State Department offers its worldwide communications network for the actual information gathering. The Commerce Department is more the digester and distributor in the United States of the Foreign Service's work. As for the personnel involved, an interdepartmental agreement provides a stepped-up commercial program within the Foreign Service. It identifies the overseas commercial attaché as a career specialist within the Foreign Service; it provides for recruitment of additional specialists from the Commerce Department and the business world, and gives the Commerce Department greater participation in the recruitment, training, assignment, and promotion of commercial officers.

Commercial Officers Overseas

When an American businessman comes into a foreign market "cold," the commercial officer there will arrange introductions and appointments with local businessmen and government officials; furnish information about import and export regulations and taxation; and provide background about market conditions and trade opportunities.

Most of the data of this kind the officer forwards to the United States as fast as it is obtained, so that it can be made available to businessmen through such media as *Commerce Today,* the weekly magazine published by the Department of Commerce. An example of an American firm benefiting from such promotion work is Tully International, Inc., Cincinnati, which reported doing an annual business of $150,000 in Hong Kong alone, thanks to trade tips turned in by the Foreign Service.

A special device used by commercial officers to help sell American firms and products is the trade information booth. Booths are used at trade fairs where there is no other United States government participation. They are manned by local commercial officers and stocked with directories of American business firms, catalogs, and other informational materials. United States firms are invited to send information and export proposals to be presented to prospective foreign buyers. One such booth, operated for ten days at the Hannover Trade Fair by commercial officers from nearby posts, produced 222 trade opportunities, many of which have since been turned into promising new business leads.

The department's commercial officers also play an important role in the overseas trade promotion activities of the Department of Commerce. The mounting of a successful trade center show, trade fair, or trade mission requires a variety of their services, including market research, personal contacts to stimulate interest, trade contact surveys to provide specific prospects for United States business participants, and follow-up action after the exhibit or mission is completed. A recent successful trade mission required 281 man-days of one post's commercial staff.

In the Washington headquarters of the State Department, several sources of help are available to the businessman. The primary point of contact is the Bureau of Economic and Business Affairs, and within that bureau, the Office of Commercial Affairs.

For information on the political climate, the businessman can go to the appropriate geographic bureau of the State Department in Washington. The department has bureaus of African, European, Far Eastern, Inter-American, Near Eastern, and South Asian affairs. These bureaus are further broken down into "desks" for individual countries; each desk includes an economic/commercial officer.

A third major source of assistance to United States firms is the Agency for International Development (AID), a part of the Department of State. Both the Bureau of Economic Affairs and AID are more fully described below.

Bureau of Economic and Business Affairs

The five areas into which the Bureau of Economic and Business Affairs is divided may all be important to businessmen in particular situations. They will be described briefly to indicate the range of services available. Rather than try to pick his way through the State Department organization chart, however, the businessman might ask the Office of Commercial Affairs, (202) 632-8097, to point him in the right direction.

The functions of this office are suggested by the names of its two divisions—Business Relations, and Foreign Economic and Commercial Reporting. Parallel to it and rounding out one of the five areas is an Office of Business Practices, which is the action office for businessmen who have problems with foreign industrial property rights, such as patents, trademarks, and copyrights.

International Finance and Development is the area of most concern to the businessman who may face a threat of expropriation in a developing country. The deputy assistant secretary for this area has stated department policy on this touchy matter as follows: "We recognize the right of expropriation, even if we do not normally find it wise, but insist on just compensation."

In the International Trade Policy area, the Office of International Trade follows up on complaints against other countries of action contrary to general trade agreement provisions, such as imposition of quotas on United States goods. It tries to eliminate restrictive foreign business practices that have harmful effects on American international commerce and access to raw materials.

A second component of International Trade Policy, the

Office of East-West Trade, has the relatively new task of fostering peaceful trade with Eastern Europe, the Soviet Union, and the People's Republic of China. Businessmen interested in these markets may obtain help here or from a similarly named office in the Department of Commerce. A concise background booklet on China, Department of State Publication 8666, is available from the Government Printing Office for $1.25.

A fourth area, that of International Resources and Food Policy, has taken on special importance for business in an era when the energy crisis is an overriding fact of economic life. Also handled here are U.S. participation in international commodity arrangements, such as the coffee agreement. Although concerned primarily with raw materials, it also deals with manufactured products receiving special attention, such as textiles and steel-mill products.

A final grouping involves transportation and telecommunications, vital channels for all foreign commerce. An Office of Aviation negotiates bilateral agreements affecting movements of air cargo and passengers, and assists in the promotion of aircraft export sales. The Office of Maritime Affairs has responsibility for shipping problems such as oil pollution and foreign regulations designed to favor ships of other nations. The Office of Telecommunications represents U.S. interests in commercial communications satellite matters and other aspects of telecommunication operations.

Agency for International Development (AID)

Through a program of development loans and technical assistance to developing countries, AID offers many opportunities for U.S. business to sell its goods and services.

AID offers many opportunities for architect–engineer, management consulting, and construction firms to obtain work overseas on projects it finances. Loan recipient countries select the firm, subject to AID approval. Where the required talent is lacking locally, lists of firms having experience in particular fields are distributed by AID to the owner or host country connected with the project. The AID office in Washington maintains an up-to-date index of professional firms that have expressed an interest in performing services in connection with the United States foreign aid program. It also uses this index to review the capabilities of firms selected by recipient countries. Firms interested in such work should write Chief, Resources Branch, Office of Small Business, AID, Washington, D.C. 20523, and ask for copies of a questionnaire that must be filled out. Personal contact may be made in Washington with the Director of Engineering or one of his principal staff officers.

American business is encouraged to participate in the export trade financed by AID loans and grants. The volume of this kind of operation can be measured in the total expenditures for economic assistance by the United States to underdeveloped countries, which in a recent year amounted to $1.3 billion. Approximately 80 percent of these expenditures are made in the United States, benefiting more than four thousand American manufacturers and suppliers.

How do American businessmen, especially those unable to maintain an overseas marketing organization, get to participate in the commodity exports financed by AID? Basically, it is a matter of being informed as to just what export opportunities exist, for AID works as a financing institution. That is, the agency is designed to encourage trade through private channels, engaging in comparatively few direct procurements itself.

This commodity financing process begins whenever AID agrees to make funds available to another government for commodity imports. It may do this through project loans for specific undertakings, such as roads or dams; program loans to finance U.S. goods such as machinery; and sector loans for broad areas such as agriculture or education. The recipient government then issues import licenses, foreign exchange, or similar authorizations to individual importers or to governmental agencies within the particular country. An example would be a local contractor purchasing American bulldozers to build an AID-sponsored road through this country. The importer would procure them through normal commercial channels and under normal trade practices, the one specification being that he notify the AID Office of Small Business in sufficient time for it to publicize his needs to the American business community.

The agency informs the American business community of AID-financed export opportunities through two kinds of circulars, described at the end of this chapter under "Publications." They do not contain information, however, about AID-financed purchases made by General Services Administration, Federal Highway Administration, Department of Defense, or Federal Aviation Administration. To be placed on the mailing lists of these Departments, address requests to: *GSA*—Business Service Center, General Services Administration, Region 3, Room 1050, 7th and D Streets, S.W., Washington, D.C. 20407. Request a mailing list application specifying exactly what materials you wish to furnish; *FHWA*—Contracts and Procurement Division, Federal Highway Administration, Department of Transportation, Room 4410, 400 7th Street, S.W., Washington, D.C. 20591. For those companies desiring to sell road construction machinery and related equipment and supplies, request a "Bidder's Mailing List Application" (Standard Form 129); *Department of Defense*—Inquiries may be addressed to Central Military Procurement Information Office, Office of the Assistant Secretary of Defense (I&L), Room 3D777, Pentagon, Washington, D.C. 20301; *FAA*—Chief, Procurement Division, Federal Aviation Administration, Room 408, 800 Independence Avenue, S.W., Washington, D.C. 20590. Standard Form 129 should be submitted.

To give the foreign purchaser wider knowledge of what our businessmen produce, AID maintains in its overseas missions libraries of United States specifications and standards and manufacturers' catalogs, and assists foreign chambers of commerce and trade associations to maintain similar libraries. Foreign importers use these libraries in deciding upon purchases and in drawing up their specifications. The AID Office of Small Business periodically checks with the missions to ascertain catalog needs, and issues such information to the particular trade in its "Small Business Memos." It urges exporters to send their catalogs to these libraries.

For information on other government agencies involved in foreign trade matters, see the chapters on Department of Commerce, Small Business Administration, Export-Import Bank and Tariff Commission, Agriculture Department, Treasury Department, and Overseas Private Investment Corporation.

Publications

The Department of State publishes a wealth of information materials potentially useful to businessmen. To be placed on a mailing list for those issued without charge, write General Publications Division, Office of Media Services, Room 4827A, Department of State, Washington, D.C. 20520.

For-sale publications may be obtained more quickly by sending a check to U.S. Government Bookstore, Department of State, Washington, D.C. 20520, rather than the main Government Printing Office. One series of particular interest is *Background Notes on the Countries of the World*. These are short factual pamphlets with a map. A set may be ordered for $16.35. Subscription for updated *Notes*, approximately seventy-five a year, is $14.50.

Since the Agency for International Development is semi-autonomous, requests to be placed on its mailing lists should be sent separately, to Marjorie M. Parker, Business and Public Inquiries, Office of Public Affairs, Agency for International Development, Washington, D.C. 20523. A major AID series is *AID-Financed Export Opportunities*. These are broken down into twenty commodity groups, shown on a mailing list application which may be obtained from Miss Parker. This series deals with formal competitive bid procurements, usually required by public agencies. To cover informally negotiated purchases by commercial firms, AID publishes Importer Lists, also available through Miss Parker.

Department of State
2201 C St. N.W.
Washington, D.C. 20520
(202)632-1394

THE TRANSPORTATION
LIFELINE

Before 1967, the government's transportation activities were scattered among more than thirty agencies. Now most of them have been brought together by the Department of Transportation (DOT) established in that year. Employing more than 100,000 people and spending over $8 billion a year, DOT is important to business in two ways:

- It provides or affects the transportation arteries that are vital to the flow of commerce.
- It purchases large quantities of goods and services.

U.S. Coast Guard

On its civilian side, the Coast Guard is concerned with the safety of the U.S. merchant marine. That concern starts with a vessel's blueprint on the drawing board and continues throughout its operating life. Coast Guard officers periodically inspect American merchant ships to make sure they conform to safety standards, and check qualifications of ships' officers and crews.

The Coast Guard establishes and maintains more than forty-eight thousand maritime navigation aids, from simple river buoys to the sophisticated LORAN network that provides worldwide service for air and marine traffic.

Recent legislation stepped up the Coast Guard's responsibilities in the area of water pollution by oil or hazardous materials. The pollution may stem from intentional emptying of ballast tanks, or accidental oil spills, estimated to number seventy-five hundred a year in U.S. waters. One way the Coast Guard is attacking the problem is through improved surveillance equipment to detect pollution as it occurs.

For these and its other activities, Coast Guard Headquarters procures vessels, aircraft, major electronics equipment, educational, research, and development services. Address requests for more information to:

Commandant (GFCP–2)
U.S. Coast Guard
400 7th St., S.W.
Washington, D.C. 20590
(202) 426–1367

Coast Guard Districts and other units listed below procure repair and replacement parts for ships and aircraft, buoys, and other items.

Commander
First Coast Guard District (f)
150 Causeway St.
Boston, Mass. 02114

Commander
Fifth Coast Guard District (f)
431 Crawford St.
Portsmouth, Va. 23705

Commander
Seventh Coast Guard District
  (f)
Rm. 1018, Federal Bldg.
51 S.W. 1st Ave.
Miami, Fla. 33130

Commander
Second Coast Guard District
  (f)

Federal Bldg.
1520 Market St.
St. Louis, Mo. 63103

Commander
Third Coast Guard District (f)
Governors Island
New York, N.Y. 10004

Commander
Eighth Coast Guard District
   (f)
Customhouse
New Orleans, La. 70130

Commander
Ninth Coast Guard District (f)
1240 E. 9th St.
Cleveland, Ohio 44199

Commander
Eleventh Coast Guard District
   (f)
Heartwell Bldg.
19 Pine Ave.
Long Beach, Calif. 90802

Commander
Twelfth Coast Guard District
   (f)
630 Sansome St.
San Francisco, Calif. 94125

Commander
Thirteenth Coast Guard District (f)
618 2nd Ave.
Seattle, Wash. 98104

* Commander
P.O. Box 48
FPO San Francisco, Calif.
   96610

** Commander
Seventeenth Coast Guard District (f)
FPO Seattle, Wash. 98771

Commanding Officer
U.S. Coast Guard Supply Center
31st St. and 3rd Ave.
Brooklyn, N.Y. 11232

Commanding Officer
U.S. Coast Guard Aircraft Repair & Supply Center
Elizabeth City, N.C. 27909

Superintendent
U.S. Coast Guard Academy
New London, Conn. 06320

Commanding Officer
U.S. Coast Guard Yard
Curtis Bay
Baltimore, Md. 21226

Commanding Officer
U.S. Coast Guard Reserve
   Training Center
Yorktown, Va. 23490

Commanding Officer
U.S. Coast Guard Training
   Center
Cape May, N.J. 08204

* Honolulu, Hawaii
** Juneau, Alaska

Federal Aviation Administration (FAA)

During the decade of the 1970s an estimated $11.5 billion from new and higher taxes on airspace users will flow into a special aviation trust fund. It will be used for airport and airways development projects and for the operation and maintenance of the system.

The airways projects—air navigation and traffic control equipment, and research and development of such equipment —are contracted by FAA itself. Airports are contracted by city, county, or state agencies, with FAA approving plans from the standpoint of a national aviation system. Each January FAA issues an annual report of operations under the Airport and Airways Development Act. It may be purchased for $3 from National Technical Information Service Center, Springfield, Virginia 22151.

The Federal Aviation Administration purchases a wide variety of equipment, supplies, and supporting spare parts in the aircraft, communications, air navigation, and air traffic control fields. These procurements are made at various locations throughout the country, depending upon the kind of item required.

The Washington, D.C., office buys major items of equipment along with the initial spare parts and test equipment needed to operate the major item. The office procures complete navigational aid systems, radar network systems, display units, aircraft, a variety of aircraft landing and aircraft traffic control systems, and computers with supporting software. Some construction contracts, primarily to support FAA-owned Dulles and National Airports, are also awarded.

The Washington procurement office conducts most of the FAA research and development contracting. This procurement covers a wide range of topics, from applied research studies through demonstration and testing of new hardware. Research studies include such subjects as automating air traffic control, weather research, and allocating airspace to prevent collisions. The hardware portion of the research and development program includes experimental equipment in the computer, radio, radar, navigational aids, and test equipment areas. Besides the Washington office, the National Aviation Facilities Experimental Center in Atlantic City, New Jersey, also awards some research and development contracts.

The Aeronautical Center in Oklahoma City, Oklahoma, purchases spare parts to maintain all FAA navigational aids, air traffic control facilities, and various types of aircraft located throughout the country.

Each of the FAA regional offices buys a wide range of items. Construction contracting is one of the major items; frequently these contracts include the installation of a complete system involving access roads, security fencing, towers, buildings, and actually installing the navigational or landing aid system itself. These construction contracts range from $2,000 to several million dollars. In addition, the regional offices buy a variety of operating supplies as well as maintenance and spare parts for emergency repairs of FAA facilities within their regional boundaries.

For further information regarding FAA procurements, contact the following:

Contracts Division
Federal Aviation Administration, ALG–380
800 Independence Ave., S.W.
Washington, D.C. 20590
(202) 426–8230

FAA Aeronautical Center
P.O. Box 25082
6400 South MacArthur Blvd.
Oklahoma City, Okla. 73125
(405) 686–4774

National Aviation Facilities Experimental Center
Federal Aviation Administration
Material and Procurement Division, NA–400
Atlantic City, N.J. 08405
(609) 641–3178, ext. 3335

REGIONAL OFFICES

Federal Aviation Administration
Alaskan Region
632 Sixth Ave.
Anchorage, Alaska 99501
(907) 265-4341

Federal Aviation Administration
Eastern Region
Federal Bldg. No. 111
John F. Kennedy International Airport
Jamaica, N.Y. 11430
(212) 995-3735

Federal Aviation Administration
Great Lakes Region
2300 E. Devon
Des Plaines, Ill. 60018
(312) 297-2286

Federal Aviation Administration
Southern Region
3400 Whipple St.
East Point, Georgia
Mailing address: P.O. Box 20636
Atlanta, Ga. 30320
(404) 526-7521

Federal Aviation Administration
Southwest Region

P.O. Box 1689
4400 Blue Mound Rd.
Fort Worth, Tex. 76101
(817) 624-6230

Federal Aviation Administration
Western Region
P.O. Box 92007
Worldway Postal Center
5651 W. Manchester Ave.
Los Angeles, Calif. 90009
(213) 670-7031

Federal Aviation Administration
Central Region
Federal Bldg.
601 E. 12th St.
Kansas City, Mo. 64106
(816) 374-3404

Federal Aviation Administration
Pacific Region
1833 Kalakaua Ave.
P.O. Box 4009
Honolulu, Hawaii 96813
(803) 955-0319

Federal Aviation Administration
New England Region
154 Middlesex St.
Burlington, Mass. 01803
(617) 223-6405

Federal Aviation Administration
Rocky Mountain Region
10455 E. 25th Ave.
Aurora, Colo. 80010
Mailing address: Park Hill Station
P.O. Box 7213
Denver, Colo. 80207
(303) 837-3476

Federal Aviation Administration
Northwest Region
FAA Bldg.
Boeing Field
Seattle, Wash. 98108
(206) 767-2777

With thousands of aircraft owned and operated by businesses, the FAA also is important as the agency that passes on the airworthiness of every aircraft and the competence of every pilot and aviation mechanic. Much of this authority is delegated to appropriate segments of the aviation industry. Thus, FAA will certify repair stations to perform required periodic checks on private aircraft, rather than attempt to make thousands of such checks itself.

Even businesses not engaged in flying may be affected by FAA rules. For example, industries with high smokestacks on air routes may have to light them so they will not be a hazard to planes. And builders would do well to check with FAA before undertaking any residential development near airports, because of noise and safety considerations.

The former may obtain a free advisory circular, "Obstruction Marking and Lighting," from Department of Transportation Distribution Unit (TAD-483.3) Washington, D.C. 20590. It should be identified as AC 70/7460-1B. Criteria for residential development near airports can be found in Parts 77 and 157 of the *Federal Aviation Regulations*, Volume II, available from GPO for $5.

Companies or individual businessmen contemplating construction of private airports may find helpful the booklet, *Utility Airports*, $1.75 from GPO.

FAA publishes a good deal of statistical material which

also can be profitably employed in nonaviation businesses. A motel chain, for example, might select locations partly on the basis of numbers of air passengers using particular airports. They can get this information every six months in *Airport Activity Statistics of Certificated Air Route Carriers*, $5, GPO. FAA's *Census of U.S. Civil Aircraft*, giving data by state and county, could be a supplementary marketing research tool. It's $1.50 from GPO. An overview of available series is given in the *FAA Statistical Handbook of Aviation*, $2.75, GPO.

Federal Highway Administration

Since virtually all movement of goods in urban areas is by truck, almost every businessman has at least an indirect stake in the activity of the Federal Highway Administration (FHWA). This is particularly true since 1970 legislation expanded its responsibilities to include aid to local governments in financing construction of streets and highways. Previously it aided the states in developing the National System of Interstate and Defense Highways. Scheduled for completion in the late 1970s, this network will carry 20 percent of the nation's traffic.

Also important to many businesses are the provisions of the 1970 act which reactivated the highway beautification program and placed new emphasis on billboard and junkyard control. In helping to plan highways, FHWA encourages multiple use of rights-of-way, creating opportunities for commercial providers of parking, recreational, business, and housing facilities.

The only direct highway construction awards by FHWA are for roads in national forests, national parks, and other federal lands. These are made by FHWA Regions 8, 9, 10, and 15, addresses of which are listed later.

FHWA's Bureau of Motor Carrier Safety has jurisdiction over the safety performance of some 125,000 motor carriers engaged in interstate or foreign commerce. It checks on driver qualifications and hours of service, makes vehicle inspections, and controls movement of dangerous cargoes.

The Contracts and Procurement Division executes all FHWA research and development contracting actions, negotiates contracts for research and analysis studies in support of the FHWA highway planning mission, procures training and related support services for the Bureau of Motor Carrier Safety, and awards data processing and computer services contracts required by FHWA program activities. The procurement office in Washington also purchases, by formal advertising or negotiation, highway construction and maintenance equipment, machinery, and materials in connection with the domestic and foreign commodity programs administered by FHWA.

All ten FHWA regions are involved in the administration of the Federal-Aid Highway Construction Program throughout the states. Each of the regions also purchases housekeeping and administrative supplies and services for its own needs.

Further information on FHWA procurement programs may be obtained from one of the following FHWA procurement offices:

Federal Highway Administration
Contracts and Procurement Division
400 7th St., S.W.
Washington, D.C. 20591
(202) 426–0724 or 0743

Federal Highway Administration
Region One
4 Normanskill Blvd.
Delmar, N.Y. 12054
(518) 472–4230

Federal Highway Administration
Region Three
1633 Federal Bldg.
31 Hopkins Place
Baltimore, Md. 21202
(301) 962–3830

Federal Highway Administration
Region Four
1720 Peachtree Rd., N.W.
Suite 200
Atlanta, Ga. 30309
(404) 526–5071

Federal Highway Administration
Region Five
18209 Dixie
Homewood, Ill. 60430
(312) 799–6300

Federal Highway Administration
Region Six
819 Taylor St.
Fort Worth, Tex. 76102
(817) 334–3219

Federal Highway Administration
Region Seven
6301 Rockhill Rd.
Kansas City, Mo. 64113
(816) 361–7565

Federal Highway Administration
Region Eight
Denver Federal Center
Bldg. 40

Rm. 242
Denver, Colo. 80225
(303) 233–6477

Federal Highway Administration
Region Nine
450 Golden Gate Ave.
Box 36096
San Francisco, Calif. 94102
(415) 556–1151

Federal Highway Administration
Region Ten
Mohawk Bldg.
222 S.W. Morrison St.
Rm. 412
Portland, Ore. 97204
(503) 226–3441

Federal Highway Administration
Region Fifteen
1000 North Glebe Rd.
Arlington, Va. 22201
(703) 557–7442

National Highway Traffic Safety Administration

Every manufacturer of motor vehicles and equipment by now is well aware of the National Highway Traffic Safety Administration (NHTSA), created by 1966 legislation. It imposes more than thirty vehicle safety performance standards for items such as tires, brakes, and seat belts.

Significant to dealers as well as manufacturers are NHTSA's

newer motor vehicle information and cost-saving programs. These include reports on damage susceptibility of different makes and models, and safeguarding consumers from turned-back odometers.

Research sponsored by NHTSA which may have important impact on the automotive industry covers crash survivability through evaluation of devices such as air bags, and development of experimental safety vehicles that will meet tougher safety criteria.

NHTSA enters into contracts with private industry, educational institutions, and nonprofit organizations for studies involving crash protection, crash avoidance, and the crash survivability characteristics of vehicles. NHTSA also contracts for the test and evaluation of vehicle components and accessories.

All NHTSA procurement activities are administered by its Washington, D.C. headquarters:

National Highway Traffic Safety Administration
Contracts and Procurement Division (Code 48–30)
400 7th St. S.W.
Washington, D.C. 20591
(202) 426-0684

Federal Railroad Administration

In spite of the declining percentage of total traffic hauled by railroads in recent years, their continued importance to business is demonstrated by the fact that they carry 75 percent of all coal, 78 percent of lumber, 86 percent of pulp and paper, and 71 percent of household appliances.

Although the mandate of the Federal Railroad Administration (FRA) does not include economic regulation, it does seek to help the rails find a place in a balanced transportation system through such channels as a major research effort into the problem of freight car shortages, and sponsorship of the Rail Passenger Service Act, which set up Amtrak.

FRA is responsible for railroad safety, and is paying particular attention to the transport of hazardous materials and improvement of grade-crossing safety at the more than 225,000 public grade crossings.

Businessmen trying to operate in our clogged cities and metropolitan corridors will watch hopefully the technological research of FRA's Office of High Speed Ground Transportation. At a test center being developed near Pueblo, Colorado, the office will test a quiet, pollution-free linear induction motor, a tracked air cushion research vehicle, and other innovative designs. Meanwhile, specially instrumented railroad cars owned by the Department of Transportation are periodically used to inspect the demonstration tracks of the Metroliner between New York and Washington and the Turbotrain between New York and Boston.

The Federal Railroad Administration contracts for research and development in railroad and high speed ground transportation, including but not limited to aerodynamics, vehicle propulsion, vehicle control, communications, and guideways. FRA also contracts for demonstrations to determine the contributions that high speed ground transportation can make to efficient and economical intercity transportation systems as well as for surveys to measure public response to changes in service.

In addition to the advanced concepts of ground transportation, FRA makes awards for research and development studies and demonstrations relating to the safety, environment, and efficiency of our national rail system.

The FRA-operated Alaska Railroad purchases all of the supplies and equipment needed to maintain and operate the railroad.

The Federal Railroad Administration procurement offices are located as follows:

Federal Railroad Administration
Room 5412 Nassif Bldg.
400 7th St. S.W.
Washington, D.C. 20591
(202) 426-0872

Procurement Officer
The Alaska Railroad
P.O. Box 7–2111
Anchorage, Alaska 99501
(206) 583-0150

Urban Mass Transportation Administration

Local public transit is important to business in terms of ability ot employees to get to work on time and in fit condition, and of its impact on the pattern of urban building development. With public transit staggering under a loss of two-thirds of its customers since World War II—18.9 billion rides in 1945, 5.3 billion in 1973—the Urban Mass Transportation Administration (UMTA) has a big rescue job to do. It can underwrite two-thirds the cost of local transit capital improvements, under a five-year authorization of more than $3 billion. The money is helping the nation's newest and oldest subway systems—in San Francisco and Boston.

It can make grants not only for purchase of equipment and construction, but for management and economic feasibility studies, research and training.

UMTA funds a wide range of demonstration projects, ranging from staggered work hours through "kiss and ride" facilities at public transit stations to "people mover" systems on downtown streets.

UMTA contracts are awarded through:

Procurement Operations Division
Office of Administrative Operations
Office of the Secretary of Transportation
Washington, D.C. 20590
(202) 426-4311

Saint Lawrence Seaway Development Corporation

Midwestern businessmen are heavy users of the Saint Lawrence Seaway Development Corporation. They ship fifty million tons of cargo a year through its facilities, which are wholly owned by the U.S. government, but jointly operated with Canada's Saint Lawrence Seaway Authority.

Millions of dollars of total income could be added to the economy of the region each year if the corporation is successful in its efforts to extend the present 8½-month season by at least one month. It is working with the Coast Guard and other agencies to explore the feasibility of such an extension. Firms interested in selling navigation equipment and other items to the corporation should direct inquiries to:

Saint Lawrence Seaway Development Corporation
Attention: Contracting Officer
P.O. Box 520
Massena, N.Y. 13662
(315) 764-0271

National Transportation Safety Board

One of the smallest agencies in the federal government, this board is concerned primarily with determining causes of civil aviation accidents. It issued some five thousand aviation accident reports in a recent year, about nine hundred based on its own investigations. The balance, dealing with less serious accidents, were based on FAA findings. The board's conclusions have brought about many changes in business aircraft operations.

It also investigates the most serious accidents in surface transportation—marine, railroad, highway, and pipeline operations. Its procurement is handled by the same office shown for UMTA.

Transportation Systems Center

This former NASA facility in Cambridge, Massachusetts, now conducts or contracts for a variety of research to meet the needs of Department of Transportation agencies. Its coverage ranges from noise abatement to nondestructive tire testing systems. For information regarding its procurement activities, contact:

Transportation Systems Center
55 Broadway
Cambridge, Mass. 02142

Information Sources

If questions arise on matters other than procurement, the department's public information officers may be helpful. They are as follows:

L. J. Churchville (APA–1)
Director of Public Affairs
Federal Aviation Administration
800 Independence Ave. S.W.
Washington, D.C. 20590
(202) 426–3883

Werner A. Siems (HPA–1)
Director of Public Affairs
Federal Highway Administration
400 7th St. S.W.
Washington, D.C. 20591
(202) 426–0648

Rose A. Benas (RA–6)
Public Affairs Officer
Federal Railroad Administration
400 7th St. S.W.
Washington, D.C. 20591
(202) 426–0881

Bobby A. Boaz (N40–42)
Director of Public Affairs
National Highway Traffic Safety Administration
400 7th St. S.W.
Washington, D.C. 20590
(202) 426–9550

T. William Swinford (UPA–1)
Director of Public Affairs
Urban Mass Transportation Administration
400 7th St. S.W.
Washington, D.C. 20590
(202) 426–4011

Capt. Terrence McDonald (GAPI/83)
Chief, Public Affairs Division

United States Coast Guard
400 7th St. S.W.
Washington, D.C. 20590
(202) 426–1587

H. David Crowther (S–80)
Director of Public Affairs
Office of the Secretary of Transportation
400 7th St. S.W.
Washington, D.C. 20590
(202) 426–4570

John Greene
Director, Office of Communications
Saint Lawrence Seaway Development Corp.
180 Andrews St.
P.O. Box 520
Massena, N.Y. 13662
(315) 764–0271 ext. 279

Edward E. Slattery, Jr. (BPA–1)
Director of Public Affairs
800 Independence Ave. S.W.
Washington, D.C. 20590
(202) 426–8787

Department of Transportation
400 7th St. S.W.
Washington, D.C. 20590
(202) 426–4570

TREASURY: TAXES PLUS

Most businessmen equate the Treasury with taxes, and certainly this function of the department is the one that has the maximum direct impact on them. They should not, however, allow the pervasive influence of the Internal Revenue Service to obscure the important role of other Treasury arms in their lives. The way the department manages financing of the national debt, for example, is a basic factor in determining interest rates, and thereby affects the whole economic structure.

The Treasury Department in a single year is likely to borrow $140 billion. An operation of this magnitude can hardly help having an impact on other security markets of deep concern to business—corporate bonds, for example, and mortgages.

Planning its borrowings with the help of advisory committees from the financial community, and keeping in close touch with the Federal Reserve on related matters of monetary control, Treasury conducts its complex debt management program with at least three national objectives in mind:

1. To maintain an appropriate level of liquidity through its decisions on the volume of short-term government securities to be issued, since these have the status of "near-money." A deli-

cate balance must be reached in arriving at a level of liquidity that serves the routine needs of the domestic economy, sustains a strong rate of economic growth, and yet does not create an inflationary hazard.

2. To permit normal functioning of the credit and capital markets and the most appropriate flow of funds into long-term private investment. The amount, manner, and timing of Treasury long-term borrowing can have important effects on that flow. Thus, when the Treasury concentrates its cash borrowings in the short-term area, the result is to reserve the flow of new long-term savings for private investment in industrial plants and equipment, commercial facilities, and housing.

3. To keep our short-term rates competitive with those abroad, in order to prevent outflow of money which would add to balance-of-payments problems and ultimately might weaken the dollar.

Under a 1973 law a Federal Financing Bank was established to market all government borrowings from the public.

Although financing of the national debt is essentially a matter for the experts, there is one phase in which every businessman can have a hand. Savings bonds account for about one-eighth of the nation's more than $450 billion debt. The volunteer help of businessmen, particularly through operation of payroll savings plans, is an important element in maintaining the volume of savings bonds at that level.

Life and Taxes

The business of collecting taxes is itself a big business. Employing sixty thousand persons and taking in more than $200 billion a year, the Internal Revenue Service (IRS) ranks with the one hundred largest United States corporations. It prides itself on being as efficient as it is big, citing an operating cost of half a cent for every dollar raised. Of course, much of the cost is borne by the taxpayer himself, under what is rightly called a "self-assessment" system, where businessmen spend large sums in record-keeping and computation for tax purposes.

Apart from this kind of cooperation, there are a number of ways in which businessmen and the IRS can work together to the advantage of both. On broad tax issues which can affect an entire industry, the commissioner will work with the trade association to effect a solution. At one point, for example, the hotel industry became concerned over a rumor that Internal Revenue was conducting a drive against conventions at resort hotels. The commissioner conferred with members of the American Hotel Association (and the Florida congressional delegation) and asked the association to submit a brief. The IRS then made a special survey of audits of convention expenses to make sure there had been no arbitrary disallowances because of a convention's site. It issued a report to this effect, and then, talking to the annual meeting of the association, the commissioner reaffirmed the IRS position that legitimate business convention expenses would not be disallowed merely because a convention is held at a resort area.

In addition to such *ad hoc* contacts, the thoughts of the business community are obtained at regular intervals through two groups. The commissioner's Advisory Group, a twelve-man body of lawyers, accountants, educators, and businessmen, meets with top Internal Revenue officials in Washington for a session of several days approximately every three months. In addition, a Forms Committee meets annually with representatives of national business, law, and accounting groups to review proposed changes in the principal tax forms. Discussion may be initiated from either side between annual meetings, as problems arise.

The Treasury is always happy to discuss with interested taxpayers the effect of contemplated legislative or administrative changes on particular industries, and to obtain their suggestions. Such information should be furnished in writing to the Assistant Secretary of the Treasury for Tax Policy.

For businessmen less interested in broad issues than in the

more immediately pressing matters of their own specific tax situation, several IRS publications may be helpful: No. 334, *Tax Guide for Small Business*, 75 cents, from GPO and many local post offices; No. 337, *Law and Regulations Relating to Employee Pension, Annuity, Profit-Sharing, Stock Bonus, and Bond Purchase Plans including Plans for Self-Employed Individuals*, 70 cents; No. 377, *Pension Trust Procedures and Guides for Qualification Under Section 401(a) and 405(a) of the Internal Revenue Code of 1954*, 35 cents; No. 448, *A Guide to Federal Estate and Gift Taxation*, 50 cents; No. 463, *Travel Entertainment and Gift Expenses*; No. 509, *Tax Calendar and Check List*; No. 511, *Sales and Other Dispositions of Depreciable Property*; No. 534, *Depreciation, Amortization, and Depletion*; No. 535, *Tax Information on Business Expenses*; No. 536, *Losses from Operating a Business*; No. 539, *Withholding Taxes From Your Employee's Wages*; No. 542, *Corporations and the Federal Income Tax*; No. 543, *Tax Information on the Sale of a Business*; No. 550, *Tax Information on Investment Income and Expenses*; No. 577, *Amortization of Pollution Control Facilities*; No. 778, *Guides for Qualification of Pension, Profit-Sharing, and Stock Bonus Plans*, 35 cents. Where no price is stated, the publication may be obtained free from IRS, Washington, D.C. 20224.

Tax practitioner institutes trained fifty-four thousand participants in a recent year. They in turn assisted nearly eight million taxpayers. This program is available to help qualify personnel of large firms to assist their fellow employees in preparation of tax returns.

When a businessman needs to know what tax liability will be involved before he decides whether to go ahead with a contemplated transaction, he can get a letter ruling—IRS issues some fifteen thousand of these a year. Although it will not rule on transactions which are primarily tax-avoidance plans, it recognizes as a fact of life that business cannot afford to move in many cases without some assurance of what the government position will be as to the tax consequences of the transaction.

If the taxpayer's question is a new or unusual one, he should address it to the Commissioner of Internal Revenue, Washington, D.C. 20224, and a ruling will be issued. Less complicated matters may be submitted to the District Director of Internal Revenue, who will issue a determination letter, applying the appropriate statute, regulation, ruling, or court opinion to the taxpayer's particular set of facts. Generally, only the national office can rule on a prospective transaction, and the district director's jurisdiction is limited to actions that have been consummated, where the taxpayer is inquiring how he should report them on his return.

Request for rulings or determination letters must be made in writing. For detailed procedures to follow see *Revenue Procedures 62-28 through 32*, CB 1962-2, 496. They set forth requirements for very complete documentation.

The taxpayer should remember that it is not safe to rely on a letter ruling for anything but the transaction on which it was issued. He certainly should not rely on a letter issued to someone else, and it is well to be cautious even about applying a letter he has received himself to some later transaction. The facts might appear to be similar, but even a slight difference could cause a different ruling.

One further caution. Although the commissioner rarely revokes a ruling, he is not bound by it, and can change it. When this occurs, however, he generally will exercise his discretionary authority to limit the retroactive effect, so that a taxpayer who in good faith acted on the strength of the ruling will not be harmed.

The businessman will find it to his advantage to know the various avenues of appeal open to him if a revenue agent asserts that he owes more than the amount of tax shown on his return. The first step is to request an informal conference with a reviewing officer in one of the fifty-eight district offices, or forty regional appellate offices. When the disputed tax is less than $2,500, the request need not be in writing.

The reviewing official will hear both sides, and has the

authority to decide for the taxpayer if he sees fit. If he does not, the taxpayer will receive a letter giving him thirty days to bring the matter to the Appellate Division. If he fails there, he will receive a ninety-day notice that the additional tax will be assessed. He can contest the tax by withholding payment and appealing to the U. S. Tax Court during the ninety days, or by paying up and filing a refund claim. If that is disallowed, or not acted on within six months, he may file suit in the United States Court of Claims or in a District Court. He may, of course, appeal on up through the Supreme Court if that body decides the case merits its attention. IRS favors administrative settlements over protracted litigation, and closes over 98 percent of all cases without trial.

In the last few years, Internal Revenue Service has made some important changes in enforcement and interpretation, with significant effects on business. Its introduction of Automatic Data Processing (ADP) systematically identifies those who do not file or who omit certain receipts.

Rules on deductions for travel, entertainment, and business gifts (set forth in Publication No. 535 listed above); greater emphasis on verification of amounts reported in inventories; and a closer look at tax aspects of foreign operations may prove burdensome to some segments of the business community. On the other hand, the recently authorized creation of Domestic International Sales Corporations (DISC) should help make American goods and services more competitive in foreign markets. IRS has widely publicized the advantages of operating a DISC.

IRS recently organized an Office of Industrial Economics, with responsibility for recommending changes in definitions of asset guideline classes and in the associated depreciation and repair norms necessary to the new Class Life Depreciation Range System. The office is staffed by economists and engineers who collect information from trade sources to serve as a basis for applying the Class Life System to various types of real and personal property, particularly computers, and such activities as shipbuilding, communications, commercial fisheries, and animal husbandry.

The Class Life System affords taxpayers the opportunity to determine reasonable allowances for depreciation on property for which the service has established guideline classes, and the use of a guideline repair allowance rule for the determination of allowable repair and maintenance expense.

IRS publications giving statistics of income can provide valuable marketing data for businessmen. For example, Publication 79, *Individual Income Tax Returns*, shows number of returns by adjusted gross income classes for states and large metropolitan areas. Business decisions can be guided by the information that in Boston the largest number of returns is in the under-$5,000 category, while in Bridgeport it falls in the under-$10,000 class. This 426-page paperback sells for $3.75. A supplement, Publication 649, provides similar information by zip code area, sectional centers, and zoned cities. It runs 130 pages and costs $1.25. Business income tax returns are analyzed by industry in Publication 438, a $4 paperback.

Ins and Outs of Customs

All merchandise imported into the United States is subject to a customs duty unless specifically exempted by law. Whether free or dutiable, it must go through certain entry procedures of the Treasury Department's Bureau of Customs. The importer, or a customhouse broker, licensed by the Department of the Treasury and paid a fee by the importer, must file entry papers. These will include: (1) an entry form showing what is believed to be the proper tariff classification and an estimate of the amount of.duty due; (2) a delivery permit; (3) an invoice from the seller; except in the case of goods dutiable by value and worth more than $500, this generally must be a "special customs invoice" rather than an ordinary commercial one; and (4) evidence of the right to make entry at the option of the importing carrier, in the form of a bill of lading, a duplicate bill of lading certified by the carrier, or a carrier's certificate. He must also post a bond.

Unless the goods are to be sent in bond from the port of arrival to another customs port, or entered for storage in a warehouse, in which cases payment of duty is postponed, they go through the following steps:

An appropriate officer in the customhouse checks the estimated amount of duty shown on the entry form, and designates on the delivery permit certain parts of the cargo for physical examination by customs officers, with instructions for weighing and gauging, if necessary. The importer then pays the estimated duties to a cashier, who stamps and signs the permit. The importer or his agent takes or sends the permit to the customs inspector, who releases all or part of the shipment to the carrier bringing the merchandise to the port.

Some of the aforementioned steps may be postponed by the importer or his agent (customhouse broker) by the use of an "immediate delivery" procedure. In this case, an application for immediate delivery (secured by an appropriate bond) is presented along with the invoice and right to make entry, when needed, directly to the customs officer on the pier. If the customs officer determines that no further examination is necessary he will perform an examination, and authorize the carrier to deliver the merchandise. The importer or his agent then has ten days to present the proper entry documents to the customhouse and pay the estimated duties. If, however, the customs officer who is conducting the examination determines that further examination is necessary he will order a public stores or importer's premises examination. If the importer disagrees with the value set on his goods, he has ninety days to file a protest with the District Director of Customs. The issue may ultimately be decided by the United States Customs Court.

After the merchandise has been examined and an entry has

been filed, the papers will be reviewed in the customhouse by an import specialist. He determines the additional amounts of duty due or excessive duties deposited that should be refunded. A percentage of all such entries are given a final audit by an auditor's staff. When review of an entry is completed, it is "liquidated," and its number is posted in the customs office as notice to the importer that duty on his merchandise has been fixed. If he is dissatisfied with the tariff classification of his goods, the computation of duties, or other matters not involving appraisal (the appeal procedure for which is given above), he may, within ninety days of the posting of the liquidation, or ninety days from the date of a decision not involving liquidation, file a written protest with the District Director of Customs. Should disagreement continue, the matter goes to the United States Customs Court.

During the entry process, the customs officers may also apply the requirements of other government agencies to products such as (but not limited to) liquor, drugs, fissionable materials, and gold, all of which must be covered by import licenses or permits.

Export control regulations are laid down by the Department of Commerce, which issues the necessary licenses. Customs examines shipping documents, including shippers' export declarations and bills of lading. Physical examination of selected shipments, which because of destination, exporter, consignee, or type of commodity, seem most likely to involve violations, is made by the Commerce Department's Office of Export Control, or by Customs. This is done not only with commercial cargo, but also with items going by mail. Shipments to the Communist bloc countries receive special attention. Vessels and planes heading to such ports must present complete cargo manifests before Customs clearance, while other vessels may submit them up to four work days after clearance.

The principal type of action taken by the Customs Service against violators of export control regulations is seizure of merchandise. During a recent fiscal year it made 121 such seizures of merchandise valued at over a million dollars. The Commerce Department can impose additional sanctions.

Helpful leaflets available without charge from the nearest District Director of Customs or the Commissioner of Customs, Washington, D. C. 20229 cover the following topics:

Alcoholic Beverages—Commercial Importations
Import Quota
U. S. Import Requirements
Customs Duty Rulings on Prospective Imports
Marking of Country of Origin

A very useful booklet, *Exporting to the United States,* may be obtained from the GPO for one dollar.

Making Money

Every businessman has said at one time or another, "I'm in business to make money." There are always a few entrepreneurs who mean it too literally, and the Treasury's Secret Service has a prime task to see that counterfeiters do not stay in business. The businessman whose operations involve handling a lot of currency should heed the advice of the Secret Service about counterfeit bills.

One dead giveaway of phony money is the portrait. The head should stand out distinctly, and the background should be a fine screen of regular lines, not too dark. If in doubt, fold the suspect bill through the portrait, and match it with the opposite half of the portrait on a good bill. You will see a distinct contrast in technique if one is bad. Do not rely on the popular device of rubbing a bill on a piece of paper—ink can come off both good and bad bills.

When you cannot make up your mind about a bill, take it

to your bank, local police department, or the nearest Secret Service field office. To help educate employees, business organizations can obtain assistance from the Secret Service, including materials which highlight the differences between genuine and counterfeit bills. Requests for such assistance can be made to any of the sixty-two field offices of the Secret Service, or to its Washington headquarters.

Even good money can wear out, although it's printed on the strongest paper that mills can make. With the constant passing from hand to hand, the average life of a dollar bill is twelve to fourteen months. The Treasury therefore asks banks to exchange old bills for new ones, and businessmen need have no hesitation about going to their banks for the same purpose.

What about torn bills? Anyone who has three-fifths or more of a bill may redeem it for full face value. A fragment that's less than three-fifths, but clearly more than two-fifths, may be redeemed for one-half of face value. Fragments of two-fifths or less cannot be exchanged unless the owner submits satisfactory proof that the missing portions have been totally destroyed. Mutilated bills may be taken to any bank, or sent by registered mail to Currency Redemption Division, Treasury Department, Washington, D.C. 20228.

The businessman should beware that he does not unwittingly violate certain laws concerning money, as he might by chance do in his advertising. It is unlawful to photograph or publish pictures of paper money, or government checks, bonds, and stamps, except for numismatic, educational, historical, or news purposes. Even in such cases, it is well to check first with the Secret Service.

The Secret Service reminds businessmen that a government check with a forged endorsement is worthless, and the one who cashes it is the loser. It recommends obtaining positive identification of the person endorsing, and making a note on the check of the identification offered—such as the number of the motor vehicle operator's permit.

The booklet, *Know Your Money,* gives additional details. It is available from the GPO, for 40 cents.

Of Special Interest to Banking and Insurance

The Comptroller of the Currency is an official of the Treasury Department, but operates with considerable autonomy in the regulation of national banks. He is appointed by the president for a five-year term, and submits an annual report directly to Congress. A 1964 presidential directive instructed the comptroller, the chairman of the Federal Reserve, and the chairman of the Federal Deposit Insurance Corporation to inform each other before issuing any banking regulations that might conflict with existing rules of one of the agencies.

The comptroller says "yea" or "nay" to the organization of new national banks, the merger of existing national banks, or their establishment of branches. The comptroller's field staff examines the financial condition of national banks at least three times each two years, and trust examiners make certain that trust departments are discharging their responsibilities.

The Treasury's Bureau of Accounts has working relationships with business and the general public in three essential areas: (1) It issues checks to suppliers dealing with all government agencies of the executive branch, except the Department of Defense and certain government corporations. The bureau's practice is to pay all vouchers within twenty-four hours after receipt from government agencies at the regional disbursing office. Any businessman experiencing delay in receiving payment should first contact the government agency to which he sold the goods or service. (2) It deals with the activities of over eleven thousand banks designated as government depositaries. For example, qualified banks may receive from employers payments of taxes withheld from wages accompanied by depositary receipt forms. (3) It passes on the qualifications of surety companies to write federal bonds—more than 250 concerns are now authorized to do so—and periodically reviews the financial statements of such companies to determine their underwriting limitations.

Department of the Treasury
15th & Pennsylvania Ave. N.W.
Washington, D.C. 20220
(202) 393-6400

The
Independent
Agencies

THE BANKING AGENCIES

Federal Reserve System

Through its influence on credit and money, the Federal Reserve System indirectly affects every phase of American commerce, even though the average businessman may never have occasion to walk through the doors of one of the twelve Federal Reserve Banks or their twenty-four branches. Set up in 1913 after a series of money crises, its original purpose was to give the country an elastic currency, provide facilities for discounting commercial paper, and improve the supervision of banking. It continues to perform these services, but today the Federal Reserve regards its primary purpose as fostering economic growth at high levels of employment, with a stable dollar and balance in our international payments.

The principal function of the Federal Reserve System, therefore, is to regulate the flow of bank credit and money. To do so, it must collect and interpret information on economic conditions. Some of this information is published and may be of interest to businessmen who are of a studious frame of mind. (See publications list at end of section.)

The Federal Reserve also examines and supervises state banks that are members of the system, often conducting examinations jointly with state authorities. (National banks are examined by the Office of the Comptroller of the Currency, part of the Treasury Department. The Federal Deposit Insurance Corporation, an independent body, examines state banks which it insures and which are not members of the Federal Reserve System.)

In addition, the reserve system provides a variety of services benefiting business, such as facilitating the clearance of checks. In one recent year, the Federal Reserve Banks handled more than $1 trillion in checks. If a manufacturer in Hartford, Connecticut, sells $1,000 worth of electrical equipment to a dealer in Sacramento, California, and receives in payment a check that is drawn on a bank in Sacramento, he is able to cash it immediately, thanks to the facilities which the Boston and San Francisco Reserve banks provide to his bank in Hartford.

Because the nation's check usage, already twenty-six billion checks a year, is increasing at a 7 percent annual rate, the Federal Reserve is participating in experiments where electronic payments instructions, instead of bundles of checks, are cleared. It is providing automated clearing houses connected by an electronic communications system. Meanwhile, it has established a nationwide system of Regional Check Processing Centers to permit overnight clearing of most of the one hundred million checks written on the average business day.

Each Reserve Bank is a regional institution as well as part of a nationwide system, and is organized to give effective representation to the views of business in its region. Three of the nine directors must be actively engaged in commerce, industry, or agriculture in the district; three others have no conditions, except that they may not be bankers; and three may be bankers.

Nearly half the nation's commercial banks are members of the system; national banks must belong, state-chartered banks may belong. Member banks hold more than three-fourths of the country's total bank deposits.

The principal means by which the Federal Reserve achieves its monetary policy objectives are through open market purchases and sales, mainly of government securities but also of foreign currencies; through discount operations, the discount rate being an important factor in credit activity; and through changes in reserve requirements for member banks, which may influence their willingness to lend to businessmen. Regulation of stock market credit is a supplementary means. The Federal Reserve limits the amount that brokers, banks, and others may lend for purchasing or carrying securities; in recent years, the limitation has varied from 10 to 50 percent of market value. The limitation does not apply to loans for other purposes, even though stocks may be pledged as collateral.

The Federal Reserve Board is also responsible for the relatively new Truth in Lending Act, which requires disclosure of the full cost and conditions of borrowing, and the Bank Holding Company Act, which governs the rights of banks to enter other fields.

The Federal Reserve System is independent of the Treasury Department, and sometimes differs with it, acting in those cases on its own judgment of the situation. The two maintain close liaison, however; the chairman of the Reserve Board of Governors and the secretary of the treasury hold a regular weekly meeting.

Among Federal Reserve publications, the following may be of special interest to businessmen: *Commercial and Industrial Loans Outstanding, by Industry; Consumer Credit; National Summary of Business Conditions; Capacity Utilization in Manufacturing.* Available from the same source at $6 a year is the monthly *Federal Reserve Chart Book on Financial and Business Statistics.* To be placed on a mailing list to receive them without charge, request should be made to the Division of

Administrative Services, Board of Governors of the Federal
Reserve System, Washington, D.C. 20551.

Federal Reserve System
20th & Constitution N.W.
Washington, D.C. 20551
(202) 737-4171

Federal Deposit Insurance Corporation

Ninety-seven percent of all commercial and mutual savings
banks in the United States are members of the Federal Deposit
Insurance Corporation (FDIC). Its mission is to assure that the
availability of the currency supply is not impaired by bank failure. This it accomplishes in two ways: by measures aimed at
preventing failures, and by steps for prompt payment of depositors in the very rare event of failure.

Preventive measures include bank examinations to determine
if any unsatisfactory conditions exist; conferences with bank
officials to obtain correction of such conditions; and actions by
FDIC leading to removal of officers, termination of insurance,
or closing of banks which fail to make corrections. This supervision is performed by FDIC for insured state-chartered banks
that are not members of the Federal Reserve System. It must
approve establishment of new branches or mergers by such
banks. Other insured banks are examined by the comptroller of
the currency (Treasury) or representatives of the Federal
Reserve System.

If a bank closes, FDIC pays depositors up to $20,000 each
and takes over their claims for a proportionate amount of the
eventual recoveries from liquidation of the bank's assets. In
some cases, it advances funds to the failing bank in sufficient
amount to enable another bank to assume its liabilities. FDIC
acts as receiver for many closed banks, including, by law, any
national bank which may be closed.

Over a thirty-nine-year period, the corporation disbursed $702 million for the protection of nearly 1.8 million depositors in 496 insured banks which closed. More than 99 percent of these depositors have received or been assured of payment of their accounts in full.

Federal Deposit Insurance Corporation
550-17th St. N.W.
Washington, D.C. 20429
(202) 389-4221

Federal Home Loan Bank Board (FHLBB)

Businessmen may be interested in the operations of the Federal Home Loan Bank Board for three reasons:

1. The board supervises the majority, both in number and in assets, of the nation's savings and loan associations, particularly those with accounts insured by the Federal Savings and Loan Insurance Corporation. Pension and business funds, as well as personal savings, may be invested in dividend-yielding accounts with these associations.

2. Whether a businessman can obtain a mortgage loan from a savings and loan association may be determined on the basis of limitations established by the board in the interest of sound and economical home financing.

3. Businessmen interested in organizing a new federal savings and loan association will require a charter issued by the Federal Home Loan Bank Board; those organizing under state law also will be concerned with meeting the board's eligibility requirements, if the association's savings accounts are to be insured by the FSLIC.

An independent, self-sustaining government agency headed by three presidentially appointed members, the FHLBB has policy-making, regulatory, and supervisory authority over the following:

The Federal Home Loan Bank System consists of Federal Home Loan Banks in twelve districts throughout the country and their 4,400 member savings and home-financing institutions. Each of the banks is a government corporation, but is owned and managed by its members and operated on a self-supporting basis. The membership consists mainly of savings and loan associations and includes mutual savings banks that also specialize in long-term mortgage financing. Serving as centralized sources of reserve credit and liquidity, the banks make advances to members to meet unusual or heavy withdrawals and seasonal needs. These advances are funded through the issuance of consolidated obligations of the banks in the money market.

The Federal Savings and Loan Insurance Corporation provides insurance protection up to a maximum of $20,000 for each saver or investor in a single insured institution. Some 4,100 FSLIC-insured savings and loan associations currently are entrusted with total savings of $249 billion for more than forty million investors. Insurance is mandatory for federally chartered associations, and available to eligible state-chartered associations upon application to, and approval by, the Federal Home Loan Bank Board. Since establishment of the FSLIC on June 27, 1934, no insured saver or investor in an FSLIC-insured institution has ever lost a single penny of insured savings. During thirty-eight years of operations, 101 associations received financial assistance from the Insurance Corporation and more than 830,000 savers in these insured institutions were protected against potential loss.

The Federal Home Loan Mortgage Corporation (FHLMC) was established in 1970 to increase the secondary market volume of sales and purchases of residential mortgages and, thus, to increase the effective supply of mortgage financing, the flexibility of mortgage investors, and the attractiveness of morgage investments.

FHLMC may purchase residential mortgages of all types, single-family, multifamily, FHA/VA, and conventional. Its purchases, however, may only be from members of the Federal Home Loan Bank System or other financial institutions, the deposits of which are insured by agencies of the United States government.

FHLMC purchase commitments in a recent year totaled over $1.6 billion, of which about half were for conventional mortgages.

The Federal Savings and Loan System consists of the privately owned and managed local savings and loan associations of the mutual type, chartered as federal associations by the FHLBB and directly under its supervision and regulation. All federal savings and loan associations are required to be members of the Federal Home Loan Bank System. They invest their funds in nonfarm real estate, primarily in first mortgages on one-to-four-family homes or combinations of home and business property located within a radius of fifty to one hundred miles of the principal association office. To a limited extent, they also can make loans on apartment buildings for five or more families, on such other improved real estate as office buildings and shopping centers, and for financing the acquisition and development of raw land into home sites.

The Office of Examinations and Supervision, through a field organization of examiners in assigned areas, performs the functions implied by its name for all federal savings and loan associations. Examination and supervision of insured state-chartered associations is conducted jointly with state authorities.

For businessmen interested in forming a new federal savings and loan association, the most important thing to do is to get in touch with the Federal Home Loan Bank of their district at the earliest possible time, even before many details in connection with the proposed association have been worked out. The bank supplies application forms, furnishes advice and suggestions in connection with filling them out, and recommends the action that should be taken on the application by the Federal Home Loan Bank Board. Major criteria used in arriving at a decision on an application are: (1) the good character and responsibility of the applicants; (2) the existence of need for the institution; (3) the reasonable probability of its usefulness and success; and (4) a showing that it can be established without undue injury to properly conducted existing thrift and home-financing institutions.

If the application appears satisfactory to the board, it will publish a notice of hearing in the locality. Ordinarily, however, if no objection is received in response to the hearing notice, the board will dispense with a hearing.

The organizers then will elect temporary officers, who will raise subscriptions to initial capital. Capital requirements are intended to assure an adequate and broad base of community support for a new institution. Currently, the minimum requirements are $300,000 from 250 subscribers and the maximum requirements are $1,250,000 from 850 subscribers. Payments on such subscriptions, the board cautions, should not be collected, nor any other expense chargeable to the association incurred, before a charter is issued. The charter will be issued after the organizing committee submits evidence that the subscriptions have been obtained and other prescribed conditions complied with.

Federal Home Loan Bank Board
101 Indiana Ave. N.W.
Washington, D.C. 20552
(202) 386-3157

Farm Credit Administration

Although its name suggests it might be part of the U.S. Department of Agriculture, the Farm Credit Administration is an independent government agency. Its task is to supervise and coordinate activities of the cooperative farm credit system, comprised of federal land banks and federal land bank associations, federal intermediate credit banks and production credit associations, and banks for cooperatives. The word "federal" in the name of some of these units reflects the fact that they were initially capitalized by the United States, but the entire system now is owned by its users, and raises funds in the open market.

Loans are made by units of the system to farmers, ranchers, producers or harvesters of aquatic products; persons engaged in providing on-the-farm services to farmers and rural home-owners; and to cooperative associations engaged in marketing, processing, supply, or business service functions for the benefit of member farmers, ranchers, producers, or harvesters of aquatic products.

The loans may be for agricultural purposes, housing, or other needs of the applicant. Housing loans are limited to towns where the population does not exceed twenty-five hundred. Length of loans varies among the different types of banks and associa-tions in the system. Applications for loans should be made to the nearest appropriate unit of the system. General information, including Pamphlet A-29 which gives a descriptive listing of publications and motion pictures on the Farm Credit Adminis-tration and the cooperative farm credit system, may be obtained by contacting:

Information Division
Farm Credit Administration
485 L'Enfant Plaza West S.W.
Washington, D.C. 20578
(202) 755-2130

National Credit Union Administration

Credit unions serve the employees of many business organi-zations, providing in-plant financial facilities. The National Credit Union Administration, an independent government agency, charters new credit unions, supervises and examines some thirteen thousand federally chartered credit unions, and insures member accounts of federal and state-chartered credit unions. It finances these activities by charges against units in this surprisingly large system—the federal credit unions alone have assets exceeding $18 billion.

Groups of employees or others with some common bond may obtain free information about starting a federal credit union.

National Credit Union Administration
2025 M St. N.W.
Washington, D.C. 20456
(202) 254-9800

FOREIGN TRADE

Export-Import Bank

The name "Export-Import Bank" is more than forty years old, and somewhat misleading as to the institution's present-day role. Currently, its thrust is almost entirely on promoting exports. And while in doing so it employs such conventional banking methods as direct loans, it also offers exporters an array of unique devices, such as loan guarantees and political risk insurance.

Its basic programs are export credit guarantees, export credit insurance, discount loans, and direct credits to borrowers outside the United States, with more than twenty variations or combinations. In a recent year it financed more than $7.2 billion through all of these means. Jet transport aircraft, nuclear power facilities, and oil rigs and related equipment were the largest categories of export items covered.

Here's how the guarantee program works: Upon receipt of an overseas order, invitation to bid, or other inquiry, the exporter goes to his commercial bank. The bank may apply to Eximbank for a guarantee against the credit and political risks of nonpayment in the transaction. Guarantees are issued subject to several conditions.

The buyer must pay the exporter 10 percent by delivery time, and give promissory notes for the balance. Of that balance, the exporter must carry at least 10 percent, and the commercial bank pays off the exporter on the rest. The commercial bank carries the commercial credit risk on the early installments, and the Eximbank guarantee covers commercial risks on the remaining installments and political risks on all installments.

Eximbank relies to a considerable extent on the credit judgment of the commercial bank. To some banks it grants discretionary authority to issue guarantees within specified limits without prior approval.

Another vehicle for financing exports is the Foreign Credit Insurance Association (FCIA), a group of fifty insurance companies working in close cooperation with Eximbank. The exporter may use FCIA policies covering commercial and political risks as collateral in obtaining bank loans.

Increasingly popular is its Master Policy, which provides coverage under a single contract for all of an exporter's short-term and medium-term sales. It includes a deductible provision for first loss on commercial risks which allows a much lower premium. A special policy has been developed for small businesses which may wish to cover sales only to certain buyers.

Discount loans make it possible for the exporter to receive 100 percent of the debt obligation arising from a sale. He gets his money from a commercial bank which has applied to Eximbank before shipment and received an advance commitment to make a discount loan or to purchase the debt obligation.

Discount loans may be medium-term—twelve months or longer—or short-term, for less than one year. On medium-term loans, Eximbank will charge an interest rate 1 percent less than the interest yield to the applicant bank, if that bank requests the loan within ninety days of making its disbursement to the exporter. On short-term loans, Eximbank charges on a sliding scale, ranging from a 2 percent spread allowed to the applicant bank on transactions of $250,000 or less down to 1 percent on transactions exceeding $750,000. The commercial bank may "package" smaller transactions, getting an advance commitment covering an estimate of all such transactions for the succeeding thirty days.

Direct Eximbank loans to borrowers outside the United States are given mainly so they can purchase heavy capital equipment from U.S. suppliers, usually on terms longer than private lenders can provide. Eximbank requires, however, that private lenders participate equally with it in such financing. It will, if necessary, provide a financial guarantee to the private lender, whether it be a U.S. or foreign institution, at a fee of ½ percent per annum on the outstanding balance.

Eximbank financial guarantees can cover not only the dollar costs of U.S. goods and services, but associated local costs, such as public utility connections, equipment installation, or employee housing. It will guarantee local costs up to 15 percent of the value of U.S. goods and services exported.

Eximbank will make preliminary commitments to overseas buyers, U.S. suppliers, or financial institutions concerning the amounts it will lend or guarantee, and the terms. This feature may be particularly useful to a U.S. exporter submitting a proposal in response to a bid invitation requiring plans for financing. Applications for preliminary commitments, direct loans, and financial guarantees may be submitted by letter (in contrast to discount loans, which require specific forms).

Exporters dealing with small and medium-sized enterprises may find the Cooperative Financing Facility plan helpful. Since these enterprises may find it most convenient to work with their own bank, Eximbank offers cooperating overseas financial institutions a loan at an attractive rate, covering half the amount of the U.S. export after a 10 percent down payment. If the overseas institution wishes to borrow its half of the financing, Eximbank can guarantee repayment to another lender. Under such guarantees, eighteen U.S. banks have extended credit lines to cooperating banks. Construction equipment, machine tools, and agricultural processing equipment account for the bulk of exports financed in this manner. On request, Eximbank will send a list of the overseas banks participating in the cooperative program.

Eximbank also makes available to selected overseas institutions lines of credit for 100 percent loans to buyers of U.S. goods and services. The relending institutions may finance only certain product lines agreed on in advance with Eximbank.

Leases of U.S. equipment outside the United States also are eligible for several forms of Eximbank coverage. These include guarantees against political risks, given at a fee of ½ of 1 percent, or comprehensive coverage of commercial and political risks for ¾ of 1 percent; direct loans or financial guarantees; and preliminary commitments.

U.S. firms undertaking engineering, planning, and feasibility studies of large capital projects for non-U.S. clients can obtain Eximbank financial assistance directed to them or their clients. If the client decides to carry out the recommendations, the study cost may be refinanced into the U.S. export portion of the resulting contract. Preliminary commitments are given for both feasibility studies and follow-on contracts.

Equipment used abroad by U.S. contractors can be protected against political risks for 75 percent of the depreciated equipment value, at a fee of ½ of 1 percent per annum.

In addition to its guarantees, insurance, loans, and credits, Eximbank offers without charge to U.S. businessmen some valuable special services. Need credit information on potential overseas buyers? A phone call to (202) 382-1785 may elicit it. Puzzled about how to find the right kind of export financing? The Eximbank vice president for export expansion offers a counseling service. Want to train members of your export department in Eximbank procedures? Eximbank gives orientation programs for this purpose. Most widely used is the day-long saturation session, tailored for a minimum of four to a maximum of ten trainees from a particular company. These should be requested sixty days in advance, giving three choices of dates, by letter to the vice president for export expansion.

Export-Import Bank of the U.S.
811 Vermont Ave. N.W.
Washington, D.C. 20571
(202) 382-1168

Overseas Private Investment Corporation (OPIC)

Services sounding very similar to those of Eximbank are offered by OPIC. The difference lies in the fact that Eximbank covers export sales, leases, or contracts, while OPIC deals with investments.

One of the newest government agencies, OPIC was organized in 1971. It offers to businessmen interested in investing overseas three services: insurance against political risks of currency inconvertibility, expropriation, and war, revolution, or insurrection; financial assistance through guaranties against loss from commercial risks, and to a limited extent, through direct loans; and partial funding of reconnaisance and feasibility surveys.

OPIC is concerned with private investment in less developed countries, complementing the work of the Agency for International Development, which helps the governments of such countries provide the necessary infrastructure of roads, electric power, and the like.

Although under the policy guidance of the secretary of state, and starting with capital provided by Congress, OPIC has a majority of private sector representation on its board of directors, and is moving toward becoming self-sustaining through fees. For example, it charges a premium of 1½ percent per annum for its insurance.

OPIC's charter limits it to assisting projects which are financially sound, competitive, welcome, and contributing to the social and economic progress of the host country. As a matter of policy, oil exploration, concession agreements, and investments in subsurface property rights are not insured.

Insurance written in a recent year amounted to $600 million, and claims paid to about $2.3 million. These were for war damage in Pakistan and Bangladesh, and expropriation and inconvertibility in Chile.

A special political risk insurance policy is available to the construction industry, in line with the policies offered by other governments to their construction companies. For details, write or call Applications Office, OPIC, Washington, D.C. 20527, (202) 632-1820.

The guaranty program is intended to help eligible projects obtain U.S. private long-term financing, particularly from institutional lenders, which might otherwise be unavailable except on prohibitive terms. The rarer direct-dollar loans are intended to assist smaller projects.

Under agreement with AID, OPIC administers "Cooley" loans of local currencies obtained by the U.S. Government through sale of agricultural commodities under the Food for Peace program.

Agribusiness and small business can get OPIC to share costs of locating investment opportunities and surveying their feasibility. OPIC will lend 75 percent of the cost of such surveys (up to certain limits) and will apply a portion of the repayment to the cost of OPIC insurance or financing if the decision is made to go ahead with the investment.

Management counseling is provided to enterprises in developing countries through the International Executive Service Corps, a private nonprofit organization of volunteer American businessmen, many of them retired. For information about

short-term assignments with IESC, write it at 545 Madison
Avenue, New York, New York 10022.

Overseas Private Investment Corporation
1129-20th St. N.W.
Washington, D.C. 20527
(202) 632-1854

Tariff Commission

Escape clauses, dumping, and other esoteric-sounding words
are the stock in trade of the Tariff Commission; to the American
businessman grappling with foreign competition, they can mean
life or death. They take on added importance as the United
States enters an era of negotiation with the countries of the
Common Market for mutual reduction of tariffs. Before any
commodity becomes a counter on the bargaining table, the Tariff
Commission offers the American businessman producing such
commodities a forum in which he can attempt to demonstrate
that a given reduction in import duty would threaten serious
injury to his industry. If he convinces the commission of the
existence of such a peril, it so advises the President. The President is not obliged to follow the recommendations of the Tariff
Commission, but the procedure provides United States industry
with an initial opportunity of stating its case publicly.

Once a trade-agreement concession has been granted, representatives of companies or unions can get the Tariff Commission
to investigate whether the product is being imported in such increased quantities as to cause or threaten serious injury to the
domestic industry. In so-called "escape clause" investigations,
the commission takes into account such factors as a downward
trend of production, prices, sales, or profits of the domestic
industry. If it finds the industry threatened, it so advises the
President, who may increase duties or restrict imports. He may

also authorize all firms in the industry to seek adjustment assistance. It is not easy to convince both the commission and the
President of injury. In a recent year the commission completed
three cases concerning injury claimed by domestic industries.
In two—umbrellas and billiard balls—the commission made a
negative decision. On nonrubber footwear, the commissioners
were equally divided on the principal types of products under
investigation and unanimously negative on the others. Even if
an industry wins tariff adjustment, the change is subject to
periodic review by the Tariff Commission, and unless specifically
extended by the president terminates after four years.

Under the Trade Expansion Act of 1962, the Tariff Commission can make a finding of injury not only to an entire industry,
as in the past, but to an individual firm or its workers. Firms
have been slightly more successful than whole industries. In
eleven completed investigations, a maker of stainless-steel table
flatware and a woven-fabrics mill obtained affirmative action.
The petitions of five other firms were voted down, and in four
cases there was a tie vote. These four, along with the two approved by the commission, later were certified by the President
as eligible to apply for adjustment assistance.

Application is then made by the firm to the secretary of commerce (or in the case of workers, the secretary of labor) for
such assistance, which can take three forms. "Technical assistance" may include market research, managerial counseling,
and aid in research and development, furnished either through
federal agencies or private sources. "Financial assistance" may
take the form of loans or loan guarantees for such purposes as
modernization or conversion of plant and equipment. "Tax assistance" can be provided through extension of the loss-carryback
period from three years to five years.

Businessmen dealing in agricultural products may find the
Tariff Commission a factor in their operations, since it may be
directed by the President to investigate whether imports of any
commodity should be restricted in order to avoid interference
with price-support or other programs of the Department of Agri-

culture. The President may then impose import quotas, as he has done in the case of certain dairy products, or he may impose import fees.

Still used, but of decreasing significance since it is inapplicable to any commodity on which a tariff concession has been made under a trade agreement, is the "flexible tariff" provision. This authorizes the President, after investigation and report by the Tariff Commission, to change an import duty in order to equate differences in cost of production between domestic and foreign producers.

If a businessman feels he is being injured by unfair methods of competition from abroad, such as use of his patents without a license, he may file a complaint with the Tariff Commission. The resulting investigation could lead to the President's issuing an order excluding the foreign products in question from the United States.

Still another possible protection is the Antidumping Act. When the secretary of the treasury advises the Tariff Commission that foreign merchandise is being sold at less than its fair value (a situation usually called to his attention by the affected United States industry), the commission determines whether such "dumping" is injuring a domestic industry. If the commission finds "injury," the treasury secretary then issues a "finding" of dumping, and special duties are collected. In ten cases out of thirteen in a recent year the commission made a finding of injury where the Treasury had reported alleged dumping.

A business that cannot find leverage for Tariff Commission action under any of the specific provisions of law so far described may use an indirect route prescribed in Section 332 of the Tariff Act of 1930. Under this legislation, the House Ways and Means Committee or the Senate Finance Committee may, by resolution, request the Tariff Commission to make a comprehensive report of the situation of an industry.

The Tariff Commission publishes a great deal of information useful to importers, exporters, and other businessmen. Most of it is available directly from the commission without charge, although a few of its publications are sold by the GPO. A booklet listing its publications, their source and price, if any, may be obtained from the commission.

The data in Tariff Commission publications come from governmental and nongovernmental sources. Some are submitted directly to the commission, some are obtained from personal visits by staff members to manufacturers, importers, and others.

Among the more important Tariff Commission publications are the *Tariff Schedules of the United States* (formerly *United States Import Duties*), published approximately every two years; *Summaries of Tariff Information*, comprised of twenty-three hundred summaries in forty-six volumes, published complete in 1948–50, but now being brought up to date gradually with several hundred revised summaries a year; monthly and annual reports on synthetic organic chemicals; and an annual report on the operation of the trade agreement program.

The extensive resources of the Tariff Commission library are open to private researchers. It contains approximately sixty-three thousand volumes and receives more than twelve hundred periodicals.

Inquiries may be addressed to:

Kenneth R. Mason, Secretary
U.S. Tariff Commission
7th & E Sts. N.W.
Washington, D.C. 20436
(202) 628-3947

GENERAL SERVICES ADMINISTRATION: BUYER, RENTER, SELLER

The General Services Administration (GSA) is important to every businessman who wants to:

- sell products to the government;
- build for the government;
- lease space to the government;
- buy surplus property, real or personal, from the government; or
- provide architectural, engineering, or transportation services to the government.

GSA's Federal Supply Service procures for federal agencies more than $2 billion worth of goods and services a year. Large as this central buying role is, GSA is not the exclusive purchasing agent for the entire government. The Departments of Defense, Health, Education, and Welfare, and Transportation, the Veterans Administration, NASA, and the Postal Service procure many of the items they use, and maintain their own bidders' lists.

For maximum sales to the government, it is necessary to contact not only these agencies, but those which rely on the GSA supply system. As GSA points out, selling to the government differs little in most respects from selling to commercial markets. "To do an effective job, businessmen must direct their selling efforts at least as much to the government consuming offices as to the buying or contracting offices."

The businessman who wants to sell to government would do well to make his first point of call one of the twelve Business Service Centers that GSA operates.

Business Service Centers

Business Service Centers help the businessman obtain government contracts and stimulate his interest in these contracts. Special emphasis is placed on assisting the minority businessman, but the service is not limited to serving minorities. The centers can also be of great assistance to firms which are too large to qualify as small businesses under the Small Business Act, but which cannot afford to employ full time contract experts to obtain government contracts.

Specialists at the centers provide information and counseling on all GSA programs which deal with purchases of goods or services. If GSA does not have a need which coincides with the potential contractor's capabilities, these specialists will provide information on other federal agencies which may be able to utilize its product or service.

According to Gordon Knight, Director of GSA's Business Services Program, more than 50 percent of the centers' staffs' time is spent in individual and group counseling, including giving assistance on contract services and contract liaison. Each year an average of 160,000 businessmen receive person-to-person counseling from the centers' specialists. Many end up with government contracts, or a subcontract from a prime contractor signed to a job.

Counseling includes information on federal procurement and disposal policies, introduction of new products to the government, disposal policies, bidding procedures and related documents, specifications, contract forms and conditions, quantities and prices of past contract awards, and names of current prime contractors from whom subcontracts might be obtained.

The centers also display current bid invitations, bid tabulations, contract awards data, and GSA catalogs and information pamphlets.

E. R. Ritchey, president of TKO Chemical Company, Inc. of St. Joseph, Missouri, is one of the thousands of small businessmen who have benefited from counseling at GSA's centers.

Ritchey's firm was about to be dropped from federal procurement schedule, when it developed a new product for use in the photographic, graphic arts, microfilm, and X-ray fields.

Ritchey turned to the Kansas City Business Service Center for advice. Center business affairs specialists counseled and steered him to the proper federal agencies. As a result, fifty-two agencies have purchased the product and are testing it. Once the product is in use government-wide, it is expected to result in savings to the taxpayers of $14 million per year.

In addition to services provided at the centers, specialists actively seek out potential buyers and suppliers, thereby providing new sources for satisfying government needs and stimulating competition for contracts.

The centers use all available means to reach businessmen. Some of the means include meetings and conferences sponsored by chambers of commerce, congressional offices, community action groups, and the Department of Commerce.

GSA representatives attended 557 such functions during fiscal year 1972, counseling over twenty thousand businessmen at the meetings. Traveling business affairs specialists seek out businessmen in cities where GSA does not operate centers. Through only recently initiated, this "circuit rider" program enabled some nine hundred contractors in eighty-four cities to take advantage of individual counseling services during fiscal 1972.

The Business Service Centers are located as follows:

Joseph P. Lawless
Regional Director of Business
    Affairs
General Services Administra-
    tion (1AB)
John Fitzgerald
Kennedy Federal Bldg.
Boston, Mass. 02203
(617) 223–2868

Connecticut, Maine, Vermont,
    Massachusetts, New Hamp-
    shire, and Rhode Island

Martin Perlmutter
Regional Director of Business
    Affairs
General Services Administra-
    tion (2AB)
26 Federal Plaza
New York, N.Y. 10007
(212) 264–1234

New Jersey, New York,
    Puerto Rico, and Virgin Is-
    lands

Richard F. Maloney
Regional Director of Business
    Affairs
General Services Administra-
    tion (3AB)
7th & D Sts. S.W.
Washington, D.C. 20407
(202) 963–4147

Delaware, District of Colum-
    bia, Maryland, Pennsylva-
    nia, Virginia, and West Vir-
    ginia

Paul J. Lieb, Manager
Business Service Center
General Services Administra-
    tion
17 N. Juniper St.
Philadelphia, Pa. 19107
(215) 597–9613

Philadelphia and Wilmington,
    Delaware

W. Q. Culpepper
Regional Director of Business
  Affairs
General Services Administra-
  tion (4AB)
1776 Peachtree St., N.W.
Atlanta, Ga. 30309
(404) 526–5661

Alabama, Florida, Georgia,
  Kentucky, Mississippi,
  North Carolina, South Car-
  olina, and Tennessee

Benjamin M. Copenhaver
Regional Director of Business
  Affairs
General Services Administra-
  tion (5AB)
219 S. Dearborn St.
Chicago, Ill. 60604
(312) 353–5383

Illinois, Indiana, Michigan,
  Ohio, Minnesota, and Wisconsin

F. Howard Whiteley
Regional Director of Business
  Affairs
General Services Administra-
  tion (6AB)
1500 E. Bannister Rd.
Kansas City, Mo. 64131
(816) 361–7203, 0860

Iowa, Kansas, Missouri, and
  Nebraska

R. Tom Ratliff
Regional Director of Business
  Affairs
General Services Administra-
  tion (7AB)
819 Taylor St.
Fort Worth, Tex. 76102
(817) 334–3284

Arkansas, Louisiana, New
  Mexico, Texas, and Oklahoma

John E. Holden
Regional Director of Business
  Affairs
General Services Administra-
  tion (8AB)
Bldg. 41, Denver Federal Cen-
  ter
Denver, Colo. 80225
(303) 234–2216

Colorado, North Dakota,
  South Dakota, Montana,
  Utah, and Wyoming

Stanley W. Anderson, Man-
  ager
Business Service Center
General Services Administration
49 4th St.
San Francisco, Calif. 94103
(415) 556–2114

Arizona, California, Hawaii,
  and Nevada

Mrs. Margaret Bayless, Manager
Business Service Center
General Services Administration
300 N. Los Angeles
Los Angeles, Calif. 90012
(213) 688–3210

Los Angeles, and Southern
  California

John J. Murphy
Regional Director of Business
  Affairs
General Services Administra-
  tion (10AB)
909 1st Ave.
Seattle, Wash. 98104
(206) 442–5556

Alaska, Idaho, Oregon, and
  Washington

Selling to the government is a subject that by itself would require an entire book to cover in detail. GSA does in fact publish a ninety-four-page book, *Doing Business With the Federal Government*, free from Business Service Centers. It also publishes a *Guide to Federal Specifications and Standards*, available free from GSA Business Service Centers. It describes the various types of specifications, discusses the role of industry in their development, and tells how to obtain copies.

Another useful volume is *U.S. Government Purchasing and Sales Directory*, which lists major federal purchasing offices and what they buy. A publication of the Small Business Administration, it may be examined at GSA Business Service Centers or purchased from GPO at $1.25.

To participate in GSA's procurement programs for standard items, ask the nearest center for forms to put your name on the appropriate GSA bidders mailing list.

New or Improved Items of Supply

GSA has established specific procedures to help businessmen present new or improved supply items. These procedures require the prospective supplier to submit inquiries to the nearest GSA Business Service Center, describing the item in detail and listing all pertinent information.

Upon receipt of the inquiry, the center determines whether the item is similar to any item currently purchased by GSA. If the item is similar, the prospective supplier is furnished the appropriate bidders' mailing list application forms, the appropriate specification, and the necessary instructions on how to submit bids on future contracts for that item.

With few exceptions, the GSA Federal Supply Service buys common use items. Specialized items are usually bought directly by a federal agency to satisfy their particular demands.

If the items are not similar, and sufficient demand can be anticipated, the prospective supplier is requested to prepare

GSA Form 1171, Application for Presenting New or Improved Articles. Each form should be supplemented by any explanatory data available; sales literature, copies of printed commercial price lists, history of sales to government agencies (document in complete detail and list names and addresses of government people who have expressed interest in purchasing your product), laboratory reports, customer testimonials, technical data, Underwriters Laboratories approval on electrical items, plus whatever the applicant feels will help the reviewing officials reach a favorable decision. In the case of detergents, applications should include the results of tests by an independent laboratory. Tests should be the type used by the Food and Drug Administration in making determinations under the Federal Hazardous Substances Act.

The applicant should compile four complete sets of his application (including copies of cover letter highlighting the advantages of the product), one set to be retained by the applicant and three sets to be submitted to the Business Service Center. Upon receipt of the completed new product application, the center will send it to the Standardization Division, Federal Supply Service, Washington, D.C. 20406. That office evaluates the merits and usefulness of the item and determines its acceptability. The center and the applicant are then notified of final action on the application. When warranted, tests may be conducted—normally at the expense of the prospective supplier—to make sure the product will measure up to the performance claimed.

The National Buying Center of GSA initiates the necessary action to add approved products to a New Item Introductory Schedule. New items usually remain on this schedule for a period of one year. If during this period a sufficient demand develops to include it in the Federal Supply System, a Federal Supply Schedule is established or the item is placed in depot inventory on a nationwide basis.

If GSA decides not to include the item under control, the prospective supplier is promptly notified by letter, which will include the reasons for rejection. Rejection of an item by GSA does not prevent a supplier from contacting other federal agencies for the purpose of selling his product. If enough federal agencies then buy the product through direct contact, a demand may develop which would justify inclusion of the item in GSA's government-wide supply system.

Sixty to ninety days are required to process new item applications.

Selling Direct to Civilian or Military Agencies

The inclusion of a product or service in the GSA Supply System is not a prerequisite to its use or purchase by other federal agencies. Prior approval by GSA is not required unless:

- The product under consideration is similar in quality, construction, and utility to a product obtainable through the GSA Supply System, and
- GSA regulations require procurement of the type of items under consideration through GSA facilities in the quantity wanted, within the time and at the place delivery is required by the buying office involved.

When prior approval by GSA is required, the agency desiring the product, not the supplier, must request GSA approval for open-market purchase. When GSA approval is not required, the agencies have full authority to make their own purchases.

Generally, a civilian or military agency can buy direct from commercial sources if:

- The product *needed* is not available from GSA supply sources. (If a *similar* product is available from GSA supply sources, prior approval of GSA *may be required* and should be requested by the agency needing the product, *unless* the agency involved is exempt from such requirement by reason of a delegation of authority from GSA, or by some provision of law or

regulation governing the agency's operations and procurement authority.)
- The activity has the requisite "local purchase" authority— "local purchase" means authority of the local activity to buy, not that purchases must be made only from "local" dealers or other sources.
- The product meets the needs of the activity in terms of economy and efficiency.

Federal agencies can always buy without regard to GSA sources of supply whenever the items are purchased for resale and/or payment and therefore do not involve the use of appropriated tax funds. Examples are purchases of articles for resale by army and air force post exchanges, navy ship stores, veterans canteens, etc., and purchases of recreational, entertainment, ecclesiastical, library, educational and many other types of items which are paid for by funds donated by the public for the benefit of military personnel, hospitalized veterans, etc., as well as from the proceeds of sales at the aforementioned post exchanges, canteens, etc.

Building for Uncle Sam

The Public Buildings Service of GSA spends close to $300 million a year on construction of government buildings. On projects of more than $500,000, a prospectus is prepared by GSA for approval of the Public Works Committees of the Congress (see chapter, "The Businessman and Congress").

As a general rule, construction contracts are awarded on the basis of competitive bids, solicited by newspaper advertising in the city where the work is to be performed, as well as notices in trade journals and in *Commerce Business Daily* ($63.50 a year, GPO).

A 1972 law authorized a new arrangement, the purchase contract program, under which a private contractor constructs a building to federal specifications, then sells it to the government over a period up to thirty years. The program involves two types of award systems:

The "package system," designed for smaller projects, calls on a builder or developer to construct the building and provide all necessary financing.

The "dual system" involves a contract for construction, with GSA providing financing.

Wherever possible, GSA tries to build on property already owned by the government. Where necessary, it will acquire private property by purchase, exchange, or condemnation. The appropriate GSA regional office will advertise in local newspapers soliciting site offers.

When a site is selected, GSA will contract with an independent appraiser to advise it of fair market value (which does not include intangibles such as good will) and will then make a written offer. If your asking price exceeds that amount, a GSA representative will call on you to negotiate.

Should you be unable to agree on a price, the government can file a "declaration of taking" in U.S. District Court, deposit with the court a check in the amount it estimates is just compensation, and take title. You may withdraw that amount, subject to determination of compensation by the judge, or if requested, by a jury. Further review may be sought in the U.S. Court of Appeals.

The law provides that business occupants of property taken by the government will be reimbursed for actual and reasonable moving expenses and for limited expenses incurred in searching for replacement property.

A booklet, *Business Relocation Assistance*, is available from GSA.

Architects and engineers seeking contracts to design federal buildings should submit Standard Form 251 and photos of completed projects to the nearest GSA regional office (see list at end of chapter). To be considered for projects of national significance, usually major buildings in the Washington area, the same material should be submitted to Office of Design and

Construction, Public Buildings Service, GSA, Washington, D.C. 20405. To help it make selections, GSA uses panels of professional colleagues from each region, and chooses from among several recommended by the panel.

Leasing to GSA

GSA leases general purpose space for all federal agencies in U.S. urban centers and in Puerto Rico and the Virgin Islands. Elsewhere, it leases such space for all agencies except the departments of Agriculture, Commerce, and Defense, which do their own leasing. For information about their activities, write the following:

*Director of Real Estate
Office of Chief of Engineers
Department of the Army
Washington, D.C. 20315

Assistant Commander for
Real Property Management
Naval Facilities Engineering Command
Department of the Navy
Washington, D.C. 20390

Chief, Real Estate Division
Office of Plant and Operations
Department of Agriculture
Washington, D.C. 20250

Director, Office of Administrative Services
Department of Commerce
Washington, D.C. 20230

* For Army, Air Force, and U.S. Postal Service

Most GSA leases are for three to five years, with options for renewal, but they may run as long as twenty years. With congressional approval, GSA may negotiate a lease on a building not yet constructed.

Leases normally are made on the basis of competitive negotiations. Owners and managers interested in offering commercial space to GSA should write to their GSA regional office (see list at end of chapter). The letter should ask to be placed on the mailing list of prospective offerors, give a general description of the space available, and indicate if interested in constructing space for lease. Regional offices announce leasing opportunities by newspaper advertising and postings in federal buildings.

One attraction of renting to GSA is that it pays automatically at the end of each month without waiting for a landlord's billing.

Surplus Sales

GSA sells off real and personal property no longer needed by the government, and manages a $6 billion stockpile of strategic materials which may involve selling or buying as the supply situation changes. In a recent year it sold $330 million of items.

To be placed on a mailing list for notices of real property sales, write the disposal officer in the GSA region. Such sales are made by sealed bid, public auction, through a broker, or under certain conditions, by negotiation.

Groups interested in promoting industrial or commercial development often are able to interest individual enterprises in bidding. GSA regional officers will meet with such groups, and to the extent practicable, coordinate GSA disposal plans with their objectives.

Brokers and appraisers interested in performing contract services should inform the GSA regional office. Appraisers should request Form 1195. If approved after submitting this form (a minimum of five years' experience is required), their names will be placed on a register to receive invitations to submit proposals.

Motor vehicles, typewriters, and a wide variety of other personal property no longer needed by civil government agencies are sold by GSA. Catalogs or other announcements may be obtained by writing the Property Management and Disposal Service in the GSA regional office and asking for a mailing list application. The announcement will indicate the method of sale, which may be by sealed bid in advance, a written spot bid during the sale, or by public auction. All offerings are on an "as-is-where-is" basis, so inspection before bidding is encouraged.

GSA seeks the advice of business on stockpiling critical materials. Its policy is to procure such materials from domestic sources where possible. In order to maintain stockpiled materials, GSA purchases storage aids such as pallets, polyethylene bags, steel drums, and burlap bags, and services such as materials handling and analyzing.

Consumer Product Information

In the course of buying $2 billion worth of goods and services a year, GSA acquires considerable information about commercial products. Since 1970, it has been publishing booklets for consumers based on this information. They cover everything from hearing aids to vacuum cleaners, and more than three million copies have been sold. Manufacturers and distributors who want to know what the government is saying about their field should request the quarterly Index of Consumer Product Information from:

Consumer Product Information
Pueblo, Colo. 81009

Regional Offices

STATES SERVED

Post Office and Court House Boston, Mass. 02109 (617) 223–2651	Connecticut, Maine, Massachusetts, New Hampshire, Rhode Island, and Vermont
26 Federal Plaza New York, N.Y. 10007 (212) 264–2650	New Jersey, New York, Puerto Rico, and Virgin Islands
General Services Regional Office Bldg. 7th & D Sts. S.W. Washington, D.C. 20407 (202) 963–3584	District of Columbia, Delaware, Maryland, Pennsylvania, Virginia, and West Virginia
1776 Peachtree St., N.W. Atlanta, Ga. 30309 (404) 526–5631	Alabama, Florida, Georgia, Kentucky, Mississippi, North Carolina, South Carolina, and Tennessee
U.S. Court House 219 South Dearborn St. Chicago, Ill. 60604 (312) 353–6045	Illinois, Indiana, Michigan, Minnesota, Ohio, and Wisconsin
GSA Administration Bldg. 1500 E. Bannister Rd. Kansas City, Mo. 64131 (816) 361–0860, ext. 7237	Iowa, Kansas, Missouri, and Nebraska
819 Taylor St. Fort Worth, Tex. 76102 (817) 334–2331	Arkansas, Louisiana, New Mexico, Oklahoma, and Texas

Bldg. 41
Denver Federal Center
Denver, Colo. 80225
(303) 234-3934

Colorado, Montana, North
Dakota, South Dakota,
Utah, and Wyoming

49 4th St.
San Francisco, Calif. 94103
(415) 556-5314

Arizona, California, Nevada,
and Hawaii

GSA Center
Auburn, Wash. 98002
(206) 833-6500, ext. 265

Alaska, Idaho, Oregon, and
Washington

General Services Administration
18th & F Sts. N.W.
Washington, D.C. 20405
(202) 343-4511

THE GOVERNMENT AND
LABOR RELATIONS

Three independent agencies of the federal government must be taken into account by businessmen concerned with actual or prospective labor disputes, as indeed most businessmen are. They are the National Labor Relations Board (NLRB), the Federal Mediation and Conciliation Service (FMCS), and the National Mediation Board. The potential role of the Equal Employment Opportunity Commission also must be considered.

National Labor Relations Board

The NLRB has two principal functions. It handles charges of unfair labor practices alleged against both unions and employers, and acts on petitions for determination of bargaining representatives which may be submitted by employers, employees, or unions.

NLRB does not act on its own motion in either category—the charge or petition must be brought by employers, employees, or unions. When NLRB was established in 1935, charges of unfair labor practices could be brought only against employers. Since the Taft–Hartley Act of 1947, it may also deal with charges against unions, and about one-third of the unfair labor practice charges it receives are now of this type.

Practices forbidden by law to management are:

1. interference with employees in the exercise of legitimate union activities;
2. company assistance, domination, or control of an employee organization or union;
3. discharge of, or discrimination against, an employee because of union membership or activity;
4. discrimination against an employee for having filed charges or given testimony against an employer under this act; and
5. refusal to bargain collectively with unions chosen by the employees.

Management in turn has recourse against unions for these six practices:

1. coercion of, or discrimination against, employees because of membership or nonmembership in unions;
2. causing an employer to violate the act by discharging an employee illegally;
3. refusal to bargain collectively with an employer;
4. inducing or encouraging strikes when an object is to (a) force employees to join unions, (b) force "neutrals" to take sides in a labor dispute, (c) force employers to recognize and bargain with "minority" unions, or (d) force employers to give work to a union when there is a jurisdictional dispute between two or more unions as to the employees entitled to the work;
5. restricting membership in unions by excessive initiation fees and dues; and
6. extorting money from employers for work which is not performed.

The Landrum–Griffin Act of 1959 also made unlawful certain kinds of organizational (or recognitional) picketing and agreements not to handle the goods ("hot cargo") of other employers.

Another NLRB duty, stemming from a Supreme Court decision, is to make work assignments in employee jurisdictional disputes when the parties haven't come up with solutions.

First step in bringing action against a labor organization or its agents is to file a charge with one of the thirty-one regional directors. This is done on Form NLRB-508, which, among other things, calls for citations of the act alleged to have been violated. The regional office staff then investigates to determine whether the charge appears to be meritorious. Approximately 30 percent of unfair practice allegations are found to have merit, while about 70 percent are dismissed or withdrawn (withdrawals, however, must be approved by the regional director).

Before issuing a complaint, the regional director works with the parties in an attempt to reach a settlement, for, to quote a former general counsel of NLRB, "The voluntary process is the speediest and least expensive way to resolve a labor dispute. It engenders respect between the parties, and respect for the parties in the minds of others who would be affected by the dispute. It furnishes a solid foundation of good relations on which to build for future dealings."

When the charge involves the secondary boycott, hot cargo, or organizational picketing provisions, and the regional director finds reasonable cause to believe it to be true, he is required to ask a district court for an injunction to provide relief for the affected party. In other cases, he may do so at his discretion.

Normally, however, the next step after issuance of a complaint will be a local hearing before an associate law judge, who makes recommendations to the NLRB. The parties may appeal his findings to the board in Washington. Less than 6 percent of charges brought finally result in board decisions. It is possible to take a case even further, to a circuit court of appeals, which also is the place the board goes to obtain enforcement action if its orders are disobeyed. Some NLRB cases eventually reach the Supreme Court.

The other major area of NLRB activity involves questions of

union representation. Usually these are raised by unions, but an employer presented with a claim by one or more unions seeking recognition may petition the NLRB regional director to hold an election.

A majority vote of eligible employees will give a union exclusive right to represent all employees in a plant or other unit determined by the regional director to be appropriate. For example, it might be decided that clerical and production employees in a manufacturing plant have sufficiently different interests to have separate representation in bargaining with the employer.

In recent years, about 55 percent of representation elections have resulted in designation of a union.

To speed up handling of its case load, the board voluntarily limits its jurisdiction to businesses with specified annual minimum volume as follows:

- nonretail operations with annual outflow or inflow across state lines of at least $50,000;
- retail enterprises, including taxicabs, with gross volume of at least $500,000 a year;
- office buildings producing gross revenue of $100,000, of which $25,000 is derived from organizations meeting the board's jurisdictional standards;
- transportation enterprises deriving at least $50,000 gross revenue from interstate operations or from services for enterprises over which the board asserts jurisdiction, and local transit systems with gross volume of at least $250,000;
- newspaper enterprises with gross volume of at least $200,000, and communications enterprises (radio, television, telephone, telegraph) with at least $100,000 volume;
- local public utilities with gross volume of $250,000, or with outflow or inflow of goods across state lines of at least $50,000;
- hotels or motels not primarily residential, with at least $500,000 gross revenue;
- enterprises affecting national defense, whether or not they meet any other standard;
- privately owned hospitals and nursing homes operated for

profit when the total annual value of revenue is at least $250,000 for hospitals, and $100,000 in the case of nursing homes;
- apartment house projects that receive at least $500,000 in gross revenues yearly;
- symphony orchestras that have a gross annual volume, from all sources, of $1,000,000 per year; and
- all enterprises in the District of Columbia.

The above standards are given in simplified form. For complete detail, the NLRB *Jurisdictional Guide* may be obtained for 15 cents from the Government Printing Office. NLRB admits that even with the help of the published standards it is sometimes difficult to say whether or not the NLRB will assert jurisdiction. Informal advice on such questions may be obtained from the board's regional offices, however, and parties to a dispute before a state court or agency, or the court or agency itself, can petition the board for an advisory opinion on jurisdiction.

NLRB regional offices are located in Boston, New York, Buffalo, Philadelphia, Baltimore, Pittsburgh, Detroit, Cleveland, Cincinnati, Atlanta, Tampa, Winston-Salem, Chicago, St. Louis, New Orleans, Fort Worth, Kansas City, Minneapolis, Seattle, San Francisco, Los Angeles, Newark, Houston, Santurce, Puerto Rico, Indianapolis, Memphis, Denver, Brooklyn, Milwaukee, and Albuquerque.

National Labor Relations Board
1717 Pennsylvania Ave. N.W.
Washington, D.C. 20570
(202) 254-9033

Federal Mediation and Conciliation Service

The Federal Mediation and Conciliation Service is probably unique among government agencies in relying entirely on the voluntary processes of moral suasion rather than the force of law or regulation. The only thing "mandatory" in its operations is a requirement of notice. If either a company or a union wants to change, modify, or terminate a contract, it must give the other party sixty days' notice, and if agreement has not been reached thirty days thereafter, the party seeking the change must notify the FMCS (and the appropriate state mediation agency) that a dispute exists.

The regional office of the Mediation Service then assigns a mediator to contact the parties to see whether or not mediating assistance will be needed. It proves necessary for a service mediator to participate in about 7 percent of all contracts negotiated, at least to the extent of conducting one joint meeting. In over 80 percent of the cases where he actually sits in negotiations, settlement is achieved without strikes or lockouts.

An employer, a union, or both may ask for a mediator to assist them in improving their relationships even when no contract dispute exists, and the service may take the initiative in offering its help. The bulk of its cases, however, originate with a notice of a contract dispute.

In such situations, the mediator (also known as commissioner) can be helpful to employer and union in several ways. If employer or union representatives fear to make new offers or counteroffers that might be used as "springboards" by the other, he can explore the area of settlement separately with the parties without committing them to official proposals. If they cannot agree on the language of a specific clause, the mediator can suggest how similar clauses have been worded, and how they have worked in other contracts. Most important, he can provide the fresh, impartial view that often serves to break a deadlock and open up a new approach to a solution.

The mediator usually begins his work by conferring with the party who filed the notice of dispute or requested mediation. Then he confers with the other party, and when he feels he understands the problem, calls a joint meeting. Here he tries to help the parties themselves reconcile their differences, for his job is not to decide issues. To make mediation as effective as possible, the service urges parties to be completely frank with the mediator in discussing the limits of their respective positions. Such disclosures are held in strictest confidence; the mediator cannot testify concerning such information in court, before boards or commissions, or in arbitration.

The whole procedure is informal and private, ordinarily. In a few exceptional cases, usually limited to strike situations of long duration or critical disputes in defense industries, mediators have made formal public recommendations.

The "preventive mediation" type of activity where no immediate dispute exists is proving valuable to employers and unions in an increasing number of cases. One mediator, for example, became aware of problems threatening the good relations between a large steel casting company and a local of the United Auto Workers. He got the two groups to agree on a series of meetings, the most significant result of which was the design of a careful program of training for both stewards and supervisors. The mediator is serving as a consultant in the operation of this program. Another mediator observed, during a contract dispute which he helped settle between a telephone company and a union, that many of the issues arose as a result of poor communication between supervisors and employees. He suggested a continuing series of panel meetings between management and union representatives. These have produced noticeably improved relationships.

Some 250 mediators are on call in seventy-eight offices. If one is not listed in the local telephone directory under Federal Mediation and Conciliation Service, a request for help may be made to the nearest regional office. These offices are located in New York, Philadelphia, Atlanta, Cleveland; Chicago, St. Louis, and San Francisco. They will arrange "mock mediation" presentations for management and other groups, to show exactly how the procedure works.

While the service itself does not undertake arbitration (where the third party decides the issue, as distinguished from mediation, where he merely helps the disputing parties reach agreement), it maintains a nationwide roster of available private arbitrators. The roster is computerized, so that a request for a panel can be filled in one day. Although FMCS prefers to submit a list and let the parties make their own selection, it will, on joint request, designate an arbitrator. Issues most frequently decided by arbitrators from FMCS panels are disciplinary; job classification and work assignment; overtime and hours of work; management rights; and seniority, in demotion and promotion.

Federal Mediation and Conciliation Service
Department of Labor Bldg.
14th & Constitution Ave. N.W.
Washington, D.C. 20427
(202) 961-3518

National Mediation Board

For the railroads, the express and Pullman companies, and the airlines, the National Mediation Board performs the same kind of functions that the National Labor Relations Board and the Federal Mediation and Conciliation Service do for other industries. Its principal duty is to mediate differences between companies and employees in these fields, growing out of their attempts to make and maintain agreements on rates of pay, rules, and working conditions. It also determines, by election or other appropriate method, who is the authorized representative of employees and so certifies to the carrier and the disputing organizations.

Disputes growing out of grievances or agreements are referred first to an adjustment board composed of equal numbers of representatives of the carriers and of national employee organizations. In deadlocked cases, the National Mediation Board may appoint a referee to sit with them. It also appoints neutral arbitrators in cases where arbitration has been agreed upon as a result of mediation and the parties are unable to agree on arbitrators.

National Mediation Board
1230-16th St. N.W.
Washington, D.C. 20036
(202) 343-8771

Equal Employment Opportunity Commission

The EEOC has the mission of prohibiting discrimination in hiring, upgrading, and all other conditions of employment because of race, color, religion, sex, or national origin.

Originally it was limited to conciliation as a means of achieving this goal. It still uses this process as a first step, but since 1972 it has had the additional power of filing suit in federal district court to achieve compliance. EEOC filed 125 such cases in a recent nine-month period.

Individual complainants retain their right to seek relief in federal court should the commission dismiss the charge or fail to file a civil action within 180 days of the filing of the charge with EEOC. Charges may be filed not only by the person aggrieved but by an individual or organization acting on his behalf.

The law now applies to all employers of more than fifteen people, so that virtually every business administrator in the country has the responsibility of insuring that company personnel practices are not in violation.

Under court decisions and commission interpretations, the major enforcement thrust is against two kinds of "systemic" discrimination. One involves employment policies that "perpetuate the effects of past discrimination." An example would be denial of promotion on the grounds of lack of required departmental seniority, if in fact the employee when hired was segregated out of that department because of his race, national origin, or sex. The other type is an employment policy that has a discriminatory "impact," because its disqualifies a substantially disproportionate number of minority persons. Thus, high school diploma requirements are seen as having such an impact (though the employer may successfully defend the "business necessity" of such a requirement if he can show its relationship to successful performance of the job).

Sex discrimination is an active EEOC front. The commission received more than ten thousand actionable charges in this category during a recent year, as compared to twenty-seven thousand involving race. It lays down three principles in this area:

- Any employment policy that disadvantages only employees of one sex is discriminatory.
- The employer has the burden of showing that such a policy is authorized by a bona fide "occupational qualification" exception.
- The only permissible basis for such an exception is in characteristics associated with *all* members of one sex and *none* of the other.

Some of the arguments it has rejected are:

"The job of outside salesman is too dangerous and unpleasant for females."

"Need to construct separate facilities."

"Our jobs require too much heavy lifting."

In its *Guidelines on Discrimination Because of Sex* (free from EEOC) it declares that help-wanted ads indicating a preference based on sex are illegal; employers may neither refuse nor terminate employment simply because of pregnancy; and state laws that prohibit or limit the employment of females are superseded.

The commission believes that the law imposes on employers a duty of "affirmative action" to end the "chilling effect" of past discrimination. It has imposed recruitment goals on employers with particularly poor hiring records.

EEOC now is focusing on cases "which affect the greatest number of people," by consolidating large numbers of charges against particular respondents.

The commission expects its conciliation process to become more effective now that it can go to court if necessary. The conciliation process has been applied in the telephone, paper, trucking, steel, railroad, and construction industries, among others. For example, a paper manufacturer agreed to provide "loss of earnings" to 145 employees, drop testing requirements, and adopt an affirmative action program to recruit minorities and women.

EEOC offers technical assistance on request, through voluntary programs officers operating from thirty-one offices around the country. It also stages educational seminars and played a role in establishing the National Council for Social Development, a coalition of trade and professional associations committed to strengthening affirmative action efforts through cooperation and exchange of ideas.

To comply with the law, every employer of more than one hundred people must file annual reports with EEOC. These must give data on the occupational status of employees broken down by minority group identification and by sex.

From these reports and other sources, the commission prepares a variety of publications. Among those which may be of general interest are: *Equal Employment Opportunity Report No. 14: Job Patterns for Minorities and Women in Private Industry*, *Guidelines on Discrimination Because of Sex*, and *Guidelines on Employee Selection Procedures*, all available free from Publications Unit, EEOC, and *Personnel Testing and Equal Employment Opportunity*, 55 cents from GPO.

Equal Employment Opportunity Commission
1800 G St. N.W.
Washington D.C. 20506
(202) 343-5621

SMALL BUSINESS
ADMINISTRATION

Imagine yourself a small businessman who operates a dairy in Maine. One night a fire of undetermined origin destroys your plant. Your insurance is not enough to rebuild the plant at today's costs. The local bank cannot help. Where can you turn?

You could apply to the Small Business Administration (SBA) for a loan. If granted, it would be at a low interest rate set by Act of Congress, and payable over as long a period as thirty years.

This would be under the Disaster Loan Program, which is only one of several types of financial assistance available from SBA. You need not have disaster strike in order to get SBA help. Through its network of eighty-five field offices and its Washington headquarters, SBA offers not only loans and guarantees, but:

- aid in leasing good locations;
- a surety bond program for contractors;
- help in selling to the government;
- guidance on purchasing government surplus;
- management counseling, courses, and clinics;
- special programs for minority enterprise.

No businessman should hesitate to ask SBA for financial or other assistance—its mission in life is to help the small businessman. Let's take a look at the variety of ways in which businessmen can obtain financial help from SBA, directly or indirectly. Every businessman at one time or another needs financing. Since about 95 percent of all business would be classified as "small business" under SBA's definition of eligibility for loan purposes (see below), the lending resources of this agency are well worth investigating.

SMALL BUSINESS CLASSIFICATIONS

Manufacturing	250 or fewer employees In certain industries, up to 1,500
Retail or Service	Annual sales of $1 million to $5 million
Wholesale	Annual sales of $5 million to $15 million
Construction	Average annual receipts of $5 million or less for preceding three fiscal years

(Consult nearest SBA field office for standards applying to your business.)

What does SBA have to offer in the way of loans? Assuming a company passes muster as a "small" business, and is not disqualified because of the type of business, such as property speculation, it may find helpful one or more of SBA's lending programs.

Business Loans

If a company needs money for purchase of equipment or supplies; for plant construction, expansion, or conversion; or for working capital; and if it is unable to secure financing on fair terms from other sources, then SBA may lend up to $100,000. Of course, it cannot claim a loan of any size as a matter of right. It must satisfy SBA that with their help it will be able to operate the business in such a way that it will repay the loan out of income. In making its decision on an application, SBA takes into account such factors as the amount of the firm's own capital in the business, the past earnings record and future prospects of the firm, and, of course, the collateral offered.

Before trying SBA, the businessman must go to two banks and see if they will make the desired loan, either on their own, with SBA putting up part of the loan funds immediately, or with SBA guaranteeing part of the loan. If the banks won't help on one of these bases, he may apply to SBA for a direct loan, documenting their refusal. If the bank is willing provided SBA comes in, the agency may do this under one of two plans:

- an immediate participation up to $150,000, at 5.5 percent, or,
- guarantee of a bank loan, to a maximum of 90 percent of the loan, or $350,000, whichever is less. The bank sets the interest rate, within certain limits laid down by SBA.

Here is the step-by-step procedure for established businesses to follow in applying for a SBA business loan (the procedure for new businesses is given immediately after):

1. Prepare a current financial statement (balance sheet) listing all assets and all liabilities of the business—do not include personal items.
2. Have an earnings (profit and loss) statement for the previous full year and for the current period to the date of the balance sheet.
3. Prepare a current personal financial statement of the owner, or of each partner or stockholder owning 20 percent or more of the corporate stock in the business.
4. List collateral to be offered as security for the loan, with your estimate of the present market value of each item.
5. State amount of loan requested and explain exact purposes for which it will be used.
6. Take this material with you and see your banker. Ask for

direct bank loan and if declined, ask the bank to make the loan under SBA's Loan Guaranty Plan or to participate with SBA in a loan. If the bank is interested in an SBA guaranty or participation loan, ask the banker to contact SBA for discussion of your application. In most cases of guaranty or participation loans, SBA will deal directly with the bank.

7. If a guaranty or a participation loan is not available, write or visit the nearest SBA office. SBA has seventy-nine field offices and, in addition, sends loan officers to visit many smaller cities on a regularly scheduled basis or as the need is indicated. To speed matters, make your financial information available when you first write or visit SBA.

For new businesses, the last two steps are the same, but the would-be entrepreneur begins as follows:

1. Describe in detail the type of business to be established.
2. Describe the experience and management capabilities.
3. Prepare an estimate of how much you or others have to invest in the business and how much you will need to borrow.
4. Prepare a current financial statement (balance sheet) listing all personal assets and all liabilities.
5. Prepare a detailed projection of earnings for the first year the business will operate.
6. List collateral to be offered as security for the loan, indicating your estimate of the present market value of each item.

Pool Loans

These are loans to corporations formed by groups of small business companies, to purchase raw materials, equipment, inventory, or supplies to use in their individual businesses; to obtain the benefits of research and development; or to establish research and development facilities. SBA, alone or with a bank, may lend up to $250,000 for each pool member, with the SBA portion at 5 percent. Maturity may be up to ten years, or if the loan is for construction, twenty years.

Economic Opportunity Loans

These are for the prospective or established businessman or woman who meets either of these conditions:

1. Total family income is not sufficient for basic needs.

2. Due to social or economic disadvantage, he or she has been denied opportunity to acquire adequate business financing.

If the applicant also shows business ability, prospect of repaying the loan from earnings, and has some of his own assets invested, SBA may lend up to $50,000 for as long as fifteen years. It also will provide management assistance.

Development Company Loans

Small businesses may obtain loans from state and local development companies (LDC) to buy land, build a new factory, acquire machinery and equipment, or expand or convert existing facilities. SBA makes loans to state development companies for the purpose, and participates with banks, insurance companies, pension funds, and others in making loans to local development companies.

SBA may lend a state company as much as its total outstanding borrowing, for as long as twenty years. It will lend a LDC a maximum of $350,000 for each small business to be assisted, on terms up to twenty-five years. The LDC usually must provide 20 percent of the project cost. LDCs must be at least 75 percent owned by persons living or doing business in the community, and must have a minimum of twenty-five stockholders or members.

A small Alabama town, for example, sold $30,000 worth of stock in a development company to one hundred residents. The townspeople also donated $10,000 worth of labor toward construction of a woodworking plant. An SBA loan of $145,000 provided the balance needed to build the plant, which now employs sixty-five men.

Disaster Loans

These may help businesses recover from several types of catastrophes, physical and otherwise.

SBA will lend up to $500,000 for rehabilitation of physical damage to businesses, either on its own or jointly with a private lending institution. Terms may run to thirty years.

Where a small firm in a disaster area suffers economic injury rather than physical damages, an SBA loan may help provide working capital and pay obligations (other than bank loans) that the borrower would have been able to meet if not for the disaster.

SBA also makes loans to small firms that have suffered substantial economic injury in so-called "product disasters." These are situations where they cannot process or market a product for human consumption because of disease or toxicity resulting from natural or undetermined causes.

Recognizing that forced relocation because of urban renewal, highway, or other federally aided construction also can be a disaster to a small business, SBA offers loans to help such firms reestablish. The funds may be used for reasonable upgrading in the process.

Small businesses affected by several pieces of federal legislation may be eligible for SBA loans. If they are affected by the Federal Coal Mine Health and Safety Act, SBA will lend an amount to correct deficiencies determined in a Bureau of Mines inspection. In the case of firms hit by the Egg Products Act, the Wholesome Poultry Products Act, or the Wholesome Meat Act, the U.S. Department of Agriculture or the appropriate state agency issues a list of required changes that govern the amount of an SBA loan. Similar help is available to make changes under the Occupational Safety and Health Act, or state standards adopted pursuant to it.

Small Business Investment Companies (SBIC)

SBICs are SBA-licensed companies that supply venture capital and long-term financing to small firms for expansion, modernization, and sound financing. SBICs may obtain some of their funds through SBA loans or loan guarantees. For SBIC financing, a firm can qualify as "small" if it falls into one of the classifications governing SBA business loans, or if it does not have assets exceeding $7.5 million, net worth exceeding $2.5 million, and its two-year average annual profits after federal income taxes did not exceed $250,000.

In addition to long-term loans, incorporated small businesses can obtain SBIC financing by selling the SBIC convertible debentures, capital stock, debt securities, or some combination.

The businessman should be able to show the SBIC how his firm will use the desired financing. The SBIC may offer management consulting service, at a fee, and may wish to put a representative on the board of directors. In seeking to protect its investment, the SBIC will want to help the company build its business.

Lease Guarantees

The small businessman may be unable to lease prime space because the landlord requires a higher credit rating. SBA may help by reinsuring a private policy that guarantees the rent, or if private insurance is not available, guaranteeing the lease directly. The guaranty may run five to twenty years on a participating basis, ten to twenty years on a direct basis.

Premiums ranging from 2.8 to 6.5 percent of total guaranteed rental are payable in advance, and the businessman must put up three months' rent, which is returned with interest if there is no default.

Surety Bonds

To help small contractors who have difficulty obtaining bonds, SBA can guarantee up to 90 percent of losses on contracts up to $500,000. It charges the contractor a small fee, and the underwriter pays SBA a portion of its bond fee.

Applications for this assistance are available from SBA field offices. They must be forwarded by an insurance agent to the surety company, which returns an agreement form to the nearest SBA regional office.

Minority Enterprise

Special services are available to potential minority entrepreneurs. Minority enterprise (ME) loans are processed under relaxed eligibility criteria. Minority-owned or -managed firms may obtain subcontracts to provide the government goods and services, with SBA acting as prime contractor. SBA also attempts to match the procurement needs of major private corporations with minority vendors qualified to satisfy those needs.

Procurement Assistance

SBA helps small businessmen both in selling to and buying from the government.

On the selling end, SBA is at work even before the businessman makes contact with it. It has procurement representatives stationed in major military and civilian procurement installations, who recommend "set-asides" of contracts for small business bidding.

Specialists in SBA field offices advise small businessmen which government agencies are prospective customers, help them get placed on bidders' lists, and assist them in obtaining drawings and specifications for specific contracts. They refer them not only to government agencies, but to companies which are prime contractors for the agencies, with a view to consideration of the small business for subcontract work.

When a government contracting officer doubts the ability of a low-bidding small firm to carry out a particular contract, SBA can be asked to make a study of the firm's resources, management, performance record, and financial status. If this investigation convinces the agency that the firm can perform the contract successfully, it will issue a "certificate of competency" that is binding on the contracting officer.

The small businessman interested in selling to the government should inquire at an SBA field office about the "contract opportunity" meetings it arranges in cooperation with other government agencies and local business groups. Here government contracting agencies and prime contractors explain their needs. (See also chapter, "General Services Administration.")

SBA also helps small business buy government surplus property, often disposed of at bargain prices. It may arrange with the appropriate government agency to set aside certain sales exclusively for competitive bidding by small business. SBA is a good starting point for obtaining information about sales of real and personal property, but ultimately direct contact with the selling agency will be needed. (See chapters, "General Services Administration" and "Defense: Our Biggest Business.")

Management Assistance

Since an estimated nine out of ten business failures are attributed to managerial deficiencies, SBA seeks to help small businessmen avoid this hazard by offering individual counseling; courses, conferences, workshops, and clinics; and a large variety of management assistance publications.

The small businessman may discuss his problems of marketing, production, accounting, or other difficulties with a Management Assistance officer in any SBA field office. In addition, SBA may match his need with the expertise of a volunteer in SCORE (Service Corps of Retired Executives) or ACE (Active Corps of Executives). These two volunteer groups are part of the ACTION agency, and are described more fully under that heading.

The assigned volunteer will visit the businessman in his establishment, make a detailed analysis of the problem, and offer a plan to remedy the trouble. The only charge is for out-of-pocket expenses.

The small businessman may attend business management courses cosponsored by SBA with educational institutions and business groups. They usually are given in the evening, over a period of weeks, and nominal fees may be charged.

One-day conferences are offered to help busy owner–managers keep up with specific management subjects, such as taxes. SBA cosponsors these with chambers of commerce and similar groups.

SBA clinics bring together small groups of businessmen for discussion of a common problem. SBA or a cosponsoring institution provides a moderator but most of the discussion arises from the experience of the participating businessmen.

For prospective owners of small businesses, SBA sets up workshops to acquaint them with capital requirements, sources of financing, choice of location, and other factors vital to success. These may be one-day sessions or a series of evening classes.

SBA also tries to help small companies acquire the latest technology for new product development and production techniques. It does this through conferences, professional assistance, or publications.

For example, a small hardboard manufacturer had unsatisfactory profit margins. SBA looked over his plant and recommended changes in layout plus switching from a two-shift to a three-shift operation, in order to eliminate start-up delays and quality problems resulting from equipment cooling off during down time.

Publications

SBA issues over 350 publications, many of them free, others for sale by GPO at nominal prices. The free publications are listed on Form 115-A, obtainable from any SBA office. They are grouped into marketing, management, and technical aids. The for-sale booklets include a "Starting and Managing" series for the would-be small businessman. The basic general booklet, *Starting and Managing a Small Business of Your Own,* (35¢ GPO) is supplemented by a series of titles for specific kinds of enterprises. Though they must be ordered from GPO, a list of the for-sale booklets is available from SBA as Form 115-B.

Field Offices

A list of SBA field offices follows. They are grouped by region, with the regional office listed first in each group.

John Fitzgerald Kennedy Federal Bldg.
Boston, Mass. 02203

326 Appleton St.
Holyoke, Mass. 01040

Federal Bldg.
U.S. Post Office
40 Western Ave.
Augusta, Me. 04330

55 Pleasant St.
Concord, N.H. 03301

Federal Office Bldg.
450 Maine St.
Hartford, Conn. 06103

Federal Bldg.
2nd Floor
87 State St.
Montpelier, Vt. 05601

702 Smith Bldg.
57 Eddy St.
Providence, R.I. 02903

26 Federal Plaza, Rm. 3930
New York, N.Y. 10007

255 Ponce De Leon Ave.
Hato Rey, P.R. 00919

970 Broad St., Rm. 1636
Newark, N.J. 07102

Hunter Plaza
Fayette & Salina Sts.
Syracuse, N.Y. 13202

Federal Bldg., Rm. 9
121 Ellicott St.
Buffalo, N.Y. 14203

91 State St.
Albany, N.Y. 12297

55 St. Paul St.
Rochester, N.Y. 14604

1 Decker Sq.
Bala Cynwyd, Pa. 19004

901 Market St.
Wilmington, Del. 19801

1113 Federal Bldg.
Hopkins Pl.
Baltimore, Md. 21201

Lowndes Bank Bldg.
109 N. 3rd St.
Clarksburg, W. Va. 26301

3410 Courthouse & Federal
    Bldg.
500 Quarrier St.
Charleston, W. Va. 25301

Federal Bldg.
1000 Liberty Ave.
Pittsburgh, Pa. 15222

Federal Bldg.
400 N. 8th St.
Richmond, Va. 23240

1310 L St. N.W.
Washington, D.C. 20417

1401 Peachtree St., N.E.
Atlanta, Ga. 30309

908 S. 20th St.
Birmingham, Ala. 35205

Addison Bldg.
222 S. Church St.
Charlotte, N.C. 28202

1801 Assembly St.
Columbia, S.C. 29201

245 E. Capitol St.
Jackson, Miss. 39205

2500 14th St.
Gulfport, Miss. 39501

Federal Office Bldg.
400 W. Bay St.
Jacksonville, Fla. 32202

Federal Office Bldg.
600 Federal Pl.
Louisville, Ky. 40202

Federal Bldg.
51 S. W. 1st Ave.
Miami, Fla. 33130

Federal Bldg.
500 Zack St.
Tampa, Fla. 33602

500 Union St.
Nashville, Tenn. 37219

502 S. Gay St.
Knoxville, Tenn. 37902

Federal Bldg.
167 N. Main St.
Memphis, Tenn. 38103

Federal Office Bldg.
219 S. Dearborn St.
Chicago, Ill. 60604

502 Monroe St.
Springfield, Ill. 62701

1240 E. 9th St.
Cleveland, Ohio 44199

50 W. Gay St.
Columbus, Ohio 43215

5026 Federal Bldg.
550 Main St.
Cincinnati, Ohio 45202

1249 Washington Blvd.
Detroit, Mich. 48226

201 McClellan St.
Marquette, Mich. 49855

36 S. Pennsylvania St.
Indianapolis, Ind. 46204

25 W. Main St.
Madison, Wisc. 53703

735 W. Wisconsin Ave.
Milwaukee, Wisc. 53203

510 S. Barstow St.
Eau Claire, Wisc. 54701

12 S. 6th St.
Minneapolis, Minn. 55402

1100 Commerce St.
Dallas, Tex. 75202

Federal Bldg.
500 Gold Ave., S.W.
Albuquerque, N.M. 87101

1015 El Paso Rd.
Las Cruces, N.M. 88001

808 Travis St.
Houston, Tex. 77002

377 P.O. & Courthouse Bldg.
600 W. Capitol Ave.
Little Rock, Ark. 72201

1205 Texas Ave.
Lubbock, Tex. 79408

109 N. Oregon St.
El Paso, Tex. 79901

505 E. Travis St.
Marshall, Tex. 75670

124 Camp St.
New Orleans, La. 70130

30 N. Hudson St.
Oklahoma City, Okla. 73102

301 Broadway
San Antonio, Tex. 78205

219 E. Jackson St.
Harlingen, Tex. 78550

701 N. Upper Broadway
Corpus Christi, Tex. 78401

911 Walnut St.
Kansas City, Mo. 64106

New Federal Bldg.
210 Walnut St.
Des Moines, Iowa 50309

Federal Bldg.
215 N. 17th St.
Omaha, Neb. 68102

Federal Bldg.
210 N. 12th St.
St. Louis, Mo. 63101

120 S. Market St.
Wichita, Kan. 67202

721 19th St.
Denver, Colo. 80202

300 N. Center St.
Casper, Wyo. 82601

653 2nd Ave., N.
Fargo, N.D. 58102

Power Block Bldg.
Main & 6th Ave.
Helena, Mont. 59601

2237 Federal Bldg.
125 S. State St.
Salt Lake City, Utah 84111

National Bank Bldg.
8th & Main Ave.
Sioux Falls, S.D. 57102

Federal Bldg.
450 Golden Gate Ave.
San Francisco, Calif. 94102

Federal Bldg.
1130 O St.
Fresno, Calif. 93721

1149 Bethel St.
Honolulu, Hawaii 96813

Ada Plaza Center Bldg.
Agana, Guam 96910

849 S. Broadway
Los Angeles, Calif. 90014

300 Las Vegas Blvd. S.
Las Vegas, Nev. 89101

532 N. Mountain Ave.
San Bernardino, Calif. 92401

1016 W. 6th Ave.
Anchorage, Alaska 99501

503 3rd Ave.
Fairbanks, Alaska 99701

122 N. Central Ave.
Phoenix, Ariz. 85004

Federal Bldg.
Juneau, Alaska 99801

Federal Bldg.
155 E. Alameda St.
Tucson, Ariz. 85701

216 N. 8th St.
Boise, Idaho 83701

110 W. C St.
San Diego, Calif. 92101

921 S.W. Washington St.
Portland, Ore. 97205

710 2nd Ave.
Seattle, Wash. 98104

Courthouse Bldg., Rm. 651
Spokane, Wash. 99210

Small Business Administration
1441 L St. N.W.
Washington, D.C. 20416
(202) 382–1891

A NOT QUITE
TO Z

ACTION

ACTION is a conglomerate of seven government volunteer programs, two of which (ACE and SCORE) are entirely business-oriented.

More than two thousand men and women from business, industry, trade associations, the professions, and educational institutions work as part-time volunteers in the Active Corps of Executives (ACE). They give their time to assist small businessmen, often from minority groups, either on a one-to-one basis or by conducting workshops.

ACE counselor Milton Gensler is an example of a businessman giving individual help. The owner of his own record store and president of the Association of Record Dealers, Mr. Gensler has been advising Rene Morety, a wholesale dealer in Spanish records in New York City.

Providing assistance through workshops is Bertel W. Daigre, of Chicago, who operates both an insurance company and a taxicab company.

Executives interested in this kind of public service may call toll-free to (800) 424-8580, or write ACTION–ACE, Washington, D.C. 20525, or contact any Small Business Administration field office.

The retired executive may use the same channels to get information about serving in SCORE—Service Corps of Retired Executives. Some forty-eight hundred retirees are putting their business expertise to work through SCORE, giving help to such varied "clients" as a soft-drink bottler, an Indian silversmith, a day-care center, and a hardware store. SCORE was originated by the Small Business Administration, but its services are not limited to SBA borrowers.

Other ACTION components are Peace Corps, VISTA, Foster Grandparents Program, Retired Senior Volunteer Program, and University Year for Action. Managements that encourage employees and their families to "get involved" might want to find out more about these programs and make the information available. Peace Corps involves two years of overseas service, and is especially interested in persons with vocational skills. VISTA volunteers work one year in the United States, full time. Although many of the Peace Corps and VISTA volunteers are young, there are no age limits for a person in good health. For details, write:

ACTION
806 Connecticut Ave. N.W.
Washington, D.C. 20525
(202) 382-5266

Administrative Conference of the United States

If a businessman feels there is room for improvement in the procedures by which federal agencies fix the rights and obligations of private persons and business interests, he may ask the chairman of this conference to make an inquiry.

He should understand, however, that the purpose of such an inquiry would not be to review the results in the businessman's particular case. Rather, it would be to determine whether the problems it illustrates should be made the subject of conference study in the interests of developing fair and effective procedures for all such cases.

The conference might then recommend changes in administrative procedures by affected agencies. While its recommendations are not mandatory, a substantial number have been implemented.

For further information, contact:

Executive Secretary
Administrative Conference of the United States
2120 L St. N.W.
Washington, D.C. 20037
(202) 254-7020

American Revolution Bicentennial Administration (ARBA)

Many business tie-ins with the nation's two-hundredth anniversary should be possible—they are limited only by ingenuity and good taste. All three bicentennial themes set by ARBA have potential, for a period that logically extends to 1989.

Heritage '76 calls for "all groups within our society . . . to take pride in our accomplishments and to dramatize our development."

Festival USA, which stresses special events, offers special opportunities to travel-related industries.

Horizons '76 presents the challenge of developing projects that will improve the quality of life. ARBA cites the example of the petroleum industry starting to build a comprehensive research and information center in Tulsa, and says, "Other industries are encouraged to develop comparable centers in appropriate cities." Another example is Dallas, where the business community used the bicentennial as a vehicle for a renewal and goal-setting program for the entire city.

To businessmen who want to participate but feel a need for some help, ARBA extends this invitation:

"The Director of Program Development and Coordination is available to share with you the ideas and plans of others, to assist you in adapting and/or developing programs suited to your particular needs, and to provide general advice and guidance on the development of Bicentennial programs."

ARBA,
736 Jackson Place N.W.
Washington, D.C. 20276
(202) 382-1776

Appalachian Regional Commission

Business can participate profitably in the economic development of the thirteen-state Appalachian area, which has been a major goal of the Appalachian Regional Commission since its establishment in 1965. That the commission's efforts are bearing fruit is indicated by the report that six hundred new manufacturing establishments were set up in the region during one recent year.

The commission has a unique, hybrid structure: it is managed by an executive committee composed of a federal cochairman, the states' regional representative, and a nonvoting executive director. A program or project proposal can be brought before the commission only by the state member involved. Anchoring operations even more firmly to the grass roots, local development districts (LDD) formulate development plans that are incorporated into the state plan.

These LDDs bring together counties and towns that once competed against each other. They now work jointly to secure tracts of land for industrial parks, sites for commercial activity, and provide other elements necessary to attract job-creating enterprises.

The commission received appropriations of $298 million in a recent year, of which $175 million was for highways, considered the biggest problem in economic development of the region. Other programs included vocational educational facilities, health demonstrations, and housing, all of which play a supportive role in attracting new industry.

Among the commission's publications, some that may be of special interest to business are:

Industrial Location Research Studies 9–16, $2.50, covering the chlor-alkali industry, materials-handling equipment, the mobile home and special-purpose vehicle industries, the instruments and controls industry, the noncellulosic synthetic fiber industry, the metal stampings industry, the aircraft and aerospace parts industry, and the primary aluminum industry.

Research Report No. 11—Capitalizing on New Development Opportunities Along the Baltimore–Cincinnati Appalachian Highway, $2.50.

Research Report No. 2—Recreation as an Industry, $2.50.

For more information, contact:

Public Affairs Office
Appalachian Regional Commission
1666 Connecticut Ave. N.W.
Washington, D.C. 20235
(202) 967-4721

U.S. Arms Control and Disarmament Agency

The U.S. Arms Control and Disarmament Agency is a source of information for the businessman interested in problems of conversion from a defense-oriented economy to a more civilian-oriented economy.

Publications which may be of interest to businessmen: (1) the agency's annual report, *Arms Control Report*. This can be ordered from GPO, 65 cents postpaid; (2) *The Economic Impact of Reductions in Defense Spending*. This can be obtained from the same source for 25 cents.

Inquiries should be addressed to:

Public Affairs Adviser,
U.S. Arms Control and Disarmament Agency
Department of State Bldg.
Washington, D.C. 20451
(202) 632-0392

U.S. Commission on Civil Rights

The U.S. Commission on Civil Rights is a factfinding rather than an enforcement agency, but information it has developed through hearings and other means played a part in the development of the civil rights legislation of the 1960s (it was established by the Civil Rights Act of 1957).

Under its mandate to look at denial of equal protection of the laws, it gets into the areas of employment, housing, and more recently, women's rights, all of which have impact on business.

As one method of gathering and disseminating information, it sponsors national, regional, and state conferences, which bring together representatives of business, labor, and the community to consider civil rights matters.

Three commission publications which may be of interest to business are: *Equal Employment Opportunity Under Federal Law*, 25 cents from GPO; *Employment Testing: Guide Signs, Not Stop Signs,* which includes reports on successful efforts by industry to reform job testing procedures, 20 cents GPO; and

The "System" Can Work, a case study of change in understanding and procedures within one large industrial firm, 35 cents GPO.

Headquarters Office
1121 Vermont Ave. N.W.
Washington, D.C. 20425
(202) 254-6600

FIELD OFFICES

Central States Regional Office
Old Federal Office Bldg.
Rm. 3103
911 Walnut St.
Kansas City, Mo. 64106
(816) 374–5253

Mid-Atlantic Regional Office
Rm. 510
2021 L St. N.W.
Washington, D.C. 20425
(202) 254–6717

Midwestern Regional Office
Rm. 1428
219 S. Dearborn St.
Chicago, Ill. 60604
(312) 353–7371

Mountain States Regional
   Office
Ross Bldg.
1726 Champa
Denver, Colo. 80202
(303) 837–3424

Northwestern Regional Office
Rm. 1643
26 Federal Plaza
New York, N.Y. 10007
(212) 264–0400

Southwestern Regional Office
New Moore Bldg.
Rm. 249
106 Broadway
San Antonio, Tex. 78205
(512) 225–4764

Southern Regional Office
Citizens Trust Bank Bldg.
Rm. 362
75 Piedmont Ave.
Atlanta, Ga. 30303
(404) 526–4391

Western Regional Office
Rm. 1730
312 N. Spring St.
Los Angeles, Calif. 90012
(213) 688–3437

U.S. Civil Service Commission

As the central personnel agency of the federal government, the commission receives many inquiries from private firms that wish either to start programs of their own in certain personnel areas, or to compare their programs with the federal government's.

The Civil Service Commission conducts extensive programs of job classification and qualification standards. These are covered in the following publications, for sale by GPO: *Handbook X-18 (Qualification Standards)*, $21 for basic document and supplements; *Handbook of Occupational Groups and Series of Classes*, $8 for basic document and supplements; *Position Classification Standards*, $54 for basic document and supplements; and *Job Grading System for Trades and Labor Occupations*, $23 for basic document and supplements.

Other commission-administered programs involve retirement, health benefits, group life insurance, incentive awards, and other features of modern personnel operations. These are briefly described in the "Federal Employee Facts" series of leaflets, 10 cents each from GPO.

Also available from GPO is a personnel bibliography series. Some titles that might be useful to personnel executives in private business are: *Self-Development Aids for Supervisors and Middle Managers*, $1.75; *Managing Human Behavior*, $1.50; *Manpower Planning and Utilization*, 60 cents; *Executive Manpower Management*, $1; and *Planning, Organizing and Evaluating Training Programs*, $1.25.

U.S. Civil Service Commission
1900 E. St. N.W.
Washington, D.C. 20415
(202) 632-4588

Environmental Protection Agency and
Council on Environmental Quality

Government's new concern about ecology, expressed in the establishment of the Environmental Protection Agency (EPA) and the Council on Environmental Quality (CEQ) in 1970, holds both a threat and a promise for business.

The threat: federal legislation and regulation could impose on the private sector $60 billion in capital investment expenditures during the ten years ending in 1981, according to CEQ.

The promise: government and private expenditures for various types of pollution control equipment, such as municipal waste water treatment facilities, could be a bonanza for the pollution control industry. CEQ estimates capital cost of all such facilities at $112 billion for the same period.

EPA establishes and enforces environmental standards for air, water, solid wastes, pesticides, radiation, and noise.

Establishment of standards is essential to the whole pollution control effort to determine what is and is not good for the environment. The standards set by EPA, or in some cases, by EPA in conjunction with the states, have the force of laws. Enforcement of these standards is, under certain laws, shared with the state and local governments, the federal government acting only when the states fail to do so. In all other instances, the federal government has primary enforcement authority.

Effective action in the area of standard-setting and enforcement requires that EPA have some sound data on which to base its actions. This brings up the essential scientific foundation for EPA activities—research and monitoring. Scientific studies are conducted to analyze the causes and effects of pollution, the techniques of pollution control, and the environmental consequences of man's actions. These diversified research programs are carried out through four major facilities—the National Environmental Research Centers.

While all are engaged in pollution problems, each has its particular specialty area. The NERC in Cincinnati, Ohio 45268, (513) 871-6201, gives particular attention to pollution control methods; the center in Research Triangle Park, North Carolina 27711, (919) 549-8411, concentrates on health effects of environmental stresses; at the Corvallis center, 200 Southwest 35th Street, Corvallis, Oregon 97330, (503) 752-4221, studies are made on the ecological effects of environmental pollution and control; and the facility in Las Vegas, Nevada 15027, (702) 736-2969, serves as the national environmental monitoring center. The four main facilities direct and coordinate research at satellite laboratories and field stations across the country.

Grants and contracts are frequently given by EPA to assist in research projects that add a significant new dimension to research problems connected with environmental protection concerns.

Disposal of solid waste—each year we throw away forty-eight billion cans, twenty-six billion bottles and jars, seven million cars and trucks, and thirty million tons of paper—is one of the most troublesome of these problems. Among demonstration projects of EPA is an advanced recycling plant in Franklin, Ohio, which mechanically sorts the city's garbage and trash, and salvages paper pulp and some metals. Another project, at St. Louis, is demonstrating the use of solid wastes as auxiliary fuel to generate electricity.

Information about grants is available from the Research Programs Public Affairs Officer, Office of Public Affairs, EPA, Washington, D.C. 20460, (202) 755-0710.

Volunteers are sometimes used to take samples in monitoring programs. For information concerning volunteer programs contact the monitoring staff specialist at the nearest EPA regional office.

One particularly important EPA program for municipalities and industries faced with taking pollution control actions is the Technology Transfer program. This brings up-to-date information to potential users on the details and costs of new control processes developed under EPA research. This program enables business and government to incorporate the best available technology into their pollution control systems, helping to avoid investment in systems that might soon become obsolete. Inquiries on specific problems should be directed to the Technology Transfer Committee Chairman at one of the EPA regional offices, or write Technology Transfer, EPA, Office of Research and Monitoring, Washington, D.C. 20460, (202) 522-0851.

Hundreds of technical reports generated by EPA-sponsored research and monitoring are available to the public, generally through the U.S. Government Printing Office. EPA periodically issues bibliographies of these new technical reports, which may be obtained at the Technology Transfer office mentioned above.

AIR POLLUTION

Industrial processes, according to EPA, account for 17 percent of the wastes released into the air over the United States. In addition, certain businesses, such as airlines, buses, and trucking, account for a part of the 51 percent attributable to transportation, and others, such as electric utilities, produce a share of the 21 percent that arises from burning fuel in furnaces and power generators.

To deal with these various sources of air pollution, EPA established national air quality standards in 1971. The "primary" standards stipulate the maximum amount of each pollutant allowable without danger to health; "secondary" standards set limits to prevent other undesirable effects.

The states have until mid-1975 to meet the primary standards through plans they develop and EPA approves, with extra time to meet the secondary standards. If they don't do the job, EPA can step in.

In addition to these general standards, EPA prescribes some specific emission standards. For certain industries, EPA requires that new plants and factories, or those being enlarged or changed, use the best possible methods to hold down pollution.

In industries emitting extremely harmful pollutants, such as asbestos, beryllium, and mercury, all plants, old or new, must observe EPA emission standards. And of course, EPA establishes emission standards for all new automobiles.

In suggesting how state plans might deal with air pollution episodes that threaten significant harm to human health, EPA has outlined a four-stage procedure. In the second stage, factories and power plants are directed to cut emissions in accordance with prearranged schedules, and in the fourth stage, "nonessential" office, retail, wholesale, and commercial operations are directed to close. EPA lists many of the nation's largest cities as vulnerable to air pollution episodes which could require such measures.

WATER POLLUTION

The largest amount and the most poisonous of water pollutants come from industrial plants, EPA says. Under a tough 1972 law, it is concentrating its efforts on some "2,700 major dischargers, whom we believe account for the vast majority of all industrial wastes discharged into our waterways." In all, some forty thousand industrial water users are subject to regulation.

Industrial (and public) dischargers of pollutants must obtain a permit from EPA or from a state with an EPA-approved plan. The permits place specific pounds-per-day limitations on effluent from each plant, and establish firm dates for completion of abatement programs.

Industries discharging waste into a municipal treatment plant will be required to pretreat the effluent, and if the municipal system gets federal funding, EPA will expect industrial users to pay a fair share of the system's capital and operating costs. EPA declares that "industry should not find this expense too burdensome, as the repayments will extend over 30 years, and no interest will be charged."

Another act passed in 1972 prohibits ocean dumping without a permit. The Corps of Engineers issues permits for dredge spoils, EPA for all other materials, including industrial wastes, of which five million tons a year were being dumped in the oceans. The EPA administrator designates dumping sites, usually beyond the Continental Shelf, where marine life is concentrated.

The laws provide strong enforcement sanctions. EPA may seek an immediate court injunction, and penalties for violations may run as high as $50,000 a day and two years in prison. Citizens also may bring civil suits.

PESTICIDES

Although the federal government has regulated pesticides to some extent since 1910, legislation passed in 1947 and substantially amended in 1972 arms EPA with much greater authority. As the law now stands, EPA will register pesticides that meet its standards, and classify them for "general" or "restricted" use. The latter may be used only by or under direct supervision of an applicator certified by a state with an EPA-approved certification program.

Some thirty-two thousand pesticides are registered with EPA, but EPA has canceled most major registered uses of the once heavily marketed DDT, as well as all predator control with chemicals. It also has moved to cancel all uses of aldrin, dieldrin, and mercury pesticides. The law provides for indemnifying certain owners of pesticides for which registrations are suspended as an imminent public health hazard, then canceled. It also sets up a system whereby test data submitted in support of an application for registration may be used by a second applicant upon payment of reasonable compensation to the original applicant.

RADIATION

EPA has authority to establish environmental radiation standards that limit the amount of radioactivity in the environment.

The Atomic Energy Commission enforces these standards. EPA also reviews proposals for location, construction, and operation of nuclear facilities to make sure they will not adversely affect people and the environment. To avoid "thermal pollution" by discharge of cooling water, it has served notice that it may require a monitoring system, and if necessary, off-stream cooling.

NOISE

In EPA's vintage year 1972, it also received a mandate from Congress for noise control and abatement. EPA was empowered to set noise-emission standards for construction equipment, transportation equipment (except aircraft), and those motors and engines, electrical and electronic equipment, and other products that could affect health and safety. It may require labeling of products as to noise-generating characteristics. Manufacturers must issue warranties that their products comply with EPA standards, and are subject to fine or imprisonment for nonconforming or mislabeled products. The same penalties apply to importers.

EPA will be prescribing noise-emission standards not only for new products, but in the case of trucks, buses, and railroads for vehicles currently in operation. It points to new muffler designs, engine enclosures, slower speed fans, and other devices for construction equipment as hopeful for the future, at an additional cost of perhaps 1 to 3 percent.

Companies selling to the federal government should note the directive in the law that agencies will, wherever possible, buy products certified by EPA as low in noise emission.

ASSISTANCE IN COMPLYING

Several programs are available to help firms adjust to environmental regulations.

Small Business Administration (which see) lends or guarantees up to $350,000 at maximum interest of 5.5 percent, and in the case of small businesses facing substantial economic injury from federal and state water cleanup requirements, can lend up to $500,000 at 4 percent for up to thirty years. Economic Development Administration (see chapter, "Commerce: The Businessman's Home in Government") can make loans to industry or for water and sewer systems in industrial parks in "depressed" areas.

Internal Revenue Service regulations permit five-year amortization of pollution control equipment certified by EPA and added to plants constructed before 1969. More than thirty states offer tax credits for pollution control.

Municipal tax-exempt bond financing, which permits a company to save substantially on interest costs, is available for pollution control facilities. Eastman Dillon estimates that such financing totaled $1 billion in 1973.

IMPACT STATEMENTS

The inclusion of environmental concern in the federal decision-making process now requires each agency to submit to the president's Council on Environmental Quality (CEQ) an environmental impact statement on any proposal for legislation or other major action significantly affecting the quality of the human environment. The statement's primary purpose is to disclose the environmental consequences of a proposed action.

EPA reviews the impact statements, but it has no authority to stop a project sponsored by another federal agency; it acts only in an advisory capacity to other agencies, CEQ, and the president.

Each impact statement must be made public by the responsible agency not less than ninety days before the proposed action. Statements are announced in the *Federal Register*, available by subscription for $45 a year from the Superintendent of Documents, Government Printing Office, Washington, D.C. 20402. Most public libraries receive copies of the *Register*.

CEQ also publishes a monthly list of environmental impact statements filed with it in the "102 Monitor," available from the Government Printing Office for $6.50 per year.

The increasing awareness and concern for the environment is reflected in the ever-growing number of citizen groups who direct their energies toward the conservation and improvement of the environment. These groups include international, national, regional, state, and local organizations who work to obtain information and advice as well as to give direction to concerted citizen participation.

For the names and addresses of international, national, and state organizations, see the *Conservation Directory* published annually by the National Wildlife Federation, 1412 16th Street N.W., Washington, D.C. 20036. The cost is $2. Also available is *Groups That Can Help* from the Environmental Protection Agency, Circulation Branch, Office of Public Affairs, Washington, D.C. 20460.

Another helpful EPA publication is *Finding Your Way Through EPA*, which has a breakdown of the agency organizational structure listing whom to see in each specific area. This is also available from EPA Public Affairs in Washington.

Good sources for information and advice concerning environmental problems are the EPA regional offices:

EPA
Rm. 2303
John F. Kennedy Federal
  Building
Boston, Mass. 02203
(617) 223–7210

EPA
Rm. 908
26 Federal Plaza
New York, N.Y. 10007
(212) 264–2525

EPA
6th and Walnut St.
Curtis Bldg.
Philadelphia, Pa. 19106
(215) 597–9801

EPA
1421 Peachtree St. N.E.
Atlanta, Ga. 30309
(404) 526–5727

EPA
1 N. Wacker Dr.
Chicago, Ill. 60606
(312) 353–5800

EPA
Suite 1100
1600 Patterson St.
Dallas, Tex. 75201
(214) 749–1962

EPA
1735 Baltimore Ave.
Kansas City, Mo. 64108
(816) 374–5493

EPA
Suite 900
1860 Lincoln St.
Denver, Colo. 80203
(303) 837–3895

EPA
100 California St.
San Francisco, Calif. 94111
(415) 556–2320

EPA
1200 6th Ave.
Seattle, Wash. 98101
(206) 442–1220

EPA Washington Headquarters
401 M St. S.W.
Washington, D.C. 20460
(202) 755-2700

Foreign Claims Settlement Commission

An independent, presidentially appointed group, it determines the claims of United States nationals against foreign governments for injuries or losses, and allocates to them a share of any lump-sum settlement made by the governments with the United States. Substantial sums may be collected by businesses under this procedure. Singer Sewing Machine Co., for example, was awarded $2,375,037.57 for losses incurred through nationalization of its Czechoslovakian branch.

Additionally, the commission is currently responsible for administering the Micronesian Claims Act of 1971 which is designed to compensate the citizens of the Trust Territory of the Pacific Islands for losses, including death and physical injury, arising as a result of the hostilities of World War II and subsequent to the dates that the various islands were secured by United States forces. The chairman of the Foreign Claims Settlement Commission is responsible under the act for operation of the Micronesian Claims Commission including the appointment of the five members. The Micronesian Claims Commission functions throughout the Trust Territory of the Pacific Islands and has its headquarters at Saipan, Mariana Islands.

Although its proceedings are like those of a court, the Foreign Claims Settlement Commission takes note of the fact that many claims are difficult to substantiate, because records are unavailable or the foreign government involved won't cooperate, and therefore attempts to assist claimants in securing necessary documentation.

After it is filed with the commission, a claim is examined by a staff attorney, or if substantial, by a member of the commission. The commission then issues a proposed decision, from which the claimant may appeal by filing objections and requesting an oral hearing before the commission. Final decisions of the commission are exactly that; they are not subject to court review.

Further questions may be directed to:

Office of the General Counsel
Foreign Claims Settlement Commission
1111-20th St. N.W.
Room 400
Washington, D. C. 20579
(202) 382-3125

General Accounting Office (GAO)

The U.S. General Accounting Office is a nonpolitical, nonpartisan agency created by Congress to act in its behalf to help bring increased economy and efficiency to the federal departments and agencies. As taxpayers, businessmen benefit from the fact that in the last five years alone, savings of over a billion dollars have resulted from improvements in federal agency operations based on GAO findings and recommendations.

Of particular interest to the business community are the many reforms in government contracting practices and procedures that have resulted from GAO reviews. Work in the area of negotiated contracts led to the enactment of the Truth-in-Negotiations Act, which requires Defense contractors to provide adequate records to support the costs and prices on which they base their proposed contract price.

GAO has also been instrumental in the development and work of the Cost Accounting Standards Board and the Commission on Government Procurement. Recommendations from both of these panels will have a profound effect on regulations governing the award and administration of government contracts in the future.

Finally, the review of bid protests is one of the important, but not well-known, functions of GAO of direct concern to businessmen.

GAO issues a decision in the form of a letter ruling when a contractor decides to protest the selection of a competitor for award of a government contract.

Protest decisions are the result of weeks of analysis and review of the legal grounds of the protest, and of conferences by GAO lawyers, the federal agency issuing the award, and corporation lawyers for all parties involved. GAO plays an ombudsman's role in watching over the best interests of the government, as well as the contractors in the case.

GAO issues about one thousand decisions each year on protests from losing bidders for government contracts, principally smaller companies.

Correspondence concerning bid protests should be addressed to the GAO's Office of General Counsel.

Publications of interest to businessmen include the *Monthly*

List of GAO Reports, summarizing findings of reports issued by the office, available through GAO's distribution section.

General Accounting Office
441 G St. N.W.
Washington, D.C. 20548
(202) 386-6471

Library of Congress

Most sections of the Library of Congress have a potential usefulness for the business community. Four units have a particular, regular usefulness for at least part of that community. These are the Science and Technology Division and its National Referral Center in the Reference Department, the Law Library, the Copyright Office, and the Photoduplication Service.

The extensive collections of the Science and Technology Division are definitive in these areas except in technical agriculture and clinical medicine, and include 3 million books, nearly 20,000 journal titles, and some 1¼ million technical reports. These are available for use in the library.

Trained reference specialists answer without charge brief technical inquiries calling for a bibliographic response. Extensive searches of the collections for the preparation of bibliographies on a one-time or continuing basis also are conducted for a fee of $11 an hour and a minimum fee of $88. Nongovernmental customers pay for bibliographic services through a cooperative arrangement with the National Technical Information Service in the Department of Commerce. Cost estimates are provided in advance. Inquiries should be directed to the Assistant Chief for Reference and Referral Services, Science and Technology Division, Library of Congress, Washington, D.C. 20540, (202) 426-5687.

The National Referral Center for Science and Technology assists individuals and organizations wishing information in science and technology to reach the actual individual or organizational sources of that information. The referral service is free. Requests should be addressed to the National Referral Center for Science and Technology, Library of Congress, Washington, D.C. 20540, (202) 426-5670.

The Copyright Office provides free information about the copyright law, the method of securing copyright, and the procedures for registering copyrights. Anyone may determine the status of a copyright by using the card catalog in the Copyright Office, 1921 Jefferson Davis Highway, Arlington, Virginia. Copyright searches are conducted for individuals and organizations for a fee of $5 an hour. Write or call the Copyright Office, Library of Congress, Washington, D.C. 20540, (703) 557-8700.

The Law Library holds in its voluminous collections information about the laws, legal systems and practices, legal history, and judicial branches of almost every country in the world. Inquiries should be sent to the Law Library, Library of Congress, Washington, D.C. 20540, (202) 426-5079.

The Photoduplication Service reproduces and makes available, upon request, copies of manuscripts, prints, photographs, maps, and book materials in the library's collections that are not subject to copyright or other restrictions. Order forms and a schedule of prices are available from the Photoduplication Service, Library of Congress, Washington, D.C. 20540, (202) 426-5650.

Library of Congress
10-1st St. S.E.
Washington, D.C. 20540
(202) 426-5108

President's Commission on Personnel Interchange

What do Marvin L. Bell of General Electric, Thomas Camp of Sears Roebuck, and Lee K. Singer of Mobil Oil have in common? They are among the sixty businessmen assigned to work in government agencies during a recent year, under the President's Executive Interchange Program. Reverse "lend-lease" took place with eighteen federal careerists spending the year in industry.

The commission which manages the program sees great value for both sides, citing these examples:

- A business executive headed an interagency task force that recommended reducing reporting requirements of the Civil Service Commission, with resulting savings in excess of $2.5 million.
- A government executive made studies showing how external factors could affect the long-term growth and profitability of a major corporation.

Participants must be nominated by the chief executive of their organization, which pays moving expenses of candidates selected. Nominations are made to the Executive Director of the Commission (address below), on forms available on request.

Executives usually are in the thirty to forty age bracket. Their earnings in industry tend to be in the $22,000 to $36,000 range, which the host agency generally can match, though some take temporary salary reductions to participate.

Backgrounds are varied, and include management, marketing, finance, accounting, engineering, etc. They must have records of accomplishment and high potential for advancement.

The commission reviews the nominations, selects candidates to be interviewed (ordinarily in Washington), and pays travel expenses for the interviews.

In making assignments, the staff of the President's Commission takes great care to screen out any conflicts of interest. The host organization is expected to place the "Presidential Executive" in a challenging, managerial post with specific responsibilities. In addition to performing the normal functions of such a job, the executive participates in an educational program. This begins with a three-day structured group session at or just before the executive starts work in the federal agency; continues with periodic group sessions during the assignment; and concludes with a one-to-two-day session at the end of the assignment. To cover part of the cost of this education program, the sponsor is asked to contribute $1,000 for each executive it places.

The President's Commission feels that the program gives both the federal government and the private sector the advantage of fresh thinking and a broader perspective; a transfer of innovative and effective management techniques; and the opportunity for professional and personal growth for the participants.

President's Commission on Personnel Interchange
1900 E. St. N.W.
Washington, D.C. 20415
(202) 632-6834
(Jay Leanse or Jack Nease)

Renegotiation Board

Statutory renegotiation of defense contracts and related subcontracts dates back to 1942, and since 1951 has been administered by an independent agency, the Renegotiation Board. Its purpose is to eliminate "excessive profits," determined not with respect to individual contracts, but on the basis of the contractor's total annual receipts or accruals from renegotiable contracts.

Not all government business is subject to renegotiation. The act applies only to contracts with the departments of Defense, Army, Navy, and Air Force; the Maritime Administration, the

Federal Maritime Board, General Services Administration, National Aeronautics and Space Administration, Federal Aviation Agency, and Atomic Energy Commission. Even with these agencies, some contracts are or may be exempted—for example, those for raw materials or agricultural commodities; those with common carriers and public utilities; competitively bid construction contracts; contracts for new durable productive equipment, and for commercial articles or services.

The subcontractor is expected to take all reasonable steps to determine the extent to which his sales are subject to renegotiation. He may find that his customer's sales ratio affords a convenient indication of the percentage of subcontract sales which is subject to renegotiation, without going into the individual sales one by one. For example, a subcontractor of castings for a prime contractor of aircraft engines may find, on inquiry, that 70 percent of the engines sold during the year were on military order and 30 percent went to the civilian market. He would be justified in assuming that 70 percent of his sales of castings to the engine maker were renegotiable.

Reporting is compulsory only for those with renegotiable receipts of more than $1 million a year. By the first day of the fifth month after the end of the fiscal year, they must file with the board a report showing sales, costs, and profits, divided between those that are renegotiable and those that are not. Nearly forty-nine hundred contractors and subcontractors filed required reports in a recent year, while some two thousand more who were "below the floor" did so voluntarily.

All reports are examined by the board. Those showing renegotiable profits obviously not excessive are disposed of by a clearance, and the contractor is so notified. This happens to about 90 percent of the reports. Reports showing a possibility of excessive profits are assigned to a regional board in Los Angeles or Washington. It seeks additional information from the contractor and holds meetings with his representatives. If the regional board reaches a tentative opinion that the contractor has realized excessive profits, he is so informed, and may request a meeting with the board before it makes a determination.

When the renegotiable profits are $800,000 or less, the regional board's decision is final if the contractor agrees with it. If he disagrees, he may request review by the Renegotiation Board, or the latter may on its own motion review the regional order.

Where renegotiable profits exceed $800,000, the Renegotiation Board itself must concur in any regional agreement, or complete the case if an impasse occurs.

In cases reaching the Renegotiation Board from the region, the contractor has the opportunity of conferring with designated members, and submitting additional information, before a final decision is made. In about 86 percent of the cases involving 68 percent of the excess profits determinations, an agreement is reached. If not, an order for payment of the excessive profits is issued. Within ninety days, the contractor may (more than 50 percent do) petition the Court of Claims for a redetermination. The court takes a fresh look at the case rather than reviewing the board's determination.

The board has no fixed formula for determining excessive profits; each contractor is treated as an individual case. The law does call for six rather broad standards to be applied: (1) efficiency, with particular regard to quantity and quality production, cost reduction, and economy in use of materials, facilities and manpower; (2) reasonableness of costs and profits; (3) net worth, with particular regard to amount and source of public and private capital employed; (4) extent of risk assumed; (5) contribution to the defense effort, including invention and development; and (6) character of business.

Applying these standards the board made 178 determinations of excessive profits during a recent fiscal year amounting to some $40 million before adjustment for federal income and excess profits tax credits. Voluntary refunds and price reductions reported in connection with renegotiation proceedings that year amounted to approximately $9 million. Total net profits of contractors whose filings were reviewed that year came to just under $1 billion on sales of $31.2 billion.

Renegotiation Board
2000 M St. N.W.
Washington, D.C. 20446
(202) 254-8266

River Basin Commissions

Business located in the basins of the Delaware or Susquehanna rivers may be affected by the commissions set up under compacts between the U.S. government and the bordering states.

Within the basin areas, these commissions are responsible for ground and surface water supplies for industrial and other uses; abatement of stream pollution; development of hydroelectric power potential, and of water-related recreational facilities.

The Delaware River Basin Commission involves New York, New Jersey, Pennsylvania, and Delaware. For further information, contact either the U.S. Commissioner, Room 5625, Department of Interior Building, Washington, D.C. 20240, (202) 343-5761, or Executive Director, P.O. Box 360, Trenton, New Jersey 08603, (609) 883-9500.

The Susquehanna River Basin Commission is concerned with areas in Maryland, New York, and Pennsylvania. Information may be obtained either from:

U.S. Commissioner
Rm. 2353
Interior Bldg.
Washington, D.C. 20240
(202) 343-4091
or

Executive Director
5012 Lenker St.
Mechanicsburg, Pa. 17055
(717) 737-0501

Smithsonian Institution

The Smithsonian Institution offers many business-related opportunities of service and participation.

The Smithsonian, which is both federally and privately funded, established its Corporate Associates in 1971 to offer services to members while assisting the institution. Corporate Associate membership is based on contributions at convenient levels rather than fixed fees.

Gifts in kind also are welcome. Many companies have furthered understanding and gained prestige through donations of products and objects for display in the National Museum of History and Technology. However, nothing should be sent to the Smithsonian without advance inquiry.

Another Smithsonian activity, but separately located, is the Science Information Exchange, 1730 M Street, N.W., Washington, D.C. 20036. It provides for the national research community a comprehensive, computerized source of prepublication information about research programs that are planned or actually in progress in the biomedical, social, behavioral, physical, and engineering sciences. More than 100,000 notices of research projects are received and processed annually, from such sources as the federal government, private foundations, professional organizations, industries, and local governments. Both federal and nonfederal users pay a nominal fee for printouts.

Further information is available from:

Director of Development
Smithsonian Institution
1000 Jefferson Dr. S.W.
Washington, D.C. 20560
(202) 381-5622

Tennessee Valley Authority (TVA)

Headquarters in Knoxville, TVA is especially significant to the seven-state area through which the Tennessee River and its tributaries flow, but some of its activities are of interest to businesses everywhere.

TVA dams have created a continuous channel 630 miles long, deep enough so that today's big inland barges and tow-boats can travel the year around instead of being blocked by low streamflow during dry weather. Shippers using this water-way saved over $51 million on transportation charges in a recent year, moving steel from the North, grain from the Mid-west, and petroleum products, chemicals, and ore from the Gulf Coast, as well as giant rockets too large to travel overland.

TVA develops new and improved fertilizers, primarily for educational programs, but also sold to manufacturers to be tried in new processes and products. Its facility at Muscle Shoals, Alabama, is the nation's only large-scale laboratory of fertilizer development. New equipment and manufacturing tech-niques are tried out in pilot installations there. More than 475 fertilizer and chemical plants around the country are licensed to use TVA developments. Industry visitors may see the opera-tion, or write for technical information to address given below.

The dams TVA builds for navigation and flood control also serve to produce electric power, as do the coal-fired and nuclear plants it has been building in more recent years. TVA sells bonds and notes in the open market to obtain capital for the power program. Although TVA gives preference to munici-palities and cooperatives in the disposition of power, it also sells to industrial customers. TVA has contracts for bulk sales to about forty large industrial concerns, and has arrangements for purchase, sale or interchange of power with several private power companies.

Industrial development of the region is one of TVA's missions, and it will provide economic and marketing research data, maps of potential sites, and other information useful in planning for economic growth. The tabulation below lists sources of specialized information.

Industrial Development and River Transportation	TVA Division of Navigation Development and Regional Studies, Knoxville, Tenn.
Contract Information	TVA Division of Purchasing, Chattanooga, Tenn.
Electric Power Supply, Rates	TVA Division of Power Marketing, Chattanooga, Tenn.
Environmental Protection	TVA Division of Environmental Planning, Chattanooga, Tenn.
Fertilizer Research	National Fertilizer Development Center, Muscle Shoals, Ala.
Flood Hazard Information	TVA Division of Water Control Planning, Knoxville, Tenn.
Forest Resource Information	TVA Division of Forestry, Fish and Wildlife Development, Norris, Tenn.
Map Information	TVA Maps and Surveys Branch, Chattanooga, Tenn.
Shoreline Development	TVA Division of Reservoir Properties, Knoxville, Tenn.

Shoreline development creates many opportunities for private investors to provide boat docks and other recreation facilities on the ten thousand miles of shoreline on TVA lakes.

And commercial fishermen take about three thousand five hundred tons a year of catfish, buffalo, carp, and other rough fish. Industries proposing to locate along shorelines where TVA has landrights must provide air pollution controls and effective wastewater treatment.

For other subjects, contact:

TVA Information Office
New Sprankle Bldg.
Knoxville, Tenn. 37902
(615) 637-0101

U.S. Information Agency

The U.S. Information Agency (USIA) encourages activities of American business that will contribute to its objective of making the rest of the world know and understand the United States better. These activities may involve direct collaboration with USIA—for example, donating merchandise as prizes in contests conducted by the agency's Voice of America—or independent operations by the company that will enhance the American image overseas. Anything that United States business does overseas affects not only its own welfare but also the standing of the United States with the people of other nations. For this reason, Information Agency personnel in foreign posts are anxious to advise and assist United States firms doing business in their areas. The Office of Policy and Plans (IOP/C) in USIA will put businessmen in touch with the appropriate personnel overseas, and indicate the scope of help that may be expected.

U.S. Information Agency
1776 Pennsylvania Ave. N.W.
Washington, D.C. 20547
(202) 655-4000

U.S. Postal Service

Mail service, the vital central nervous system of our economy, has until recently been taken for granted by businessmen. The postman emptied his sacks several times a day, and all it meant to the average businessman was a higher pile in his "In" basket.

New forces, however, are compelling more widespread business interest in the operations of the U.S. Postal Service. In 1972, for instance, the Postal Service extended service to another 1.3 million city dwellers, 23,000 more businesses, and 440,000 new rural addresses. Not only is our population rising, but every one of our 210 million citizens is sending more mail! On the average, each American now gets 419 pieces of mail every year. Add and multiply, and the resulting volume flooding the nation's 31,686 post offices exceeds 87 billion pieces of mail a year. This volume has made itself felt by businessmen in three ways. Combined with increasing services and wages, it has created larger deficits (the postal people prefer the word "deficiency" but it's in red ink, whatever the name), forcing rate increases on businessmen and other users of postal services. Publishers and direct mail advertisers have asserted that additional rate increases could force them out of business.

It has produced delivery delays, even though the Postal Service has made strenuous efforts to improve service through better use of machines and men, and has increased its productivity, one index of the success of management improvements, more during fiscal 1972 than any year since 1955.

It has spurred the Postal Service to seek the active cooperation of businessmen in developing mutually advantageous solutions to mounting problems. In the years ahead, this is likely to reach the point where the businessman is, in a literal sense, the working partner of the Postal Service. He will presort the mail he sends—large mailers do this now—and if he is the owner of a large office building he will install facilities for individual tenants to get their mail faster.

IMPROVING MAIL SERVICE

Postal Customer Councils, composed of large business and industrial mailers, have been established in some seven hundred cities. Some sixty-five thousand executives use these councils to discuss with postal representatives ways to speed their mail and handle it more efficiently.

Mail Early is a customer cooperation program designed to get first-class mailers to deposit their mail with the post office before the end of the business day. It often involves an analysis of a customer's mail operation to work out a schedule for mail deposit. If more customers deposit their mail early in the day, the Postal Service claims they will receive better service.

A self-service program provides around-the-clock, seven-day basic postal service enabling customers to purchase stamps, post cards, envelopes, and minimum parcel post insurance from vending equipment. Letters may be deposited at all hours and information and facilities for weighing, rating, and mailing packages are a part of each unit.

These automated units are encased in three types of housing, depending upon function and location. Screenline units are installed in post office lobbies. Those in shopping areas and on campuses are identified as mail or kiosk units. Drive-up units are in shopping centers.

"Plant Loading" defines an operation in which the Postal Service accepts large-volume mail shipments at the customer's plant, thereby eliminating transport by the mailer to a post office. This procedure is applicable in instances in which large mailers, such as publishers and direct mail advertisers, generate sufficient mail volumes to justify full truck loads to destinations other than the local post office. Mutual benefits accrue to both the customer and postal service through reduced handling requirements.

Lightweight plastic trays are used to carry letter mail between large volume mailers and the post office. These trays are provided by the Postal Service and replace the conventional mail sack where practicable. Mail is faced in one direction. Sack dumping and bundle cutting operations are thereby eliminated in preparing mail for processing in the mail system. Creased or "dogeared" envelopes cannot be machine-processed in post offices and require more costly manual handling. Traying mail eliminates this problem.

Benefits to mailers include a more efficient mail dispatch operation; a cleaner mail room with more efficient utilization of workroom space (trays stack and require much less space than do mail sacks); and improved service to the extent that postal processing is expedited.

ZIP

Emphasis is on customer coding and presorting of mail, largely through Zoning Improvement Plan (ZIP). Large-volume mailers who process mailed items on punch-card equipment and computers are using their machines to code mail by sectional center, city, and postal zone, and where possible to separate and bundle it mechanically. This presorted, bagged mail goes directly to the sectional centers from the mailer, bypassing a number of post offices and manual handlings along the way, cutting delivery time by from twenty-four to forty-eight hours.

It is estimated that 80 percent of all first-class mail now bears a ZIP Code in the address. To assist the large mailer to include ZIP Codes in his address file, the Postal Service has arranged for computerized mailers to ZIP Code their lists by means of computer tapes, which it loans free of charge.

Smaller mailers using manual methods may submit mailing lists on cards to postmasters, who, for $1.50 per thousand, will arrange to have them separated by ZIP Code numbers and returned to the customer.

Customer Service Representatives in the field also advise

mailers how best to arrange their lists to maximize the service benefits obtainable.

VERTICAL MAIL

Another area for speedup of mail is now being explored through the so-called Vertical Improved Mail (VIM) service, envisioning a more efficient distribution of mail in large office and department buildings. Until recently, all high-rise buildings were served on a door-to-door basis by several men in blue-gray uniforms. Under the VIM program a postal carrier is provided full time in eight hundred large office buildings equipped with a basement mail room and a vertical conveyor for delivering mail. (Nine hundred more buildings will have VIM installations within the next year.) Under these conditions this one man can deliver mail faster than several men in the older buildings. The tenant, moreover, selects his own time to have mail shot up to his floor.

Postmasters are receiving excellent cooperation from building owners, some of whom are installing mail rooms and loading docks. Many designers of future high-rise buildings are cooperating by including mail rooms and vertical conveyor systems in their plans.

VIM has three variations—VIM Conveyor Systems, VIM Lock Box Systems, and VIM Mail Room Systems. The conveyor system is the most sophisticated form. In this system, VIM provides ten-to-fifteen-minute delivery of mail from a lower-floor mail room to all other floors, via vertical conveyors operated from each floor by the touch of a button. Usually, this system can be utilized only if it is included in the architectural-engineering design of the building.

The VIM Lock Box System consists of a mail room in the lobby, or some other easily accessible location within a building, equipped with lock boxes for each tenant. The mail room and boxes are provided by the building owner and the post office assigns a carrier to distribute the mail to the boxes, provide other services (registry, parcel delivery, etc.), and advise tenants on special mailing problems. The lock box program enables tenants to pick up their mail as they enter the building in the morning, and permits frequent outgoing dispatches during the day.

The VIM Mail Room is a conveniently located room provided by the building management, where tenants may pick up their mail in the early morning. If a tenant has not called for his mail by about 9:30 A.M., a carrier, on part-time duty at the mail room, personally delivers it to the tenant.

Other experimental programs of special interest to businessmen include:

- Mailgram, a combination letter-telegram, which is sent by wire and delivered by letter carrier, making it cheaper than a telegram, faster than a letter; presently over 35,000 mailgrams are sent daily.
- Express Mail Service, which provides (1) courier-type guaranteed delivery service on a contract basis for large-volume mailers, and (2) downtown-to-downtown overnight service for the public in thirty-six selected cities, with a money-back guarantee.
- Facsimile Mail Service, which is designed to transmit electronically exact copies of letters, charts, graphs, blueprints, or artwork between post offices at rapid speeds.
- Controlpak, which is designed to provide added security to credit-card mailers by transmitting credit cards in heat-sealed bags through the registry system to destination post offices.
- "Speedy" bags, which are designed to speed Special Delivery mail by transmitting it in special plastic pouches, keeping such mail separate from the rest of the mail stream.
- Stamps-By-Mail, under which small stamp orders may be placed by mail and paid by check.
- "Night Owl" collection service. Mail is picked up between 6:30 P.M. and 8:00 P.M. from boxes identified by two stars on the sides.

COMPLAINTS

When, in spite of Postal Service efforts, situations arise that give businessmen reason to complain, they can now hope to get greater returns for taking the trouble to write in about their problems. Their letters go to the Consumer Advocate's Office, established in 1971, which not only tries to straighten out the postal customer's particular problem, but also classifies complaints to discover if any general deficiency patterns are developing. Should such patterns appear, the office can generate action for changes in policy or procedures.

Businessmen are being invited to furnish the Postal Service with certain items that can help make the mail system more efficient, and at the same time return a profit to the businessman for his endeavors. A big leasing item is motor vehicles—the Postal Service hired 39,265 motor vehicles in 1972 to be used by their own carriers full time. In addition, they used another 31,517 nongovernment vehicles for rural and star-route delivery under contracts requiring each carrier to supply his own vehicle.

LOTTERIES

Businessmen may find the post office to be an important factor in their promotion schemes. What on first thought might seem a brilliant prize contest may on closer examination turn out to be a lottery, subject to the law banning announcement of a lottery through the mails.

The Postal Service defines a lottery as "a scheme where a *consideration* is furnished for a *prize* that is dependent upon *chance*." All three italicized elements must be present to have a lottery. If a box top or other evidence of purchase must be submitted, this is regarded as consideration; on the other hand, if there is an optional method of entry without regard to purchase, or the copying of trademarks from the advertisement or the product, this may take the scheme out of the lottery class. There seldom is any question as to whether a prize is offered, but whether its award is based on chance may be a sticky point. If the winning depends even in part on chance—for example, a drawing is held from the names of all who solved a problem correctly—the whole scheme may be a lottery.

Further complications may arise on the question of mailability. A lottery advertisement is nonmailable even though it does not give the full story of the scheme's operation. Thus, an announcement of a bingo game that said nothing more than "games," but was understood by the reader to give notice that games of chance would be played, could not be mailed.

The businessman who is in doubt about a contemplated promotion scheme, may, before going ahead, describe it fully to the Law Department, Consumer Protection Office, U.S. Postal Service, Washington, D.C. 20260. The office says it will furnish a ruling "as promptly as circumstances permit." In nonlegal questions, local postmasters are called upon by businessmen for advice and service on such matters as mailability of items, handling mail (especially airmail) in the least expensive way, and correcting mailing lists at a nominal charge.

One of the most romantic services of the Postal Service is the Inspection Service, charged with preventing, detecting, and investigating postal crimes. The businessman generally has little awareness that in safeguarding the public against postal crimes the inspector moves into areas of prime concern to business. The businessman must maintain public confidence or go under. The inspector who acts in criminal frauds perpetrated by, or against, small business—such as advance fee rackets, phony vending machine schemes, fraudulent real-estate promotions, and savings and loan associations—is acting simultaneously for the Postal Service and for the best interests of the solid merchant or manufacturer. The businessman, if less directly, also benefits from the inspector's investigations of thefts from mail receptacles, diploma mills, medical quackery, and extortion.

In 1972, the Postal Inspection Service investigated over ten thousand alleged cases of consumer mail fraud, the most celebrated involving the arrest and conviction of Clifford Irving, after postal experts proved letters allegedly written by Howard Hughes to Irving and McGraw-Hill were in Irving's handwriting.

United States Postal Service
L'Enfant Plaza West S.W.
Washington, D.C. 20024
(202) 245-4000

Veterans Administration (VA)

The VA has three programs of special interest to business: the GI Home Loan Guaranty program, the On-the-Job Training program, and the Vocational Rehabilitation program.

In the Home Loan program, more than 8.7 million mortgages have been guaranteed or insured by VA—one out of every five homes built in the United States since World War II has been financed with GI Loans. Lenders—savings and loan associations, banks, mortgage brokers, etc.—are guaranteed by VA against loss up to 60 percent of the loan with a maximum guarantee of $12,500. Loans are made for purchase of homes, condominium units, refinancing of existing mortgage loans or liens. Loans on mobile homes are also guaranteed with different rates and limits from those on permanent homes.

Businessmen may also be interested in VA's sales of vendee accounts. These are properties that have reverted to the VA after foreclosure. VA also sells, through real-estate dealers, certain homes on an individual basis. One need not be a veteran to qualify. Information on vendee accounts and sales may be had from the loan guaranty officers in VA regional offices in each of the fifty states. (See list at end of VA section.)

On-the-Job Training is a program that has been instrumental in placing thousands of Vietnam veterans in "earn-as-you-learn" jobs with VA paying an allowance in addition to the veteran's wages. Hundreds of businesses, large and small, are taking part in this program. On request, VA representatives will call on businessmen who are interested.

Vocational Rehabilitation programs of the VA have helped thousands of disabled veterans and employers to find mutual aid and satisfaction in the Hire the Disabled Veteran programs. Information is available at VA Central Office in Washington.

In addition to the three big programs of interest to businessmen at large, VA hospital construction service makes available, through its Construction Research and Development Service, the results of its projects in testing construction concepts and materials. These may be valuable to the construction industry.

Further information may be obtained at:

Veterans Administration Central Office
810 Vermont Ave. N.W.
Washington, D.C. 20420
(202) 393-4120

VA REGIONAL OFFICES

Montgomery, Ala. 36104
Juneau, Alaska 99801
Phoenix, Ariz. 85025
Little Rock, Ark. 72201
Los Angeles, Calif. 90073
San Francisco, Calif. 94103
Denver, Colo. 80225
Hartford, Conn. 06103
Wilmington, Del. 19805
Washington, D.C. 20421
St. Petersburg, Fla. 33731
Atlanta, Ga. 30308
Honolulu, Hawaii 96801
Boise, Idaho 83707
Chicago, Ill. 60612
Indianapolis, Ind. 46204

Des Moines, Iowa 50309
Wichita, Kan. 67218
Louisville, Ky. 40201
New Orleans, La. 70113
Togus, Me. 04330
Baltimore, Md. 21201
Boston, Mass. 02203
Detroit, Mich. 48232
St. Paul, Minn. 55111
Jackson, Miss. 39216
St. Louis, Mo. 63103
Fort Harrison, Mont. 59636
Lincoln, Neb. 68508
Reno, Nev. 89502
Manchester, N.H. 03103
Newark, N.J. 07102

Albuquerque, N.M. 87101

Buffalo, N.Y. 14203

New York, N.Y. 10001

Winston-Salem, N.C. 27102

Fargo, N.D. 58102

Cleveland, Ohio 44199

Muskogee, Okla. 74401

Portland, Ore. 97204

Philadelphia, Pa. 19101

Pittsburgh, Pa. 15222

Manila, APO, S.F., Phil. 96528

San Juan, P.R. 00901

Providence, R.I. 02903

Columbia, S.C. 29201

Sioux Falls, S.D. 57101

Nashville, Tenn. 37203

Houston, Tex. 77061

Waco, Tex. 76710

Salt Lake City, Utah 84111

White River Jct., Vt. 05001

Roanoke, Va. 24011

Seattle, Wash. 98121

Huntington, W. Va. 25701

Milwaukee, Wis. 53202

Cheyenne, Wyo. 82001

The
Regulatory
Agencies

CONSUMER PRODUCT
SAFETY COMMISSION

In case any businessman has the notion that only food, drugs, automobiles, and flammable fabrics are subject to product safety regulation by the federal government, now hear this:

The Consumer Product Safety Commission (CPSC) was activated in May 1973 with authority to take off the market just about any product, from tricycles to television sets, that it finds to present an unreasonable risk of injury. The only exceptions are products already subject to such regulation by other agencies.

This new organization has plenty of muscle. In addition to a variety of sanctions against the product, the law establishing the commission provides criminal penalties of up to a year in prison for willful violations. The CPSC chairman has said that he is inclined to include the board chairman or chief executive officer in such a proceeding. He adds that "we mean business, but are certainly not antibusiness."

In fact, CPSC is actively seeking the cooperation of business in several respects. One is participation in standards-making. A section of the law requires CPSC, when beginning development of a standard, to publish an invitation (in the *Federal Register*) for any person or group to submit an existing standard or offer to develop the proposed standard. CPSC may accept such offers and help underwrite the offeror's cost. But its chairman says that if this section is to work, "we will need a commitment from industry that's never been there before. Instead of amateurs, you're going to have to send the experts to standards-making meetings. Often that will mean the engineer you can least afford to spare. If the boardroom doesn't make a commitment, we will be setting the standards ourselves."

Another form of cooperation is mandated by the law. It requires any manufacturer, distributor, or retailer who learns that a product has a hazardous defect or fails to comply with a standard to inform the commission immediately. The company that moves fast and effectively can take at least some of the sting out of such a situation.

A leading television maker, for example, found a possible fire hazard in one of its models. It telephoned CPSC about this on a Thursday afternoon, and by that night had notified its distributors by telegram of plans to inspect all such sets in the owners' homes and repair defective ones without charge. On Friday morning both the company and the commission issued press releases, that of CPSC praising the company's "immediate response" and "full cooperation."

CPSC also solicits business help in spreading the word about its activities. The Council of Better Business Bureaus has offered its assistance, and several companies have launched educational campaigns of their own.

An Advisory Council to the agency is provided for by law, with five of its fifteen members to be from consumer product industries. This can provide another channel of cooperation.

Congress has directed CPSC to minimize the disruption of manufacturing and other commercial practices consistent with the public health and safety. Its actual effect will become clearer as it establishes standards for priority items.

In deciding priorities, one tool it uses is the National Electronic Injury Surveillance System (NEISS). NEISS receives daily reports from 119 hospital emergency rooms of injuries associated with consumer products. *NEISS News,* a monthly publication, reports the injuries by product categories. To be placed on the mailing list, write:

U.S. Consumer Product Safety Commission
1750 K St. N.W.
Washington, D.C. 20207
(202) 496-7621

FEDERAL
COMMUNICATIONS
COMMISSION

Best known as the overseer of television and radio broadcasting through its power to license stations, the Federal Communications Commission (FCC) charter extends to other communications activities of more direct concern to many businessmen.

The interstate and international telephone, telegraph and data transmission rates which are a not inconsiderable item of business expense must be filed with FCC and are subject to its review, as are the adequacy and quality of these telecommunications facilities. A businessman who feels he is not getting his money's worth from his share of the more than $16 billion a year paid by the public for telephone and telegraph services may file a complaint with the FCC in Washington about services other than intrastate.

More and more businesses are establishing their own private radio communication systems, first obtaining a license from the FCC. Among the businesses most widely using this tool are petroleum, power, forest products, and transportation. It makes possible more efficient use of employee time and of equipment such as repair trucks. To make businessmen aware of the types of communications systems that are practical within the limits of the frequencies available, the commission has encouraged organization of regional advisory committees in the principal industries using radio. Its list of industrial radio services includes:

- Manufacturers Radio Service, to aid in production as well as safeguarding and handling of materials at plants;
- Special Industrial Radio Service, for use in construction of bridges and highways, for mining, and for certain other specialized activities essential to industrial operations or public health;
- Relay Press Radio Service, for quick contact with reporters and photographers traveling in automobiles on news assignments;
- Motion Picture Radio Service, used by film producers to coordinate action and to safeguard life and property on outdoor "location";
- Industrial Radiolocation Service, which aids commercial or industrial enterprises in establishing a position, distance, or direction;
- Telephone Maintenance Radio Service, the function of which is clear from its name;
- Business Radio Service, open to persons engaged in any lawful commercial activity which would be benefited by radio;
- Power Radio Service, for maintenance of electric, gas, water, and steam utilities;
- Petroleum Radio Service, for like help to the petroleum and natural gas industries;
- Forest Products Radio Service, for logging and tree-farming operations.

Land transportation radio services are available to railroads, common carrier or contract trucks and buses, taxicabs and emergency vehicles. It should be noted that the common and contract motor carrier category includes local package delivery service, but not individual delivery vehicles and sightseeing or other special charter buses.

Persons licensed in any one of the land transportation radio services may render dispatching service on a cost-sharing non-profit basis to any other person engaged in the same type of transportation activity. This permits several companies to use the same base station, reducing original investment and operating cost.

The first step for a businessman interested in starting an industrial or land transportation radio service is to order and study Volume V of the FCC *Rules and Regulations*. It is available for $12.50 from the GPO, Washington, which will mail the subscriber any later amendments. When he is familiar with the commission's requirements, he should submit an application to the Secretary, FCC, Washington.

In a separate category is Citizens Radio Service. Described by the FCC as its fastest growing service, this is available for essential personal or business *short-range* communications or radio remote control of objects such as display signs. Channels have to be shared and users are not protected from interference as they are in other types of services. Both business firms and individuals can qualify for licenses. Application is made to the FCC's Gettysburg, Pennsylvania, office, except for the more powerful Class A stations which are handled by the Washington headquarters. The rules and regulations for Citizens Radio Service are found in Volume VI, priced at $3.50, from the GPO.

Businessmen who do not even dream of using radiocommunications may find themselves involved with the FCC. For example, an industrial activity such as arc welding, or a business activity such as operation of an electrical sign, may cause interference with radio or television reception. In such cases, the unwitting offender may hear from an FCC field engineer or from one of the more than 740 local or regional interference committees established with FCC's blessing. The best way of avoiding this kind of difficulty is to take advantage of the FCC's readiness to test or type-approve certain equipment in advance of manufacture, to make sure that it will not cause interference when put into operation.

As advertisers, as competitors of advertisers or as citizens, businessmen may at some time have a complaint about a radio or TV station. It is their right to submit it to the FCC, which may investigate it and take it into account when the station's license is up for renewal. The complaint, if substantiated, will be weighed in light of the licensee's obligation to operate in the public interest. Since few stations are willing to risk loss of their license, legitimate complaints ordinarily can be settled by direct discussion with the station management.

Federal Communications Commission
1919 M St. N.W.
Washington, D.C. 20554
(202) 632-7260

FEDERAL POWER
COMMISSION

Two new facts of life in the mid-1970s are exerting a push-pull effect on the Federal Power Commission (FPC). The energy crisis, in which the demands of an affluent society for electricity and natural gas are outrunning the supply, is pushing FPC toward encouraging exploration and development by allowing increased rates. On the other hand, concern for the environment, expressed in the National Environmental Policy Act, compels FPC to consider policies from a standpoint other than the purely economic.

Although FPC does not have all-encompassing jurisdiction over the interstate sector of natural gas, it does exert controls over about two-thirds of the annual gas production in the United States. Under this authority, it has acted in recent years to increase supplies through such steps as increasing rates on sales in interstate commerce for resale; permitting pipelines to make advance payments to producers in return for drilling commitments and dedication to the interstate market of gas that may be found; and allowing short-term emergency purchases at prices above ceiling rates.

If shortfall makes it necessary to curtail or cut off some customers, FPC has issued a policy statement on priorities of deliveries by interstate pipelines. It stresses protection of "human needs" customers, i.e., residential. Industries using natural gas for boiler fuel will feel the pinch first.

FPC authority over natural gas begins at the well, gathering point, or processing plant when it is sold for resale in interstate commerce. Then, it has authority to determine whether the sales should be permitted as in the interests of public convenience and necessity, and if so, at what price and on what terms.

The interstate pipeline companies and their more than $22 billion in plants also are regulated by FPC. They require the commission's prior approval for construction, and operation of facilities; of the prices at which they buy gas; and the prices at which they sell it for resale.

FPC authorizes import of natural gas, large volumes of which have come in by pipeline from Canada. With the development of liquefied natural gas (LNG) and special ocean tankers to carry it, FPC has received a number of applications for large-volume LNG imports.

On electric power, FPC regulates the rates and services of public utilities selling electricity in interstate commerce at wholesale (the states regulate retail sales). Such business represents less than 7 percent of their annual dollar volume.

Where the source of power is hydroelectric, FPC issues licenses for construction and operation of projects on waters or lands subject to federal jurisdiction. It inspects such projects for safety and environmental impact.

It promotes voluntary interconnection, which has been made more attractive by the development of extra-high–voltage, long-distance electric transmission lines. Under certain circumstances, it may direct interconnection.

It regulates the merger of electric public utilities (although the Securities and Exchange Commission has jurisdiction over utility holding companies).

FPC enforces a uniform system of accounts for both electric power and natural gas pipeline companies under its jurisdiction, which facilitates rate regulation at both federal and state levels.

The effect of FPC on the business world radiates outward from the two industries it regulates directly. All businesses use electricity, and many use natural gas as well. In the production of aluminum, magnesium, and titanium, the most important economic factor is the supply and cost of electric power.

An FPC publication, *National Electric Rate Book,* is helpful to businessmen in this regard. It shows power rates for every community of more than twenty-five hundred. Individual books for each state may be bought for 25 cents from GPO. A yearly subscription for all revisions as they are made costs $8.

The commission published a comprehensive National Power Survey in 1970, which it updates with reports as needed. The survey laid out a long-range guide for efficient development of the nation's electric power industry through 1990. In the original survey and in its updating, FPC is drawing on the advice of all segments of the electric industry, as well as utility customers, conservation groups, and others.

A corresponding National Gas Survey is nearing completion. It is designed to obtain an overview of the prospective growth of the natural gas industry, its markets, and the gas supplies needed to meet them.

The central source of information on the commission's activities is its Office of Public Information. Here copies of the reports filed by regulated companies may be inspected; applications and files of formal proceedings may be studied; and copies of formal documents issued by the FPC may be obtained. Mailing lists for various needs are also maintained by this office.

One major problem of businessmen dealing with the Federal Power Commission—as with any regulatory agency—is ex parte or "off-the-record" communications with commissioners or staff members involved in the decision-making process. Under FPC regulations any communication, oral or written, with a commissioner or key staff member involving the merits of a particular case is made a matter of public record and is excluded by the commission in its consideration of the case.

This rule, however, is not intended to discourage businessmen or representatives of an industry from seeking the help of the commission in connection with any problem which has not yet reached the stage of formal commission proceedings. Through its publications and through personal contact and letter the commission staff stands ready to provide assistance to industry in connection with its energy requirements.

All formal decisions of the commission, like those of other regulatory agencies, are appealable to the United States Court of Appeals, and general guidelines for commission decisions are available in an extensive body of law established over the years in such decisions, including many by the Supreme Court.

Federal Power Commission
441 G St. N.W.
Washington, D.C. 20426
(202) 386-6102

FEDERAL TRADE
COMMISSION

Once upon a time the Federal Trade Commission (FTC) could be regarded as a paper tiger by monopolists, price-fixers, and deceptive advertisers. It squandered its limited manpower resources on a seven-year antitrust action against a toothpick manufacturer, and a lengthy battle about the use of the word "liver" in the name of a pill.

Now it is a more formidable adversary, selecting its targets on the basis of economic analysis and cost-benefit studies of where it can have the broadest impact. Thus, it has launched an investigation of the giant petroleum industry, looking toward structural changes that could force major oil companies to divest themselves of the production, refining, or marketing function.

It also is invoking new legal weapons, as in its action against four leading breakfast cereal manufacturers. Here it is attacking an alleged monopoly structure of the industry which it says has resulted from unfair and deceptive practices, but it is not claiming that the four firms conspired.

FTC authority over business derives from thirteen pieces of legislation, starting with the original FTC Act of 1914 and continuing through the Fair Credit Reporting Act of 1970. Under these laws, the FTC can act against:

- unfair methods of competition;
- activities which tend to lessen competition or create a monopoly, especially mergers and acquisitions;
- price discrimination between large and small customers;
- deceptive acts against consumers;
- mislabeling and false advertising of wool, fur, and textile fiber products;
- flammable wearing apparel and fabrics;
- deceptive packaging and labeling as in the case of "cents-off" and other reduced-price claims on the package;
- incomplete disclosure of credit terms (truth in lending—see also "The Banking Agencies, Federal Reserve System");
- inaccurate or improperly disclosed credit reports.

A businessman's letter or call to the nearest FTC regional office (see list at end of section) may trigger an FTC investigation, or the application for issuance of a formal complaint may come from a trade association.

Depending on what it finds out, FTC may close the case, handle it informally by accepting an assurance that the questioned practice will be discontinued, or issue a complaint and a cease-and-desist order.

The company involved may sign a consent order, or contest the complaint before an FTC hearing examiner. His decision may be appealed to the commission, a U.S. district court of appeals, and ultimately the U.S. Supreme Court.

FTC acknowledges that "action simply cannot be brought against all offenders." It seeks the help of "reputable businessmen who voluntarily stay abreast of and obey trade rules and laws" and "advertising media and advertising agencies that maintain high ethical standards."

Acting on the assumption that "many violations result from ignorance and that the best way to enforce the law is to educate businessmen," FTC attempts to do this by issuing industry guides and trade regulation rules.

Industry guides are advance statements to business of the position likely to be taken by the commission in the event of litigation. Advisory only, they may cover single-industry concerns or practices that occur in many industries. An example of the former is *Guides for the Decorative Wall Paneling Industry,* dealing with disclosures in advertising and labeling that relate to the construction, composition, or appearance of industry products. The latter type is exemplified by *Guides for Use of the Word "Free" and Similar Representations.* Most of the guides are free—see FTC list of publications, itself available without charge.

Trade regulation rules, in contrast, are legally binding. They are issued only after full open hearings at which businessmen may voice their views. Examples are *Posting of Octane Numbers on Gasoline Dispensing Pumps* and *Care Labeling of Textile Wearing Apparel.* Adoption of such rules allows all companies that may be engaging in a banned practice to abandon it simultaneously, without loss of competitive position.

Each of the FTC's three major operating bureaus is opening up new ground that warrant the close attention of business. The Bureau of Consumer Protection has become especially active against deceptive advertising, with an increase of more than 60 percent in the number of complaints issued during a recent year. It is developing innovative remedies that go beyond the traditional cease-and-desist order. Notable is "corrective advertising," where companies have been required to devote 25 percent of their annual advertising budget to insertions containing a corrective message. It also is making greater use of the requirement of "affirmative disclosure," as, for example, the presence of common ingredients such as caffeine and aspirin in many analgesic products.

Another new program requires advertisers to file data that substantiates objectively their claims of safety, performance, efficacy, and comparative price. Major advertisers have received orders to file such reports on automobiles, television sets, air conditioners, cough and cold remedies, and toothpastes, among others. These reports are placed on the public record, for the benefit of both consumers and competitors, and may become the basis for complaint action.

Within this bureau is an Assistant Director for Consumer Education, whose stated duties include helping "business develop its own programs designed to inform and educate consumers."

The Bureau of Competition handles the complaints of businessmen and others about illegal restraints on trade—more than fourteen hundred in a recent year. It has staff attorneys who attempt to advise and assist small businessmen.

It, too, is getting into new areas. Shopping centers, for example, which account for about one-third of U.S. retail sales, were the subject of two complaints against lease agreements that restrict the entry of competitors.

In challenging mergers and acquisitions as restricting competition it has been especially active in the auto parts, food, drug–cosmetic, and metals industries.

When corporations with assets of $250 million or more acquire a firm with assets of at least $10 million, they are required to file a special report with the Bureau of Economics. This may lead to a challenge. The bureau's own studies may be the forerunners of complaints, so its examinations of electrical machinery, prescription drugs, and the energy sector bear watching, as do others which may be launched in the future.

The Bureau of Economics also publishes information useful to business, such as quarterly statistics on sales, profits, operating ratios, and other balance sheet items of manufacturing corporations.

Confusion sometimes arises over the overlapping roles of FTC and the Justice Department in antitrust actions. Under an agreement, FTC generally acts in price-discrimination matters, those involving the food industry, and cases with wide economic ramifications. Justice takes price-fixing cases and those involving apparent criminal violations, and represents FTC in court.

The regional offices are a good starting point for business contact with FTC. It should also be noted that they have worked with other federal, state, and local agencies in setting up consumer protection committees in major cities to receive and refer consumer complaints to the agency having authority. Grouped under some regional offices are field stations to serve the public in additional cities.

Federal Trade Commission

Pennsylvania Ave. at Sixth St. N.W.
Washington, D.C. 20580
(202) 962-7144

REGIONAL OFFICES

Rm. 720
730 Peachtree St., N.E.
Atlanta, Ga. 30308

Rm. 2200-C
John F. Kennedy Federal
  Bldg.
Government Ctr.
Boston, Mass. 02203

Rm. 600
22 W. Madison St.
Chicago, Ill. 60602

Rm. 1339
Federal Office Bldg.
1240 E. 9th St.
Cleveland, Ohio 44199

Rm. 452-B
500 S. Ervay St.
Dallas, Tex. 75201

Rm. 2806
Federal Office Bldg.
911 Walnut St.
Kansas City, Mo. 64106

Rm. 13209
Federal Bldg.
11000 Wilshire Blvd.
Los Angeles, Calif. 90024

Rm. 1000
Masonic Temple Bldg.
333 St. Charles St.
New Orleans, La. 70130

22nd Floor
Federal Bldg.
26 Federal Pl.
New York, N.Y. 10007

Box 36005
450 Golden Gate Ave.
San Francisco, Calif. 94102

Suite 908
Republic Bldg.
1511 Third Ave.
Seattle, Wash. 98101

6th Floor Gellman Bldg.
2120 L St. N.W.
Washington, D.C. 20037

FIELD STATIONS

Rm. 206
623 E. Trade St.
Charlotte, N.C. 28202

Rm. 105
995 N.W. 119th St.
Miami, Fla. 33168

Rm. 209
Federal Office Bldg.
P.O. Box 568
Oak Ridge, Tenn. 37830

333 Mt. Elliott Ave.
Detroit, Mich. 48207

San Antonio Federal Ctr.
  Bldg. 3
630 Main Ave.
San Antonio, Tex. 78212

Rm. 18013
Federal Office Bldg.
1961 Stout St.
Denver, Colo. 80202

Rm. 828
Amerco Towers Bldg.
2721 N. Central Ave.
Phoenix, Ariz. 85004

Rm. 1132
Bank of America Bldg.
625 Broadway
San Diego, Calif. 92101

Rm. 221
Federal Bldg.
111 W. Huron St.
Buffalo, N.Y. 14202

Rm. 605
Melim Bldg.
333 Queen St.
Honolulu, Hawaii 98613

231 U.S. Courthouse
Portland, Ore. 97205

Rm. 1406
Bankers Security Bldg.
1315 Walnut St.
Philadelphia, Pa. 19107

POSTAL RATE COMMISSION

When Congress transformed the Post Office Department into the U.S. Postal Service, it also created a Postal Rate Commission, independent of USPS. Requests by USPS for rate changes or establishment of new classifications must be reviewed by the Postal Rate Commission.

The commission holds public hearings, where business mail users and other interested parties can make their views known. (Or, they may submit written statements.) It then makes recommendations to the Board of Governors of the Postal Service. These can be modified only by unanimous vote of the governors.

Actions by the Board of Governors may be appealed to any federal court of appeals, which may sustain the decision or order further consideration, but may not modify it.

At time of writing, the commission is holding its first classification hearings, considering such matters as allowing credit for presorting. Once a new mail classification schedule is established, the commission on its own initiative may submit recommendations for additional changes.

Postal Rate Commission
Rm. 500
2000 L St. N.W.
Washington, D.C. 20268
(202) 254-3800

SECURITIES AND
EXCHANGE COMMISSION

The securities business has undergone considerable change and turmoil in recent years, and the Securities and Exchange Commission (SEC) has been taking steps to cope with these new problems. To understand these programs, we must first look at its basic, continuing programs.

A great many businessmen invest in securities. A smaller, but substantial number, are issuers of securities, or dealers in them. In the first case they are protected by the Securities and Exchange Commission; in the second, regulated by it.

The SEC was set up in the wake of the 1929 stock market crash. The commission's basic philosophy was that investors should be given complete and truthful information about securities to enable them to make buying decisions intelligently, or at least with the full awareness of the risks involved.

Registration Statements

In working toward this goal, a primary tool of the SEC is its requirement that before securities are publicly offered, a registration statement must be filed. It must disclose all material facts about the issuer's property, its management and operation; a balance sheet and earnings data must be given. A prospectus summarizing this information must be delivered to would-be purchasers. If the commission does not take exception to the statement, it becomes "effective," and the securities may be sold.

A small business planning an offering up to $300,000 need not file the more elaborate registration statement, but can satisfy the commission with a simpler "notification" to an SEC regional office and the distribution of an offering circular containing certain basic information. And issuers with an established record of earnings and continuity of management who already file reports with SEC may use a new short form, S-16, for registration.

More than thirty-seven hundred registration statements, covering securities valued at $62.5 billion, became effective in a recent year. Though a prospectus provides the investor with data essential to make an informed evaluation of the securities, additional underlying information may be obtained from registration statements, which he can inspect in SEC offices or buy in photocopy form. (Much of the information also can be found in commercially published securities manuals.) He should understand, however, that the only standard for registration the SEC has power to impose is limited to an adequate and accurate disclosure of the material facts concerning the company and the securities it proposes to sell. Clearance of a registration statement does not mean that the commission approves the price of the securities or believes the issuing company has reasonable prospects for success. The investor must decide this for himself.

The registration statement does, however, provide the investor with a legal weapon if he suffers a loss on the security, and can prove there was incomplete or inaccurate disclosure of material facts. Under these circumstances, he can sue in court (not before the commission) to recover his loss.

The commission has taken steps to improve disclosure by

requiring that "boiler plate" language in new offering prospectuses be made more meaningful. Especially with so-called "hot issues" it is seeking to clarify the elements of risk and potential gain. For older companies, it is seeking faster reports on company insider transactions and, when a company changes auditors, an explanation if the change results from a conflict of views.

The commission has adopted a rule that it will defer processing registration statements by issuers who are delinquent in their periodic reporting.

The information provided to investors by the registration statement must be kept current through filing of periodic reports, which are available to the public for inspection or purchase of photocopies, in the same manner as registration statements. Similar requirements for periodic disclosure of financial and other data apply to all companies whose securities are listed on the New York Stock Exchange, or on other stock exchanges.

When proxies are solicited from holders of listed securities, proposed proxy-soliciting material must be filed in advance with the commission. The materials are examined to be sure that they disclose all material facts concerning the matters on which holders are asked to vote. More than sixty-five hundred proposed proxy solicitations are filed annually.

The investor is protected not only through disclosure of information, but also by rules designed to keep "insiders" from misusing corporate information that is not generally available to the investor. Officers and directors of companies listed on stock exchanges, and persons holding more than 10 percent of their securities, must file monthly reports showing changes in their holdings of the company's stock. They are prohibited from selling the company's stock short, and if they take a profit on company stock they have held for less than six months, the company, or a stockholder acting for it, can recover that profit by an action in a United States district court.

Broker–Dealers

The investor almost invariably buys and sells securities through a broker–dealer firm. Such firms must register with the commission and conform in their business practices with provisions of the law and with SEC rules designed to protect investors against abuses. The SEC may revoke the registration of any broker–dealer if it finds, after a hearing, that the firm is engaged in fraudulent activities, or otherwise violated its rules or the law.

Most broker–dealers are members of the National Association of Securities Dealers (NASD), one of the nation's stock exchanges, or both. These groups, over which the SEC has partial review authority, exercise regulatory and disciplinary powers over members, and are designed to maintain equitable principles of trade in the industry.

Following a wave of broker–dealer failures, SEC tightened up its rules in this area, requiring among other things that broker–dealers set up reserve bank accounts covering customer assets and distribute quarterly balance sheets to all customers. Congress created a Securities Investor Protection Corporation (SIPC) to insure cash and securities in accounts of broker–dealer customers. While SIPC is funded primarily through assessments of its broker–dealer and exchange members, it has access to emergency financing of up to $1 billion from the U.S. Treasury. After eighteen months of operation, SIPC was involved in the liquidation of forty-three broker–dealers.

Mutual Funds

SEC protection of investors involves regulation not only of companies issuing securities and brokers dealing in them, but also of mutual funds and investment advisers. Mutual funds have grown tremendously in number and size since the SEC began regulating them in 1940. There now are more than thirteen hundred with assets of perhaps $80 billion. The statute under which SEC operates requires, among other things, that management and advisory contracts be submitted to security holders for their approval, and prohibits transactions between the investment companies and their officers, directors, and affiliates without the approval of the commission. It also has directed NASD to put an end to reciprocal practices of mutual funds rewarding broker–dealers for sale of fund shares by directing commission business through them. The SEC has taken note of the importance of the funds by setting up a Division of Investment Company Regulation.

Investment advisers, with some exceptions, must register with the SEC, and comply with its rules concerning advertising, segregation of clients' funds and securities, etc. More than thirty-eight hundred advisers are registered.

When corporations are reorganized in district courts under Chapter X of the Bankruptcy Act, the commission may participate, paying special attention to the interests of public security holders. In one recent year, it was active in 113 such proceedings, involving indebtedness of $1.2 billion, owed by debtors ranging from an automobile race track to a cement manufacturer.

The SEC has largely completed the task assigned it by Congress of reorganizing the public utility holding-company systems which, when it entered the field in 1935, controlled 98.5 percent of all transmission of electric energy across state lines. It expects about seventeen systems to continue indefinitely, however, subject to its regulations on issuance and sale of securities, purchase and sale of physical properties, etc. These systems have aggregate assets less valuation reserves of about $26.5 billion; they meet the law's standards of physical integration and corporate simplification under which Congress saw possibilities of operating efficiencies to justify holding-company control.

Accounting

Since a good deal of the commission's work hinges on financial statements filed with it, the SEC cooperates closely with accounting and related trade groups to improve accounting and auditing standards for preparation of such statements. The commission has adopted a basic accounting regulation, Regulation S-X, and other Accounting Series Releases, which govern the form and content of most of the financial statements filed with the SEC. These are available from GPO at 75 cents for Regulation S-X, $2.50 for a compilation of Releases 1-112.

Companies planning to register a securities issue should be aware of the commission's cautionary statement that "difficulties often arise in connection with initial filings because accountants and other advisers . . . have not had any prior experience with the Commission." Verification of inventories and receivables by the auditor certifying a financial statement has been a particularly thorny problem. A "Guide to the Preparation and Filing of Registration Statements" (Release 33-4666) should prove helpful. It is available free from SEC Publications Unit, Washington, D.C. 20549.

An SEC *Policy Statement on the Future Structure of the Securities Markets*, published in 1972, undoubtedly foreshadows many changes in SEC regulatory practices and in industry self-regulation (just as a 1963 SEC study forecast the requirement, adopted somewhat belatedly in 1972, of a broker's reserve account to cover securities or funds left with him by customers). In essence, the statement calls for a central market system, where communications would tie together all competing markets so that investors can see where the best price is available.

Three industry advisory committees have been developing recommendations to SEC for implementing such a system. The industry already has activated two programs that could be elements of an ultimate central system. One is the National Clearing Corporation, which clears over-the-counter trades, starting on a pilot basis with New York, Boston, and Philadelphia–Baltimore–Washington. The facility is subject to SEC review of any refusal or limitation of access by customers, issuers, brokers, or dealers.

A related development of significance to the over-the-counter market is NASDAQ, the automated quotations system sponsored by NASD. It now quotes more than 3,350 securities valued at more than $140 billion, and receives some 1.15 million interrogation requests daily. NASD cooperates with the SEC surveillance staff in looking into any unusual market activities in NASDAQ securities.

Sometimes SEC deals with new market phenomena by applying old legislative authority. Thus, when "pyramid" sales plans of selling multilevel distributorships burgeoned as a get-rich-quick scheme in the early seventies, SEC held that the agreement between the offering company and the investor might be a security, subject to SEC registration. Moreover, a person distributing such securities might have to register with SEC as a broker.

Thousands of reports and registration statements containing information of interest to investors, and for that matter, to competitors, are filed with the SEC each year. All of it is available for inspection in the Public Reference Room of the commission's Washington office, and some of the more current material at SEC regional offices. For those who prefer to purchase copies, a *Compilation of Documentary Materials Available in the SEC* and estimates of the cost of photocopying such materials may be obtained from the Branch of Records and Service, Securities and Exchange Commission, Washington, D.C. 20549.

Those who wish to keep right on top of SEC developments should subscribe to its daily *News Digest*. Available at $33 a year from the GPO, it provides a résumé of commission orders, decisions, rules, and proposals, plus a summary report of each stock offering and financing proposal requiring a registration statement.

Other SEC periodicals that should be useful to investors are its weekly *Statistical Bulletin* and its *Quarterly Financial Reports*. The *Bulletin* presents stock price indexes and round-lot and odd-lot trading on the New York and American Stock Exchanges; current assets and liabilities of United States corporations; secondary distributions, etc. It costs $17 a year through the GPO.

Investors should have no hesitation about making inquiries or complaints to the SEC, for this is one of the commission's primary sources for detecting law violations in securities transactions. Contact one of the regional offices listed below or its Washington headquarters.

And in the unfortunate event of getting into difficulty with SEC, the commission points out that it has "informal procedures to provide persons under investigation with the opportunity to present their positions prior to authorization of an enforcement proceeding."

SEC Headquarters Office
500 N. Capitol St.
Washington, D.C. 20549
(202) 755-4846

Regional Offices

Kevin T. Duffy   New York, New Jersey
26 Federal Plaza
New York, N.Y. 10007

Floyd H. Gilbert   Massachusetts, Connecticut,
Suite 2203   Rhode Island, Vermont,
John F. Kennedy Federal   New Hampshire, Maine
  Bldg.
Boston, Mass. 02203

Jule B. Greene
Suite 138
1371 Peachtree St., N.E.
Atlanta, Ga. 30309

Tennessee, Virgin Islands, Puerto Rico, North Carolina, South Carolina, Georgia, Alabama, Mississippi, Florida, part of Louisiana

John I. Mayer
Rm. 1708
Everett   McKinley   Dirksen
   Bldg.
219 S. Dearborn St.
Chicago, Ill. 60604

Illinois, Indiana, Iowa, Kansas City (Kansas), Kentucky, Michigan, Minnesota, Missouri, Ohio, Wisconsin

Robert F. Watson
503 U.S. Court House
10th & Lamar Sts.
Fort Worth, Tex. 76102

Oklahoma, Arkansas, Texas, part of Louisiana, Kansas (except Kansas City)

Donald J. Stocking
7224 Federal Bldg.
1961 Stout St.
Denver, Colo. 80202

Wyoming, Colorado, New Mexico, Nebraska, North Dakota, South Dakota, Utah

Gerald E. Boltz
Rm. 1043
U.S. Court House
312 N. Spring St.
Los Angeles, Calif. 90012

California, Nevada, Arizona, Hawaii, Guam

James E. Newton
900 Hoge Bldg.
Seattle, Wash. 98104

Washington, Oregon, Idaho, Montana, Alaska

William Schief
Rm. 300
Ballston Ctr. Tower #3
4015 Wilson Blvd.
Arlington, Va. 22203

Pennsylvania, Maryland, Virginia, West Virginia, Delaware, District of Columbia

Branch Offices

Rm. 899
Federal Office Bldg.
1240 E. 9th at Lakeside
Cleveland, Ohio 44199

1044 Federal Bldg.
Detroit, Mich. 48226

Rm. 2606
Federal Office & Courts Bldg.
515 Rusk Ave.
Houston, Tex. 77022

Suite 701
DuPont Plaza Ctr.
300 Biscayne Boulevardway
Miami, Fla. 33131

Rm. 108
U.S. Customs Bldg.
2nd and Chestnut St.
Philadelphia, Pa. 19106

Rm. 1452
210 N. 12th St.
St. Louis, Mo. 63101

Rm. 6004
Federal Reserve Bank Bldg.
120 S. State St.
Salt Lake City, Utah 84111

450 Golden Gate Ave.
Box 36042
San Francisco, Calif. 94102

THE TRANSPORTATION
AGENCIES

Five government agencies have a major impact on transportation, and are therefore important both to the transportation industry and to all other industries which use it for shipment of goods or movement of executives, salesmen, and other personnel. The Interstate Commerce Commission deals with railroads, motor carriers, domestic water carriers, oil pipelines, and freight forwarders. The Civil Aeronautics Board and Federal Aviation Agency divide jurisdiction over air transportation. The independent Federal Maritime Commission and the Commerce Department's Maritime Administration (treated in the Commerce Department chapter) handle the waterborne foreign commerce. In addition, the Department of Transportation exercises an overall planning function.

Interstate Commerce Commission

The Interstate Commerce Commission (ICC) regulates some twenty thousand carriers in economic matters. Those subject to its economic regulation have annual operating revenues of about $30 billion. They include common and contract motor carriers, but not the private. The water carriers under ICC jurisdiction are those operating in interstate commerce coastally, intercoastally, and on inland waterways.

Significant to businessmen as shippers is the ICC requirement that carriers publish their rates and file them with the commission thirty days in advance of their becoming effective. This allows time for shippers or competing carriers to protest. The commission may suspend the proposed rates or direct changes. It has held, for example, against surcharges on less-than-truckload shipments, heeding the plea of small businesses that they could not compete with larger concerns able to take advantage of the economy of volume shipments.

The ICC has launched a comprehensive investigation of railroad freight rate structure, and separately of railroad freight service. Shippers' views are welcome in these proceedings.

More informally, through correspondence or conferences, ICC will attempt to adjust complaints. In a large number of cases, it has obtained refunds for shippers and passengers who were overcharged, adjustments of charges when shipments were misrouted by carriers, and adjustments of claims for damage to freight. Letters on such matters may be addressed to Informal Cases Unit, Interstate Commerce Commission, Washington D.C. 20423.

Businessmen anxious to achieve greater economy and speed of shipping through new methods such as "piggybacking" of trailers on flatcars have been helped by ICC rulings. The number of railroad cars loaded in this manner more than tripled in five years following an ICC declaratory order on the subject. The order laid down broad lines of authority, but specific questions on rates for coordinated services continue to come before the commission.

ICC surveillance also helps to maximize availability of freight cars, shortages of which have from time to time seriously hindered the movements of goods.

Shippers or other users of railroads who may be affected by a proposed abandonment of a line or a substantial change in service can obtain a public hearing by ICC. Although no railroad can be compelled to continue an operation at a loss, ICC may approve or disapprove changes short of complete cessation of the enterprise. It has on occasions prevented abandonment of a branch line where users showed they would be seriously injured. Environmental considerations, e.g., possible increases in highway traffic, now must be taken into account.

Other economic matters handled by ICC include mergers, which it considers from a public interest standpoint, taking into account the probable effect on service to shippers and other users, on competing carriers, on employees and, of course, on stockholders. ICC also passes on issuance of securities of railroads and of common and contract motor carriers and participates in court reorganization of insolvent railroads.

In order to operate in the motor transportation field, common carriers need to obtain an ICC certificate of convenience and necessity; contract carriers, an ICC permit; and brokers, an ICC license. Even after issuance of certificates and permits, ICC must settle many questions between competitors as to operating rights.

Firms that must arrange for shipment of employees' household goods in transfer of station benefit from ICC requirements that estimates of charges be given in writing, and that carriers furnish a statement outlining shippers' rights and carriers' duties.

Limited reference service on matters within the jurisdiction of ICC will be provided by its Reference Services Branch in response to requests by telephone or letter.

Interstate Commerce Commission
12th & Constitution N.W.
Washington, D.C. 20423
(202) 343-4141

Federal Maritime Commission

The Federal Maritime Commission (FMC) is a regulatory agency, completely separate from the Commerce Department's Maritime Administration, whose functions are primarily promotional—subsidies for construction and operation, and sponshorship of research.

It has broad authority over rates, particularly in the domestic offshore trade, that is, between the United States and Alaska, Hawaii, and Puerto Rico. There, it may suspend rates for up to four months. Carriers have been known to cancel proposed increases following service of an order of investigation by the commission.

In the foreign trade, it may not suspend rates, but can order a hearing. Then, if it finds the rate unjustly discriminatory between shippers or ports, or unjustly prejudicial to U.S. exporters as compared with their foreign competitors, or so unreasonably high or low as to be detrimental to the commerce of the United States, it may alter the rate.

A publication, *Ocean Freight Rate Guidelines for Shippers*, is available without charge from FMC. Rates must be filed with the commission by all carriers and conferences of carriers, and by marine terminal operators.

When the commission finds disparities in rates that are harmful to U.S. trade, as for example, when it costs more to ship from here to another country than from a third country to the same destination, it attempts to negotiate adjustments, often with considerable success. Thus, it was able to persuade a conference to reduce rates for shipment of seven commodities from Great Lakes ports to the Mediterranean, bringing them in line with their charges from Canadian ports to the same area.

Businessmen may file informal complaints about rates with the FMC Bureau of Compliance (or with its Bureau of Enforcement on other matters), sending copies of any correspondence they have had with carriers.

FMC exercises surveillance not only over rates, but over agreements among carriers. Agreements approved by the Commission are exempt from anti-trust laws. It will step in when it considers conference rules contrary to public interest, as it did, for example, on rules limiting the number of terminals in the San Francisco Bay area at which conference members could call.

FMC authority also extends to licensing of ocean freight forwarders. A recently added responsibility is to make vessels prove they are financially able to meet liability to the United States for the costs of cleaning up any oil pollution of U.S. waters or shoreline. FMC previously was given a similar task with regard to financial responsibility of passenger vessels for paying personal injury or death judgments or indemnifying ticket-holders for non-performance of a voyage.

The Commission tries to keep on top of new trends, such as containerization and intermodalism, which it calls "the biggest thing in the transportation industry since the changeover from sail to steam." It now permits carriers to file through-rates either unilaterally or jointly with carriers of other modes, and has approved modification of 16 conference agreements extending their application to inland points. Formation of a Steamship Operators Intermodal Committee has been given FMC approval.

Finally, in recognition of the huge capital investments required to establish a steamship container service, FMC has approved a number of mergers and other forms of unified operations.

Federal Maritime Commission
1405 I St. N.W.
Washington, D.C. 20573
(202) 393-3111

FIELD OFFICES

Rm. 4012
26 Federal Pl.
New York, N.Y. 10007

P.O. Box 30550
Room 945
610 South St.
New Orleans, La. 70130

Rm. 2302
Federal Bldg.
100 McAllister St.
San Francisco, Calif. 94102

Rm. 108A
Old San Juan Post Office Bldg.
Comerico and Tanca Sts.
P.O. Box 3168
San Juan, P.R. 00904

Civil Aeronautics Board

The Civil Aeronautics Board (CAB) is an independent regulatory commission that is responsible for the economic aspects
of America's civil aviation industry. As such, it is important to
businessmen when it acts to assure adequacy of air service—
passenger, cargo, or mail—for their communities and market
areas; when it passes on fares and cargo rates; when it authorizes route changes; and when it assists shippers and others who
may have problems in their dealings with air carriers.

For the businessman based in a smaller community that cannot generate enough air traffic to meet the costs of service, the
board's policies on subsidizing local service carriers have special
impact. In recent years it has been spending more than $65
million annually for this purpose. Noting growing defects in the
system, the board has proposed that it be given authority to
award contracts, on a competitive bid basis, for provision of
specific services, rather than subsidize a carrier's entire system.

Air taxis and other special services used by business are given
either blanket authority or individual permits when the board
feels they perform a useful function without adversely affecting

regular airline operations. In a recent year, nineteen hundred air taxi operators, including 185 commuter air carriers, registered with the board.

If a group such as an employee recreation association wishes to charter a plane for a vacation trip to Europe, it can do so either with a scheduled airline or with one of the six supplemental carriers holding transatlantic charter service authority from the CAB. In all, there are thirteen supplemental carriers authorized to fly charters to various foreign areas. Seats must be limited to members of the association and their immediate families.

Air freight forwarders, often used by businessmen to achieve expedited service or lower rates through consolidation of shipments, are licensed by the board on a showing that they have the capital, experience, and plans for a service in the public interest. About 250 companies have this authority, and they gross about half a billion dollars a year.

The CAB regulates travel agents indirectly, by passing on agreements among the air carriers relating to selection and retention of travel agents and the sales commissions paid to them.

If the businessman, either in his capacity as passenger or as shipper, has a problem that he cannot settle with the carrier, he may write the Director, Office of Consumer Affairs, CAB, or phone (202) 382-7735. Where he alleges a violation of laws, tariffs, or operating authorizations, he may file a complaint with the board's Bureau of Enforcement.

In a recent year, the Office of Consumer Affairs received more than nine thousand complaints. They covered such matters as schedule irregularities (flight cancellations, late operation, early departure, unscheduled stops, omission of scheduled stops, and termination of flights before reaching scheduled destinations); reservation difficulties (oversale of space, substitution of class of service other than requested, and reservation cancellation); tariffs (nonpayment of refunds, overcharges, etc.); baggage (loss, damage, delay and dilatory handling of claims); and charters (failure to perform according to contract and leaving passengers stranded).

Air carriers are required to file in advance any proposed schedules of cargo rates or passenger fares. Should a businessman object, he may ask the board to review such filings to determine whether they are lawful.

The following publications that may be of interest to businessmen are available without charge on request to CAB Publications Services Section, B-22, Washington, D.C. 20428: *Air Travel in the Seventies—The Economic Potential; Forecast of Scheduled Domestic Cargo for the 50 States, 1971–1975; Forecast of Scheduled International Air Traffic of U.S. Flag Carriers 1971–80.* Other free and for-sale publications are shown in a list available from the same source.

Although the CAB is small as government agencies go, spending about $13.5 million a year for salaries and expenses, anyone wishing to provide it with goods or services may contact the CAB Office of Facilities and Operations.

For any other information, contact the CAB Office of Information, (202) 382-6031.

Civil Aeronautics Board
1825 Connecticut Ave. N.W.
Washington, D.C. 20428
(202) 393-3111

The
Science
Agencies

ATOMIC ENERGY
COMMISSION*

No industry is more thoroughly enmeshed with government than atomic energy—if it may be called an industry. Some 154,000 persons are employed directly in nuclear activities at industrial establishments (or AEC facilities operated by contractors) and are dependent on the Atomic Energy Commission either for grants, contracts, purchase of their output (uranium, plutonium, thorium, etc.), or licenses.

Licenses are required for construction and operation of nuclear facilities, and possession and use of radioactive materials. Issuance is based on both radiological and environmental factors. Fees are substantial. To apply for a construction permit on a power reactor plant costs $70,000; the permit itself $300,000; and the operating license fee $400,000.

In establishing regulatory standards, AEC has recruited hundreds of industry people for voluntary work on standards com-

---

* The Atomic Energy Commission as such was abolished by a bill signed in October 1974. In its place were established an Energy Research and Development Administration, and a Nuclear Regulatory Commission. The former will handle development of atomic and other energy sources. The latter, under a chairman and four commissioners, will perform the licensing and regulatory functions formerly handled by AEC.

mittees. AEC also has called on the utility industry to take the lead in standardization of nuclear power plants and their components. Among other benefits this could make possible generic licensing hearings.

In the course of its operating and developmental activities, AEC generates a great deal of nonnuclear technology which has wide application throughout industry. It is so eager to share this information that it has established three Offices of Industrial Cooperation as focal points for industry. They are as follows:

Argonne National Laboratory
Office of Industrial Cooperation
9700 S. Cass Ave.
Argonne, Ill. 60439

Oak Ridge National Laboratory
Office of Industrial Cooperation
P. O. Box X
Oak Ridge, Tenn. 37830

Sandia Corporation
Office of Industrial Cooperation
P. O. Box 5800
Albuquerque, N.Mex. 87115

Examples of AEC technological output would include many in the energy development field, since Congress gave the agency an expanded mission of providing additional options to meet the nation's growing energy needs. Thus, development of a lithium/sulfur high power-density storage battery is under way at Argonne National Laboratory. It could be used by utility systems for electricity storage during off-peak periods, and in a smaller version, to power pollution-free electric automobiles.

In the life sciences, a new X-ray intensifying screen which can reduce medical X-ray exposures to a fraction of the present dosage has been developed under AEC sponsorship at Lockheed Missiles and Space Co. The screen will lead to longer X-ray generator life and could make possible new radiographic procedures where detection speed and X-ray tube power are limiting factors.

Of course, AEC continues active with nuclear devices, many producing beneficial byproducts for industry and the nation. Thus, AEC, in cooperation with industry, has conducted several successful experiments in stimulating recovery of natural gas by nuclear detonations. It is hoped that this phase of the Plowshare project eventually may provide significant relief of the natural gas shortage.

Anticipating a need for more enriched uranium to fuel nuclear power plants in the 1980s, AEC is encouraging private industry participation. It has accepted proposals from seven U.S. firms for access to its classified uranium enrichment technology.

While AEC generally identifies its own needs for research and development and solicits competitive proposals, it encourages submission of ideas for research and development work. Such unsolicited proposals may become the basis for negotiated contracts. The procedure to follow is clearly spelled out in the AEC booklet *Guide for the Submission of Research and Development Proposals by Individuals and Organizations*. It may be obtained from Director, Division of Contracts, U.S. Atomic Energy Commission, Washington, D.C. 20545.

How can the businessman find out what's going on in the government's atomic energy work that might be useful to him? In spite of what he might assume about the closely guarded nature of information in this field, a surprising amount is readily available in published form. In a recent year the AEC declassified—that is, removed security restrictions from—200,000 documents useful to industry and science. A free booklet, *What's Available in the Atomic Energy Literature* may be obtained from the AEC Division of Technical Information Extension (DTIE), P. O. Box 62, Oak Ridge, Tennessee 37830.

Nuclear Science Abstracts, published by AEC, comprehensively abstracts and indexes atomic energy literature. Annual domestic subscription rate for the twenty-four issues is $42 from GPO, but sets are available in many libraries. If any unclassified information that may be desired cannot be located through this journal, a request may be made to the Division of Technical Information Extension for a literature search.

Publications

New materials are published all the time. Through the Department of Commerce's National Technical Information Service (NTIS), 6,750 new report titles were offered for sale in a single recent year. As AEC research proceeds in fields of such broad industrial application as materials to withstand high temperatures and physical and process metallurgy of elements, a substantial part of the findings will be released. It is even possible to buy engineering drawings through NTIS. These describe irradiation instruments and processes, etc. An Engineering Materials List of what is available may be obtained free by writing to the Oak Ridge DTIE office (see above) and asking for TID-4100.

Another way in which the businessman may tap the treasure of AEC is through its patents. The commission owns a portfolio of some forty-six hundred U.S. and thirty-five hundred foreign patents which are available for licensing. Licensing procedures are set forth in the brochure *USAEC Patents Available for Licensing*, available free from DTIE, Oak Ridge. From time to time, listings of patent abstracts are issued by the AEC Office of Information Services, Washington, D.C. 20545.

Should the needed AEC material be classified for security reasons, it may still be possible to obtain an access permit for civilian applications under appropriate security protection. More than 240 such permits are in effect. The booklet *Questions and Answers on USAEC Access Permits* may be obtained from the

AEC Division of Industrial Participation, Washington, D.C. 20545. This division acts as the commission's focal point in promoting civilian applications. Its telephone number is (301) 973-5151.

Participation in AEC Activities

Companies contemplating civilian application of nuclear processes are offered an opportunity by AEC to have qualified employees obtain specialized work experience in AEC facilities. The commission emphasizes that the program is designed "to familiarize participants with nuclear processes applicable to specific uses, not to provide basic instruction or generalized experience in nuclear science." The company continues to pay the employee's salary and expenses while he works at the AEC facility.

Three-day seminars on uranium mining and related problems are held at AEC's Grand Junction, Colorado, office. Representatives of industry or financial institutions who wish to attend should write that office. Its telephone number is (303) 242-8621.

The AEC also has made provision for companies lacking the necessary equipment to have research and development work done at government-owned facilities "in the interests of furthering private participation, including small business, in the development of the field of atomic energy." Full cost of the work must be paid, of course.

In a letter to the United States Chamber of Commerce, the National Association of Manufacturers, and the Manufacturing Chemists' Association, the commission has declared its "firm policy to procure goods and services from private industry wherever practical." Steps implementing this policy include withdrawal from land-burial of low-level wastes at AEC sites in favor of using state-owned sites operated by private enterprise, and arrangements for private facilities to perform chemical reprocessing of spent fuel from commercial reactors. The director of AEC's Division of Industrial Participation has said that "private capability now exists to provide on a commercial basis nearly all the materials, equipment and services needed to support the peaceful uses of atomic energy." Increasingly, businessmen will find opportunities to use this capability, and the AEC may be expected to encourage this trend.

Atomic Energy Commission
Germantown, Md. (actual location)
Washington, D.C. 20545 (mailing)
(301) 973-7754

NATIONAL AERONAUTICS AND SPACE ADMINISTRATION

Apart from its overriding significance to businessmen in the aerospace and related industries, which look to it for several billion dollars a year in contracts, the National Aeronautics and Space Administration (NASA) in its far-ranging activities generates much in the way of information and techniques that can be applied in other industries. Photographs taken from space by its Earth Resources Technology Satellite, for example, have yielded such diverse benefits as:

- a land-use map of the cities of Chicago, Indianapolis, and Minneapolis;
- locations of new nickel deposits in Canada and South Africa, and large copper ranges in Pakistan;
- identification of every smoke plume rising from the state of Virginia.

NASA-developed computer programs are available at far below original costs, and can save the industrial user valuable development time. An inventory of nearly twelve hundred programs, including some contributed by the Department of Defense and the Atomic Energy Commission, is maintained at the Computer Software Management and Information Center (COSMIC), University of Georgia, Barrow Hall, Athens, Georgia 30601, (404) 542-3265. It distributed 4,150 software packages in a recent year, and one user alone reported $80,000 savings in design of a nuclear power plant. A directory of COSMIC programs, plus updating announcements, costs $10 a year. If a subscriber orders at least one program, his subscription is renewed without charge.

Recognizing that the entire industrial community has the right to benefit from innovations flowing out of the agency's expenditure of public funds, NASA has a $4-million-a-year technology utilization program aimed at identifying potentially valuable developments and making information about them readily available. The transfer to industry takes place via four major channels—application teams, regional dissemination centers, publications, and patents.

The NASA application teams serve as principal links between NASA technology and the potential users. In tandem with these nonaerospace clients, the application teams carefully define those technical problems that are important to the user and which appear to lend themselves to aerospace-derived solutions.

Once the problem is identified, the application teams search aerospace technology files (the NASA data bank stores over one million reports) for relevant technology. At the same time, specialists at NASA laboratories and field centers are systematically canvassed for potential solutions.

A successful search is followed by experimental efforts to prove out proposed solutions. In some cases, NASA actually develops prototype devices to be tested by the user.

The teams work primarily with the public sector, but often come up with applications that have industrial spillover. An example is the "Complex Coordinator," a device originally used by NASA to test astronaut performance skills. It then was tried out for the Environmental Protection Agency, to ascertain the effect on driver skills of exposure to carbon monoxide. Now it is seen as a means of testing motor skills related to operating equipment or machinery. And as a final result, after a Small Business Administration-funded market study, a minority business offers the equipment for sale.

NASA's most active program for dealing with the private sector is a network of six regional dissemination centers, which work on a one-to-one basis with industrial users. In a recent year, they served about 2,150 industrial units, almost half being small businesses.

Whenever NASA research results can be applied to the solution of an industrial problem, the center furnishes the information, and it may also arrange direct contact with the NASA scientist or engineer who can give expert personal guidance or comments on the problem.

One repeat user of the center in Indiana is Franklin Electric Co., a small manufacturer. Recently it was experiencing problems with carbon bearings in its line of gasoline submersible motors. Franklin was able to achieve a rapid solution by applying methods NASA had used in a similar situation.

Regional Dissemination Centers

Aerospace Research Applications Center
Indiana Memorial Union
Bloomington, Ind. 47401
(812) 337-7970

Knowledge Availability Systems Center
University of Pittsburgh
Pittsburgh, Pa. 15213
(412) 621-6877

New England Research Application Center

Mansfield Professional Park
Box U-41N

University of Connecticut
Storrs, Conn. 06268
(203) 429-6421

North Carolina Science and Technology Research Center
P.O. Box 12235
Research Triangle Park, N.C.
(919) 549-8291

Technology Application
    Center
University of New Mexico
Albuquerque, N.M. 87106
(505) 277-3118

Western Research Application
    Center

Graduate School of Business
    Administration
University of Southern Cali-
    fornia
809 W. 34th St.
Los Angeles, Calif. 90007
(213) 746-6133

Publications

Technology utilization publications of NASA include:

TECH BRIEFS—announcements of technical innovations useful
for nonaerospace applications. In a recent year, 756 were
issued.
TECHNICAL SUPPORT PACKAGES—in-depth technical descriptions
to supplement Tech Briefs.
TU COMPILATIONS—collections of techniques, processes, and
equipment relating to a single technical field.
SPECIAL PUBLICATIONS—surveys, handbooks and conference
proceedings regarding the use of NASA technology in areas of
application such as fire safety, high-velocity metalworking, biomedical instrumentation, magnetic recording, power sources,
cryogenics, etc.

For information about any of these categories, write NASA
Scientific and Technical Information Facility, Code T1, P.O.
Box 33, College Park, Maryland 20740.

The NASA has certain well-defined channels for issuing
regular reports on its aerospace work. Twice a month it publishes *Scientific and Technical Aerospace Reports*, often
referred to as "Star." Its first section contains abstracts of
research and development information arranged in thirty-four
general subject categories for ease of scanning. Among these
categories are electronics, machine elements and processes, and

several others of potential industrial application. The second section contains indexes by subject, source, author, and report number. The subject index is useful both to those making a retrospective search and to those scanning for newly announced items of significance. All four indexes are issued in quarterly, semiannual, and annual cumulations within two to four weeks after the close of the period they cover. NASA reports listed in Star usually are available in major public libraries. They may be purchased either from the Superintendent of Documents or from the Department of Commerce, as indicated in Star.

Star abstracts and indexes reports; journals and books, however, are covered in the *International Aerospace Abstracts*, privately published by the American Institute of Aeronautics and Astronautics. Under a cooperative agreement with NASA, the institute uses a format similar to Star; the two are published on alternate weeks.

For more details on bibliographies, translations and other information products of NASA, inquiries should be directed to the Office of Scientific and Technical Information, NASA, Washington, D.C. 20546.

Patents

Inventions made in NASA contract work become the exclusive property of the government unless the administrator waives patent rights to the contractor.

To foster commercial development and use of NASA-owned inventions, the agency will grant a nonexclusive royalty-free license to all who apply during the nine months after NASA obtains a patent. After this period, if the invention has not been worked, it becomes available for exclusive license.

That is what happened with a NASA-developed lightweight, non-tippable, radar-reflective life raft. It finally granted an exclusive license to Robert F. Perchard. He arranged development of a commercially feasible material and in turn licensed the Winslow Co. of Osprey, Florida, to manufacture and sell the rafts.

A list of NASA patents available for nonexclusive or exclusive licensing is published quarterly in the *Official Gazette* of the United States Patent Office. License applications should be addressed to the NASA Administrator, identifying the patent by number, title, and date. Copies of patents may be obtained from the United States Patent Office for 25 cents each. Further information may be obtained from Assistant General Counsel for Patent Matters, Code GP, NASA, Washington, D.C. 20546.

National Aeronautics and Space Administration
400 Maryland Ave. S.W.
Washington, D.C. 20546
(202) 755-2320

NATIONAL SCIENCE FOUNDATION

Business can benefit from National Science Foundation (NSF) activities both as a user of, and a participant in, its research. NSF describes itself as "the sole agency of the federal government for which the support of basic research is the principal and most important mission." But a few years ago Congress expanded its authority to allow it to undertake applied research as well, and it now spends more than $70 million a year for such purposes.

Together, the basic and applied research programs of NSF form an overflowing cornucopia of information that alert businessmen can use profitably. And although the bulk of NSF research contracts go to universities, in 1972, following a presidential directive, it issued a policy statement identifying six programs in which it encourages industry participation. An industrial concern or trade association may be the sole grantee, or it may collaborate with university researchers or with a state or local government. Unsolicited proposals will be considered on a cost-sharing basis. Awards based on solicited proposals cover full costs, including fee.

One program inviting industry participation is "Research

Applied to National Needs" (RANN). This broad grouping includes several categories. "Advanced Technology Applications" concentrates on energy systems; earthquake engineering; fire protection, prevention, and suppression; and instruments to monitor environmental pollutants. Examples of projects under way include a system aimed at economical use of solar energy for generating electric power; a process to produce economically useful supplies of hydrogen gas; a coal-gasification program; translation of earthquake engineering research into criteria, specifications, and methods usable by professional engineers and builders; and an instrument to measure in less than one minute trace concentrations of heavy metals such as mercury in samples of tuna, possibly preventing large losses in the fishing and canning industries.

Under the heading of "Environmental Systems and Resources" are a study of probable demands for water by chemical industries in the next three decades, and a study in southeastern Missouri—the world's largest lead mining and smelting district—of pollution processes. The latter is being conducted in collaboration with the mining industry.

A study in the category of "Social Systems and Human Resources" has had great impact on builders in San Jose, California, where it resulted in restriction of development in five areas to avoid a drain on the resources of the city.

Finally, an example of "Exploratory Research and Problem Assessment" is the collaborative effort of the Gleason Works and the University of Rochester toward improved efficiency of small and medium-scale manufacturing by automating parts programming.

The publication *Research Applied to National Needs* describes guidelines for proposal preparation in the RANN programs. For further details, address the four division offices at National Science Foundation, Washington, D.C. 20550.

The International Decade of Ocean Exploration (IDOE) is another of the six programs inviting industry cooperation. Grants and contracts are awarded for work bearing on a number of long-range goals, including better management of ocean mineral exploitation and exploration. It is of interest that preliminary results from IDOE studies of the continental margin off the west coast of Africa have identified several large geologic structures with great potential for future petroleum exploitation. Information about submitting proposals is contained in the publication *International Decade of Ocean Exploration—A Guide to the Preparation of Proposals,* or may be requested from the Office for IDOE, NSF, Washington, D.C. 20550.

Two programs open to industry are in the computer field. "Computer Applications in Research" includes innovative and effective approaches to resource sharing, projects to transfer advances in computer science into new computer-based methodology for research, and software quality research. "Computer Impact on Society" embraces such aspects as application of computers to management and decision-making, to law and economics, to traffic flow, and impact on the individual. Companies interested in making proposals should request the brochures, *Grants for Computing Activities, Grants for Scientific Research,* and *Expanded Research Program Relative to a National Science Computer Network* from Office of Computing Activities, NSF, Washington, D.C. 20550.

Two other programs open to industry are in the preliminary planning stage. They deal with "Experimental Research and Development Incentives" and "National R & D Assessment." Write the NSF offices bearing those names for more details.

Other NSF programs and projects of value to industry include a plan under which an engineering faculty member may spend two summers with industry in order to relate his research activities to real-world problems, and university–industry workshops. Subjects of such workshops in a recent year ranged from "Industrialized Building Processes" to "Glass Processing."

NSF's wide-ranging research support generates innumerable by-products for business. Some recent examples:

- To prevent vessel collisions in harbors, which cause hundreds of millions of dollars in losses yearly, air traffic control methods are being adapted for marine use.
- Chemical process dynamics are being studied, and it is thought that dramatic improvements in plant efficiency may be achieved.
- In the field of materials research, noteworthy advances have been made in the art of purification and filtration using magnetic fields. Thus, a new filter employing magnetized steel wool has furnished a more economical method of removing impurities in kaolin used for white paper coating. It was an outgrowth of an esoteric physics research project—a search for the magnetic "monopole."

In the near future, NSF hopes to explore such fascinating possibilities, with obvious implications for industry, as:

- Creating steam to run generators by finding formations of stone that are hot from volcanic activity, drilling holes to them, and pouring water down the holes.
- Turning human and animal wastes into methane gas fuel by burning them.
- Cooling electric cables to absolute zero so there would be very little loss of energy in transmission.

NSF offers many free publications, others are for sale by GPO. For an NSF publications list covering both types, write Distribution Section, NSF, Washington, D.C. 20550.

National Science Foundation
1800 G. St. N.W.
Washington, D.C. 20550
(202) 632-5704

Now
That
You Know

NOW THAT YOU KNOW

After surveying this vast panorama of services, it becomes clear that a businessman could easily spend his entire life in Washington trying to get help from the government. This would be neither good use of one's time nor good economics; indeed, it would be a fundamental philosophical violation of the free enterprise system.

We need a well-balanced point of view toward our relationship with the federal government, neither leaning on it too heavily nor ever overlooking the governmental dimension that so often is involved in our decision-making and in our problem-solving. It is wasteful for us not to get help where it is available; it is imprudent for us not to make our requirements and our points of view known to the legislative and executive branches. It is foolish for us to assume that when the chips are down and we have a crisis on our hands, we can rush down to Washington and, at the drop of a hat, find just the right responsive ear and get the help we need.

So, we must do three things. The first step is to analyze our business operations so that we have a clear understanding of what portions of our business are or might be affected by the federal government for better or worse. The second step is to look over the governmental landscape in order to understand where decisions are being made and where resources are available that can help us. The third step is, in some orderly way, to make a start at becoming familiar with the people and the organizations and the techniques for reaching into this great repository of resources for help, counsel, and understanding. Now, let's take a look at each one of these three steps.

It would be a wise thing for you and your associates, regardless of whether you have a big business or a small business, to spend some time in thinking through each area of your operations after having gone through this book. You will quickly see how many different sources of information, data, actual business opportunities, federal government sources of funds, restrictions, and possible potential for federal involvement there is in your operation. Once you have done that you can begin to draw a road map for yourself.

Then, check the lists of Department of Commerce field offices or Small Business Administration field offices to see where the nearest one to you might be. The likelihood is that there is one within 150 miles of your operation, at the maximum. It would be a good idea to call in to either one of these two offices and to arrange a meeting between one of their key people and yourself. Feel free to bring along any of your associates that you might want with you. Sit down with the Commerce or SBA people; tell them about your business; tell them about some of your problems in marketing, production, transportation, and financing; ask them what kinds of publications and other help are available through the field office. They may also be able to refer you to local field offices of other government agencies who can help you right in your own community.

On another level, write to your representative and to at least one of your senators—the one who lives nearest you—and tell them that you would like to meet them. Indicate whether you have a specific problem, but don't delay seeking their acquaintance until one arises. Ask them when they are going to be back in their home territory and suggest that they let you know when it might be convenient for you to pay a call on them. When you do see them, put your visit in an information-giving framework. Because of your economic role in the community, you feel it is important to share with them some firsthand knowledge of yourself and your business.

The next step might be to make sure that you spend the $19.35 a year it will cost to receive the monthly catalog of the GPO. This will keep you informed on new publications coming out of the government. After you have looked over a few issues, you will find that you can scan the catalog very rapidly. It's worth the few minutes a month to spot items that might be important for you to see. You already know from the listings in this book that government literature is inexpensive. Often it's worth the trouble of sending a few cents for a publication to find out if it's as promising as it sounds. Perhaps you'll find it is not exactly applicable in your particular case, but just as often there may be a chapter or a few paragraphs or even an entire publication that can save you, or help you make, thousands of dollars.

Depending on how large your organization is, you might want to designate one person as your government relations man. It would be up to him to constantly maintain some kind of overview (as your staff adviser, not as a line supervisor) of all the activities in your company that could use help from the government or that have problems affected by the government. It would also be this person who goes over the *Commerce Business Daily*, who reviews the catalogs from the GPO, who makes an annual trip to Washington for three or four days and sits down and talks to all the people with whom you want to maintain relationships. This same man would mail your annual report and other appropriate company literature to the people in government who should see it. He would check your various industry trade journals as well as the general consumer press (and to be really thorough, each day's *Congressional Record* and *Fed-*

eral Register,* which publishes new regulations of all government agencies) for information concerning legislation or administrative actions that would influence the success of your business. He would draft letters expressing your company points of view (probably for the signature of the president of your company) to members of Congress or members of the executive branch of government.

When anyone in your company says, "I wish I knew about . . . ," or "I wish I could get my hands on such and such," it would be useful to thumb through the index of this book, find the agency that seems to have something to do with the question in your mind, and write to them. Ask them whether or not there is anything that they can do to be helpful to you. Again, always bear in mind the easy alternative of calling a local field office of the agency involved. If you don't know which agency is involved, remember that you can start off with the Small Business Administration or the Department of Commerce field offices because they maintain entree into all other agencies of government.

A word of caution. Let us always remember that the government is of necessity big. Each one of us may have a different point of view as to exactly how big it ought to be; still, we all recognize that it is the largest single enterprise on the face of the earth. Therefore, we may not be able to take absolute dead aim at the right target in government on the first shot. However, as each of us gets a little bit more knowledgeable in finding his way through the maze of government, getting good answers—the right answers—will take less time.

Nothing in personal or business life is ever 100 percent perfect. There will be times when the right answer can't be found. There will be times when an uncooperative person is encountered. There will be times when the information you seek is unavailable. There will be occasions on which your point of

---

* *Federal Register*, $45 a year; *Congressional Record*, $45 a year; GPO.

view will not prevail in the halls of Congress or in a decision-making procedure inside one of the executive departments. Don't despair—this is predictable; nobody gets his way all the time; nobody is successful all the time. In this facet of our business lives, let's remember that we are playing for the percentages, "for the batting averages," just as we do in the rest of our business. We want to be successful as often as we possibly can. We look for 100 percent, we strive for it even though we know we will never quite make it.

The government establishment changes just as does your own organization. In order to maintain familiarity with it, in order to understand how to use it, one has to look at government relations as somewhat like a muscle. One can't permit it to atrophy. One has to keep it in constant use. This means that it has to be worked at; when it's worked at, it can be productive for you.

A final recommendation: The federal government establishment is not the beginning and end-all of your relationship with government; the same process has to be gone through at the state and local level. Do you know your mayor? Do you know your city councilmen? Are you up to date on proposed local ordinances that will have an impact on your business? Do you participate in civic affairs? If there is a bond issue, how is it going to affect your taxes? If they are going to go up, is it a worthwhile investment for your business that will make your community a better one to live in, and consequently a better place for you to do business in? If not, what are you doing about it?

There are three levels of government in this country. All three need the same kind of understanding and building of communication bridges. This is just sensible "preventative maintenance," a prudent activity required of the businessman.

In terms of getting active help, information, and assistance from government, the federal level probably outweighs by far the other two in its potential productivity for you. Don't discount the other two, however. They are loaded with surprises and with good programs that can be important and useful to you. This will be even more true as revenue-sharing progresses.

So, happy hunting in your quest for the helpful services from government that are every businessman's due, and good luck in building a productive and cooperative relationship with your biggest partner—the United States government.

THE WASHINGTON MEDIA

The businessman who comes to Washington on a mission that puts him in the public eye had better know something about the Washington-based news media and how to deal with them.

Except for New York, Washington has the largest corps of newsmen and women in the world. The reason they are there is that Washington is a rich source of news. For the businessman who wants news coverage of his activities, that means he has plenty of competition.

The converse is not necessarily true, however. The businessman who would like to avoid attention—if, for example, he is testifying before a hostile congressional committee—should make his plans on the assumption that the newshawks will be there for at least a while, no matter what other stories are breaking.

Some Rules

Either way, there are certain basic principles and procedures the businessman should follow:

1. Be frank and truthful with the media. Recent events have amply demonstrated how counterproductive attempts at coverup can be.

2. Tell your story clearly, in layman's language. Reporters who have to plow through gobs of government gobbledygook will appreciate it.

3. Keep your news releases brief. If you're going to present a fifty-page statement before a hearing, top it with a two-page summary.

4. Make your material readily available. Congressional committees generally will ask for at least seventy-five copies, some of which they will put in the hands of the press. Other steps you can take on your own are to place about fifty copies in the rack at the National Press Club, a gathering place for correspondents; hire Chittenden Press Service (RE 7-4434) or Heiss Press Service (628-8224) to deliver your releases to about three hundred media representatives on their regular run; or retain Press Relations Wire (347-5155) to get your release to Washington media via teletype.

The channels listed in Item 4 are appropriate when you have "hard news" for general distribution. If what you have to offer is more in the nature of a point of view, and if it presents a new and interesting perspective on current developments, then you may want to try the "exclusive" route. This could involve approaching one of the columnists syndicated out of Washington. To avoid wasting your time and theirs, familiarize yourself with their "slant" by reading some of their columns (the Library of Congress has an extensive collection of newspapers). What will appeal to Marquis Childs probably will not appeal to Holmes Alexander, and vice versa.

Other specialized avenues to remember are the correspondents for the trade magazines of your industry and for newspapers of the principal cities in which your company operates. A good source for the names of these correspondents is *Hudson's Washington News Media Contacts Directory,* (703) 522-5177. The government-published *Congressional Directory* also contains a listing of correspondents accredited to the press galleries of Congress.

Much network television and radio news originates in Washington, usually involving government people. Occasionally, however, a business executive who can provide a significant perspective on a developing news story—say, an oil company president when the energy crisis is in the forefront—may be considered appropriate for an interview. All three major networks have news bureaus in Washington. If you think you have something of interest, call their assignment editors at these numbers: ABC, 393-7700; CBS, 296-1234; NBC, EM 2-4000.

A less obvious channel for getting on the air is through your representative or senator. Many tape shows in Washington for distribution to stations in their districts; senators use a recording studio in the Capitol, representatives have access to a facility in the Rayburn Building. Call your congressman's administrative assistant, or press secretary if he has one, about the possibility of being interviewed.

News Conferences

In a limited number of cases, it might be advisable for you to call a news conference. Before doing so, ask yourself if your subject can be better clarified by such a conference than by distribution of a news release. Correspondents work on a tight time schedule, and will avoid conferences that do not seem likely to be productive.

If you decide you have justification for calling a conference, the best way to get the word about it to the Washington news corps is via the local wires of Associated Press and United Press International (the latter calls its local wire Washington Capital News Service). They begin each morning's transmissions with a calendar of the day's newsworthy events, and a calendar for the week ahead is carried on Friday. A short written notice is preferred, but if time does not permit, they will accept telephone notification. Associated Press is at 1300 Connecticut Avenue N.W., Washington, D.C. 20036, (202) 833-5300. Washington Capital News Service is in the National Press Building, 14th and F Streets N.W., Washington, D.C. 20004, (202) 628-6621.

An ideal place for a news conference is the National Press Club, if you can meet its requirements. Check with the club office (202) RE 7-2500. If you are able to work several weeks ahead, it's worth exploring with the club's program chairman whether he'd like to have you as a luncheon speaker or as the interviewee at one of the club's newsmaker sessions. You're competing against the world's statesmen, so the odds are long.

As a general rule, avoid turning your news conference into a social event, with elaborate food and beverages. If you're holding it midmorning, coffee and rolls might be in order, but that's about it. Best times for news conferences are midmorning or early afternoon. Beyond 2:30 you begin to run into deadline problems.

Use of the word "you" in this section is not intended to suggest that do-it-yourself public relations is necessarily the best way. A knowledgeable Washington PR man may save you a lot of grief. If your firm has a public relations agency, it will be able to line up competent Washington assistance for you. If not, ask the Washington chapter of the Public Relations Society of America for names of accredited members who might be able to help. The chapter does not have a telephone listing. Try its 1974 president, Edwin L. Stoll, at (202) 466-8200.

THE LOGISTICS OF WASHINGTON

The section that follows does not purport to be an encyclopedic listing of every hotel, restaurant, and other service available in Washington. That can be found in the yellow pages of the telephone directory, which might be awkward for the businessman to put in his pocket.

We have attempted to give only a representative selection, adequate for the businessman's needs during his typical Washington stay of a week or less. The authors believe the facilities listed are reliable, but can offer no guarantees. Indeed, in a transient city like Washington, one cannot even be sure they all will still be in operation by the time of publication.

Some very fine services may well have been omitted. We invite readers who discover a gem of a restaurant, or a crackerjack secretarial service, or a marvelous small hotel to let us know about it for possible listing in the next edition of this guide.

All telephone numbers are area code (202) unless otherwise stated.

Hotels

Our first four listings are all relatively new on the Washington hotel scene—three to nine years. The next two are older hotels of distinction to which many top-drawer businessmen remain loyal.

EMBASSY ROW—Just outside the downtown area, at 2015 Massachusetts Avenue N.W. 265–1600.

MADISON—15th & M, N.W., in the business section. 785–1000.

WASHINGTON-HILTON—1919 Connecticut Ave. N.W. 483–3000. By far the largest of the six, with extensive convention and exhibit facilities. Not to be confused with the Statler-Hilton, an older member of the family.

WATERGATE—2650 Virginia Ave. N.W. 965–2300. Close to State Department and Kennedy Center. Lively shopping mall.

MANGER-HAY-ADAMS—800-16th N.W. 638–2260. Overlooking the White House.

SHERATON-CARLTON—16th & K N.W. ME 8–2626.

The businessman who is bringing his family along might want to stay in a residential or close-in suburban location. In the former category are two hotels off upper Connecticut Avenue within a block of each other:

SHERATON PARK—2660 Woodley Road N.W. 265–2000.

SHOREHAM—2500 Calvert N.W. 234–0700.

Both are large hotels with a lot of convention business, but they also go after family trade. Ask about special family rates in summer.

Ringing the city are a number of motels. Nearest to downtown and to Washington National Airport are three in Virginia run by Marriott:

CRYSTAL CITY—U.S. 1. (703) 521–5500.

KEY BRIDGE—Rosslyn. (703) 524–6400.

TWIN BRIDGES—U.S. 1. (703) 628–4200.

Two other chains recently opened motels in Rosslyn:

HOLIDAY INN—1850 N. Ft. Myer Dr. (703) 522–0400.
RAMADA INN—1900 N. Ft. Myer Dr. (703) 527–4814.

The Rosslyn location is handy to shopping in the Georgetown boutiques, while U.S. 1 is a straight run to Department of Commerce and other government buildings.

Washington hotels are heavily booked in the spring, when tourists and high school graduating classes descend en masse. Make sure you have reservations then and also in September and October, favorite convention months.

As in any big city, walking around Washington at night has its risks. Whichever hotel you choose, we'd advise doing your walking by day, and using taxis at night (or buses when the service is door-to-door).

Transportation

Before detailing Washington's transportation facilities, let's compare the options.

Use of your own or a rented car is not recommended unless your objectives are in the suburbs—e.g., National Institutes of Health in Bethesda, Maryland, or Fort Belvoir, Virginia. Downtown parking and traffic in Washington are a hassle.

Taxis are cheap, and plentiful except in rain or rush hours. The bus system is fair, but its new management, the Washington Metropolitan Transportation Authority (METRO) promises improvement. Chauffeured limousine service may be worth considering if you have a number of stops and a tight schedule (especially if several people are traveling together, since taxis charge by the person). Keep in mind that all ground transportation will take a little longer for the next few years because of subway construction.

Taxi rates are set on a zone system. Most government buildings and many hotels are within the first zone, which means that you can ride between any two points in the zone for 85 cents (group rate 50 cents per passenger). It's even possible to ride within a subzone of the first zone for only 60 cents. A tip of 15 to 25 cents per passenger on a first zone ride is customary. There's an additional charge of 50 cents if you telephone for a cab, but you're better off taking your chances on the street—in rush periods you could wait an hour for a cab on call, or be stood up entirely.

Greyhound (EX 3-3060) operates limousine service every 20 minutes from Washington National Airport to six downtown hotels and hourly from the Statler and Washington-Hilton Hotels to that airport. From Dulles International Airport it runs buses to downtown hotels every half hour, and follows the same procedure on the run to Dulles. Bus fare for Dulles at time of writing is $3.50. Greyhound also provides taxis for Dulles passengers; taxi service at Washington National is now unfranchised.

Airline Transport, Inc. (783-5343) provides bus service between downtown Washington and Baltimore–Washington International Airport (formerly known as Friendship).

Allow an hour to get to Dulles or Baltimore airports, half an hour to Washington National.

The Washington yellow pages lists thirty-nine limousine services. A few of the better known are:

ADMIRAL—Madison Hotel. 638–3006
CAPITOL—Watergate Hotel. 333–0383
CAREY—1522 Wisconsin Ave., N.W. 337–5400
DIAMOND—Shoreham Hotel. HO 2–4500
GRAY LINE—1010 Eye St. N.W. DI 7–0600

Service is offered by the hour, day, week, or month.

The METRO bus fare within the District of Columbia is 40 cents. A pocket route map may be obtained free from METRO at 600 5th St. N.W., Washington, D.C. 20001.

Restaurants

The executive who comes to Washington to do business with the government has two basic options of where to eat lunch. He can eat in a government building cafeteria, where the food ranges from bad to tolerable and lunch can be disposed of in half an hour. Or he can take a lot more time and choose from Washington's varied roster of good restaurants.

Most bureaucrats will welcome a chance to break the routine of cafeteria eating. An invitation to lunch takes a little advance planning. The official will need to arrange his schedule, and to get a table in the better restaurants you should call in a reservation no later than 11 A.M. For greater certainty of being accommodated, make your request for 12 sharp, or for after 1 P.M. If you're taking a government employee, chances are he'll prefer the earlier hour, so he won't return conspicuously late.

We asked some veteran Washington public relations people to list their favorite places when they take a visiting executive to lunch. The fact that four people named fourteen restaurants with no duplicate listings suggests that Washington has something to offer for every taste. Here are their nominations:

Basil Littin, Special Assistant to the Secretary of Commerce —Two Continents, 1420 F Street N.W., 347-4499, "central location, fine cuisine, nice surroundings"; Paul Young's, 1120 Connecticut Avenue N.W., 331-7000," service and food good, and plenty of room to discuss business without someone at your elbow."

Venlo Wolfsohn, Executive Director, National Auto and Truck Wreckers Association—Jefferson Hotel, 16th & M Streets N.W., DI 7-4704, "cuisine not great, but very pleasant and quiet atmosphere"; The Embers, 1200 19th Street N.W., 296-5555, "bigger and noisier"; Court of the Mandarins, 1824 M Street N.W., 223-6666, Peking-style Chinese food, but the authors suggest you ask for advice on the menu from the proprietor, Mrs. Berman, who is Chinese in spite of her name.

John Daly of the Direct Mail Advertising Association favors three French-style restaurants, and adds two for convenience when doing business on Capitol Hill—the French restaurants are Two Continents, 1420 F Street N.W., 347-4499; Le Provençal, 1234 20th Street N.W., 223-2420, where you may see CBS-TV news correspondents; Le Bagatelle, 2000 K Street N.W., 872-8677; on Capitol Hill, the Monocle, 107 D Street N.E., 546-4488, where you may ogle a senator or two;and the Rotunda, 30 Ivy Street S.E., 546-2255.

The selections of George Wells of the National Soft Drink Association cluster in the area of Connecticut Avenue and K Street N.W.: For seafood and good service, he likes Harvey's, 1001-18th Street N.W., 833-1858; Duke Zeibert's offers a varied menu at 1722 L Street N.W., 296-5030; and his choice of a steak house is Golden Ox, 1615 L Street, N.W., 347-0010.

Leonard Arzt of the National Society of Professional Engineers nominates Adam's Rib, 2100 Pennsylvania Avenue N.W., 659-1881; and for a hearty, quick, moderately priced lunch of beef, salad, and beer, Emerson's,1511 K Street N.W.,659-8170. If you want to go just beyond the downtown area into Georgetown, he thinks you might like the pub atmosphere of Clyde's, 3236 M Street N.W., 333-9180; and for greater elegance at dinner only, El Tio Pepe, 2809 M Street N.W., 337-0730, serving paella, fish, and other Spanish specialties for about $10.

If you're going to be in Washington for dinner, Georgetown offers many attractive choices to suit any taste. On the continental side, the authors can recommend Jour et Nuit, 30th & M Streets N.W., FE 3-1033, where a dinner featuring veal Marengo was well worth the tab of $11 including wine and tip. For plainer fare, Publick House, 3218 M Street N.W., 333-6605, puts out a good steak plus salad bar at a bargain $5.50. Even less expensive is Mykonos, 3066 M Street N.W., 337-8652, an informal little place that does a good job on Greek specialties.

Those who expect to do a lot of eating in Washington might want to get hold of *Check Mark Dining Guide,* which rates some three hundred area restaurants. This pocket-size book is available for $3.50 in bookstores or may be ordered from Mark Associates, Inc., 1629 K Street N.W., Washington, D.C. 20006.

After Dark

If, after a day of doing business with the government, you want to go out on the town, Washington offers rich cultural fare, but little in the way of night life.

For a city its size, Washington presents theatergoers with an exceptionally varied menu. Major plays and musicals on their way to or from Broadway, but at less than Broadway prices, can be found at the National Theatre, 1321 E Street N.W., the Eisenhower Theater in the Kennedy Center, and the American Theater, 429 L'Enfant Plaza S.W. Smaller in size but with a justified international reputation is the Arena Stage, Sixth and M Streets S.W. Occasionally coming up with a real winner is Ford's Theater, 511-10th Street N.W., a restored version of the playhouse where Lincoln was shot.

The intellectually adventurous may enjoy the avant-garde productions of the Washington Theater Club, 23rd and L Streets N.W., and theater classics are well performed at Catholic University.

In summer, a short trip to the suburbs will bring you to Wolf Trap Theater, Vienna, Virginia, where musical comedies, operas, concerts, and ballet of top quality are presented in an architecturally striking setting. Entertainment more on the pop side is featured at the Merriweather Post Pavilion in Columbia, Maryland. Shady Grove Music Fair, Rockville, Maryland, offers a mix of musical comedies and big name singers and comedians. The Carter Barron Amphitheater in Rock Creek Park leans to rock and pop music.

For symphonies and instrumentalists, there's the Kennedy

Center Concert Hall, and chamber music is performed Friday evenings at the Library of Congress, with admission free. Public concerts also are given at the National Gallery of Art Sunday evenings at 7.

You may find comedian Mort Sahl or folksinger Gordon Lightfoot performing at the Cellar Door, 34th and M Streets N.W. If you want to dance, try the Shoreham Hotel, 2500 Calvert Street N.W., with Mark Russell's devastating political satire between sets.

Sights to See

If the executive brings his family to Washington, or if he has time to spare, the town has more points of interest than most people have shoe leather and energy. This section attempts only to hit some highlights. For more detailed information, two useful pocket books are *The New York Times Guide to the Nation's Capital* and *The Washington Guidebook* by John and Katharine Walker.

The White House has to head the list of attractions. It's open to the public 10 A.M. to 12 noon, Tuesday through Saturday, but if you can plan several weeks ahead, ask your congressman to get you on the special tour at 8:45. You see more, and get briefed by a guide.

Congress to most people means the Capitol building and a session of the House or Senate, where admission is by pass, obtained readily from your congressman. The real action, however, is in committee hearings, open to anyone. Consult the *Washington Post* for time, place, and subject.

The Monuments—Facing each other across an eight-block expanse of mall and reflecting pool are the majestic Lincoln Memorial and the Washington Monument, which gives a dominating view of the city and environs. If you have kids along, they might want to climb the 898 steps to the top of the Washington Monument, but there is an elevator. In spring and summer it's open until 11 P.M., the rest of the year to 5 P.M. The Lincoln Memorial has been open to midnight the year around, but check with National Capital Parks (426-6700) for possible effects of energy conservation.

The Kennedy Center is fairly close to the Lincoln Memorial, and if you don't go to the top of the Washington Monument, the center's terrace offers a less commanding but very attractive view. The architectural merits of the Edward Durrell Stone design are the subject of wildly varying critical views; see it for yourself and decide.

Kennedy Grave may be grouped with two other historic sites just across the Potomac in Virginia—the Tomb of the Unknown Soldier and the Curtis Lee Mansion—all in Arlington National Cemetery. Even if you don't want to go through the mansion, its grounds offer an impressive view of the city.

Smithsonian Institution is a collection of buildings with something to tickle anyone's funnybone, from clocks to space rockets. Open to 4:30; check for possible later spring and summer hours. For children from about eight on up, a visit to the institution makes a good combination with the nearby FBI. The FBI is open only Mondays through Friday, to 4:15 P.M.

National Gallery is the city's leading attraction for art lovers, and when your feet give out, it has about the best cafeteria in town. Usual hours are 10 to 5 Monday through Saturday and 2 to 10 Sunday. During spring and summer weekday hours may be extended to 9 P.M. with Sunday opening at noon.

Hirshhorn Museum and Sculpture Garden is the city's newest art museum, housing a superb collection of modern art. It's open every day of the year except Christmas, and admission is free. The striking circular building is located on the Mall.

Phillips Gallery (or more properly, Collection) is a little gem, especially strong on impressionist art. Somewhat removed from the prime tourist attractions, it is near the Woodrow Wilson House, 2340 S Street N.W. (open afternoons only) and the Textile Museum, 2320 S Street N.W. Phillips is closed Mondays.

A convenient way to see many of the sights without driving and parking headaches is the Tourmobile. This concessioner of the National Park Service circulates continuously around the monuments and public buildings; you can get on and off all day for one fare (638-5371).

SERVICES JUST IN CASE

The executive who knows exactly where to turn for various logistical services when he is at home may find himself at a loss if the need arises in Washington. Below we have listed some companies providing such services. Many others, of course, can be found in the yellow pages.

Delivery: Central (589-8500), Mar-Sid (347-7262), Metro (337-6610), and Morgan (483-5151). See also press release delivery services under Washington Media.

Temporary Help: Tele Sec (223-4900), Manpower Inc. (393-8475), Kelly Girl (393-5779), and Potomac Temporaries (296-2270).

Secretarial Service: Efficient Business Service (783-0715), Office Services, Inc. (296-5212), or ask your hotel.

Convention and Meeting Services: Courtesy Associates (296-8100), Ralph Whitener & Co. (471-5761), and United Exposition Service Co. (488-3770).

Audio-Visual Equipment Rental: Conn Camera (293-5484), Wilson Gill, Inc. (462-1450), The Film Center (393-1205).

Exhibit Services: Exhibit-Aids, Inc. (920-4100), William P.

Gelberg, Inc. (882-7733), Hargrove, Inc. (773-6600), Art Designers, Inc. (549-6933).

Commercial Art: Creative Arts Studio (832-2600), Design Center (483-4461), Permut, Rappeport & Associates (530-3447).

Stationery: For engraved invitations, Brewood (347-4868) or Copenhaver (232-1200); for supplies, Ginn's (628-5000) or Chas. G. Stott & Co., Inc. (333-5200).

Clothing and Accessories: Men's Formal Wear Rentals, Scogna (296-4555) or M. Stein & Co. (659-1434). General, Men's: Arthur A. Adler, Inc. (NA 8-0131), Brooks Brothers (659-4650), Carlton's Inc. (331-8292), Rosenthal & Co. (659-4820); Men's and Women's, Garfinckel's Department Store (628-7730), Raleighs (347-7000), and Lewis & Thomas Saltz (393-4400).

INDEX

Postal Rate Commission, 326–
327
Prairie Village Commodity
Office, 64, 65
President
advisors to, 36–39
correspondence with, 34–46
See also Executive Branch
Presidential "E" awards, 76
President's Commission on Per-
sonnel Interchange, 287–
289
"Preventive mediation," 247
Price-fixing, and Justice Depart-
ment, 141–142
Price supports, and USDA, 63–
65
Proxy-soliciting material, and
SEC, 330
Public Buildings Service, of
General Services Adminis-
tration, 234–236
Public land, and Interior Department, 134–135
Public Relations Society of
America, 376
Publications,
of AEC, 351–352
of Agricultural Marketing
Service, 58, 59
of Appalachian Regional
Commission, 271
of Bureau of Customs, 199
of Bureau of International
Commerce, 74–75
of Bureau of Labor Statistics,
156, 157
catalog (monthly) of, 369
of Civil Aeronautics Board,
345
of Commerce Department, 82
on Congressional organization, 19
on day care, 106

on Defense Department purchasing, 88, 89, 90, 92
on Economic Research Ser-
vice, 69
of EPA, 282
of Equal Employment Opportunity Commission, 250,
251
of Export Marketing Service,
66, 67
of FAA, 180–181
of Farm Credit Administration, 213
of Farmer Cooperative Service, 79
of Federal Maritime Commission, 341
of Federal Power Commis-
sion, 318
of Federal Reserve, 207–208
of Federal Trade Commis-
sion, 322, 323
of Forest Service, 51, 52–53
of General Accounting Office,
285–286
of General Services Administration, 231
of HUD, 115
of Internal Revenue Service,
193, 196
of National Labor Relations
Board, 245
of National Park Service, 135
of NSF, 361, 363–364
of OSHA, 159
of Patent Office, 80
procedure for obtaining, xxi–
xxii
of Secret Service, 201
of Securities and Exchange
Commission, 33, 334–335
on sightseeing in Washington,
D.C., 384–386